TRADE MARKETING STRATEGY

Gary Davies
Post Office Counters Ltd Professor of Retailing
Manchester Business School

P·C·P
Paul Chapman
Publishing Ltd

Paul Chapman Publishing Ltd
144 Liverpool Road
London
N1 1LA

British Library Cataloguing in Publication Data

Trade Marketing Strategy
I. Davies, Gary
658.8

ISBN 1 85396 213 9

Typeset by Textype Typesetters, Cambridge
Printed and bound by Athenaeum Press Ltd, Newcastle-upon-Tyne

A B C D E F G H 9 8 7 6 5 4 3

CONTENTS

PREFACE

Thank you to all those individuals and companies whose cooperation has made this book possible, to Paul Chapman and his team for their work and advice, to Lynn Ward for her wordprocessing, to my sponsors for their financial support, to MBS for time and facilities and to my wife and family for their patience.

INTRODUCTION

Suppliers to retailers are learning to market to, rather than market through, the retail sector. This change of orientation has been made necessary by a change in the power structure between the various businesses that are responsible for growing, making or distributing goods for and to the consumer. Once the retailer felt obliged to stock mainly what had been presold to the shopper. Now the retailer decides in the main what to stock. Consumer loyalty to the manufacturer, or rather to its brand, is being superseded by loyalty to the store. Concentration in the retail sector and centralisation of buying has made the retail buyer a powerful and pivotal role in the supply chain. Manufacturers have recognised the changes facing them by re-organising their salesforces, cutting back on the numbers of staff whose role it once was to visit each retail outlet, and expanding the number of those who deal, as trade marketing managers, with the retailer's head office.

But do manufacturers treat retailers as customers? I remember the reaction from the senior management team of one manufacturer when, having ascertained that they did view the retailer as a customer, I asked whether they subscribed to the maxim that the 'customer is always right'. The answer came in the form of a wry smile: no the retail customer is not always right it seemed. There is a tension between manufacturer and retailer. Another comment from an executive of a company manufacturing branded foods, which does not market own-brands, illustrated an aspect of the problem of considering the retailer as a customer. In his view his company was now in the position of supplying its own competitors. Seeing retailers as competitors, because retailers market their own brands, is very different from seeing them as customers. Retailers can be seen as competitors in other ways, such as competing for the profit of supplying goods to the customer with the manufacturer who makes the goods.

The growth of own-brands is seen as a threat by many suppliers and as an opportunity by others. The views raised by the former group include the prediction that own-brand penetration will reach a plateau. The shopper, it is said, wants choice within a product type and will therefore only shop where there is a choice. Tell that to Marks & Spencer! The fundamental problem facing manufacturers is that the larger retailer is often better placed to respond to market demand than they are. Product marketing is often fundamentally cheaper when led by a retailer which does not have to market its wares to the shopper over the heads of the distribution channel using ever more expensive advertising. The retailer's shelves are its media, its customers are its audience for any promotion. Attitudes among consumers are changing too. One trend highlighted in Chapters 5 and 6 of this book is that of less value being placed upon branding by consumers.

This book is about how a manufacturer or supplier of consumer products should respond to the changing realities in the marketplace for consumer products. It begins with an historical perspective in Chapters 1 and 2, chosen to make the point that the changes taking place today are more radical than many perceive them to be. They are, however, no more radical than the changes that have occurred in the past in the distribution of consumer products since the days of an agrarian economy when most people grew or made what they needed themselves. The retailing and distribution of goods were less than relevant as activities, but things changed radically. They are changing again today.

Other perspectives are introduced from academic research. One body of literature, that of marketing channels or channels of distribution theory, is particularly relevant and is drawn from throughout the book. But the attitude alluded to from manufacturers, that retailing is a reactive channel for their goods pervades not only the title but also the paradigm of such research. Retailers are not just a channel that is managed by the manufacturer. An alternative academic paradigm is emerging, that of supply chain management, that at least leaves the matter open as to who has the right to control the distribution of products, and Chapter 7 deals with this issue in some depth.

The two literatures contain a number of concepts and frameworks (power, leadership, conflict, cooperation) which are highly relevant to any analysis of the strategic options facing the retailer's suppliers. But most of them assume an adversarial posture between manufacturer and retailer. To counterbalance this, the concept of relational marketing is introduced as well as chapters in the book on understanding retailing as a business in Chapter 4 and understanding the motivations of the retail buyer in Chapter 3. This allows the reader to understand how the retailer can be treated as a customer or a partner, rather than as a competitor.

A number of case studies are used throughout the book both to illustrate the points made in the individual chapters and to bring what might appear to be a clinical analysis of the issues back to practical reality. The academic frameworks offer a starting point for analysing practice, but are rarely perfect in guiding the practitioner. A lengthy study of the evolution of one of Britain's leading retailers, Marks & Spencer, follows Chapter 1 and illustrates the historical perspective referred to earlier and introduces the reader to some of the main issues in managing a retail business. Following Chapter 2 are two interviews, one with a product marketer and the other with a retail buyer focusing on the issue of forming closer relationships between supplier and retailer. By way of contrast, the case study of Emma Somerset following Chapter 3 illustrates a more arm's length relationship in the retailing of fashion.

The development of own-brand is illustrated after Chapter 6 in the context of Asda's rapid development of its own brand range. The significance of EDI to interfirm relationships and the power of leading retailers is the subject of the study after Chapter 7. The role of the wholesaler is less significant in the British market today but the case study on W. H. Smith News that follows Chapter 8 illustrates how it is still possible for a wholesaler to take the lead in a distribution channel. The last two case studies preceding Chapter 10 present two very different options for the manufacturer, the marketing of a leading brand and the marketing of own-brand.

Chapters 8 and 9 present ideas on how manufacturers can or have responded to what has already happened. The final chapter contains my own views on the future facing the retailer's suppliers and on how to plan for that future. Retailer power, I submit, has not yet reached its peak. Manufacturers must respond, either by redefining their role to be suppliers to retailers or as retailers themselves or by revisiting their traditional role as innovators of brands that retailers must stock to guarantee their own customer base. Academic research needs to respond to the same and other changes in the marketplace. The final chapter argues the case for the unit of strategic analysis to be the supply chain rather than the individual firm or strategic business unit. Each chapter ends with a Keypoint Summary and, where appropriate an introduction to the case study that follows.

The context for the book is often British, although examples are included from around the world and much of the academic research cited is American. In Britain, the absence of laws designed to sustain the smaller shopkeeper has led to an acceleration in the growth of multiple retailing. The power of British retailers comes from their size and their ability to use that market power. Similar trends can be seen in other countries but most manufacturers, in the author's experience, have yet to experience the extent of what is now routine pressure from powerful retailers. Even in Britain there are many sectors where manufacturers are more powerful than the retailers who sell their goods to the public. Many will remain just as powerful in the future, but others in Britain and elsewhere will experience a significant change in their relationships with retailers, a change that needs to be managed.

This book has been written for both academic and practitioner audiences. It relies upon my own research into retailing as a business and a process and a concern to apply that knowledge for the benefit of those who work in the manufacturing sector. I hope that its publication will also stimulate further research interest into how to market to retailers, rather than market through them.

Gary Davies
Manchester 1993

1

AN HISTORICAL PERSPECTIVE

The main purpose of this book is to provide a framework for dealing with change. The change is that of a fundamental shift in the shape of the distribution system for consumer products. For the manufacturer the most obvious manifestation of this change is the rise in retailer power and the way that power has been used by many large retail businesses. The context for the book is largely that of retailing in Britain as, it will be argued, the extent of retailer influence over distribution channels is far greater than that in most other countries. The author believes that what has happened in Britain will nevertheless occur in other countries should the same economic, social and, in particular, legal environments pertain. Furthermore the author believes that what has already happened in Britain is just the beginning of a new era and that further evolution can be expected.

To argue convincingly that radical change is inevitable is never easy. It is easier to postulate a modification to an established trend rather than a step change, albeit one that is more of a gradual process, occupying perhaps half a century rather than a dramatic shift over a year or two.

To convince the reader that fundamental change is possible and that it is already in train, this chapter takes an historical perspective and looks back at what has already occurred in the distribution system. The chapter concludes that there have already been at least two dramatic shifts in the structure of the distribution channel for consumer goods, no less fundamental than the one that is happening today. One significant difference is timescale: the rate of change is faster today than before.

Markets and fairs

Following the collapse of the Roman Empire, Western Europe entered a period of economic decline and social disorder – the Dark Ages. Towns and even substantial cities disappeared and a new economic and social order gradually emerged, the Feudal System, where the vast majority of the population were subsistence farmers under the control of a ruling class. The economic and social unit was the manor. Self-sufficiency was the norm and there was little opportunity for trading any excess production either within the manorial domain or between such isolated centres of population.

Gradually, as the economy evolved, the opportunity for trade increased. Craftsworkers moved back to the rejuvenated towns and formed associations or guilds for the purpose of trade. Some basic materials such as salt and iron had always been traded between communities but the growth in trade of goods required that buyers and sellers could meet at regular intervals. The authorities at the time, and in practice this was normally the King or ruler together with the nobility and the Church, saw trade as a source of revenue via taxation (Heard, 1973). To ensure that no trade escaped taxation, where and when trade took place had to be regulated. Licences were given to operate fairs and markets, the distinction between the two being that fairs were larger, often annual events, often international, and markets were more local and frequent. Some social historians point to the social as well as economic significance of markets. They argue that a week represents the time between markets, not the phase of the moon, and they point to societies, including the Roman, where the week was not seven days long (Sorokin and Merton, 1937).

A fair deal

The concept evolved of regular markets and fairs. Tolls were levied on people coming to the market, for the rent of stalls, the use of weights and on the transactions made. An important principle was that all exchanges be carried out between supplier and customer before witnesses to ensure a 'fair deal'. Buying before the market was prohibited for two reasons: first the loss of taxes to the authorities; and second the danger that such practice might involve speculation, particularly the holding back of food from the market in times of shortage in the hope of high profit. Forestalling, as it was called, was a crime and it meant that retailing as we know it today was illegal. Trade was largely between producer and consumer.

International fairs at Stourbridge and Bury St Edmunds in England, Troyes and Bar in France and around the Rhine waterway in Germany gave the few merchants of the era the opportunity to trade goods from different countries and regions. Merchants tended to deal with each other and in large quantities but in many ways they represented the origins of modern wholesalers rather than retailers. Such fairs were well established by the 11th century and were important until the 15th century as wholesale markets.

By the 18th century fairs were more concerned with domestic trade and were seen as important social as well as business events. The Stourbridge Fair of 1725 measured 500 metres across and served as the out-of-town shopping centre of its day. But fairs only lasted a week or so and markets just the daylight hours of one day in the week. Neither contained fixed shops.

Some form of markets probably existed in prehistoric times located at religious sites, such as burial grounds, and on the main trading routes of the times. The religious connection persisted into the Middle Ages with the churchyard a common location and the cross a familiar sign to denote a market place. By 1400 there were only an estimated two or three dozen annual fairs in England (Davis, 1966). By 1748 there were 681 market towns in England and by 1792, 550 places that held regular fairs (Brown, 1986). Population and economic growth had produced a significant increase in trade, but within another century the fair would no longer be a significant element in the distribution system. Regular markets would persist as they do today, even in the most advanced of societies, but around about this time came the first retail revolution, the fixed shop.

The fixed shop

Historians differ as to when the fixed shop rather than just the market stall became a significant feature in Britain, although the debate may be more about differences in definition. Davis (1966) suggests that as early as 1400 even the smallest town would have had a genuine retail shopkeeper, keeping goods not available locally and operating very much as a shopkeeper would today. She identifies the Elizabethan era and the 17th century as the period when the fixed shop, rather than the market stall, emerged as the normal place to spend one's income.

There is a good deal of evidence to suggest that the fixed shop was commonplace in this time. The Elizabethan writer Ben Jonson in his play *The Alchemist*, written in the 17th century, lampoons a would-be tobacconist who is asking the Alchemist, a fake magician, for advice on the design and layout of his shop. To appreciate the humour the audience would have had to be familiar with a tobacconist. However Alexander (1970) suggests that this was too early an era to claim significant change and proposes instead that the beginning of the industrial revolution saw the first real division between production and distribution leading to retail shops as we know them. He implies that the largely rural and agricultural economy that prevailed until the 18th and 19th centuries had no need for investment in fixed shops, as producers and consumers of what was bought and sold were so close, geographically, together. Jefferys (1954) went further than Alexander and argued that retailing lagged behind the rest of economy in the developments that occurred at the height of the industrial revolution between 1750 and 1850. Winstanley (1983) is another to accept a date as late as 1850 for the emergence of shops on a large scale in a form that would be recognisable today. Shops existed well before this time but their role was often different from that which we accept today.

The general store was definitely important well before the industrial revolution. Blencowe and Lower (1979) abstract the diaries of one Thomas Turner, a one-time school master turned shopkeeper who sold grocery, ironmongery, crops and clothes. He also supplied the house of the then Prime Minister, the first Duke of Newcastle, acting as much as a purchasing agent for his lordship's household as anything else. Fixed premises where goods were sold directly to consumers originated in a more distant era. Amman's *Book of Trades* was first published in Nuremberg in 1568. His illustrations show a number of tradesmen at work in a room with a window looking out onto the street part-filled with a display of goods for sale. The shoemakers for example are shown working at their trade in the foreground while one of their number serves a female customer through such an open window in the background. The word 'shop', it must be recalled, can mean retail premises or place of manufacture. In 16th century Germany it meant the same place. The producer/retailer always worked and sold from such fixed premises. In the Middle Ages the guilds and the market system might have precluded them from selling on other than market days, but that may have not even been the case. By the 16th century in Britain, the general retailers referred to as chandlers had already broken the market system in selling items such as candles and soap throughout the week (Davis, 1966). By the 18th century one estimate was that a quarter of all houses in London were either shops or taverns. In some streets shop signs became a danger to the passer-by and were banned by statute in 1762. Whether there were pure retailers or not is unclear. Logically the industrial revolution would have been the time when the producer/retailer would become economically disadvantaged and would either have had to rely more on retailing products made elsewhere or risk going out of business. Up until this time the dominant distribution channels would be represented by those in Fig 1. 1.

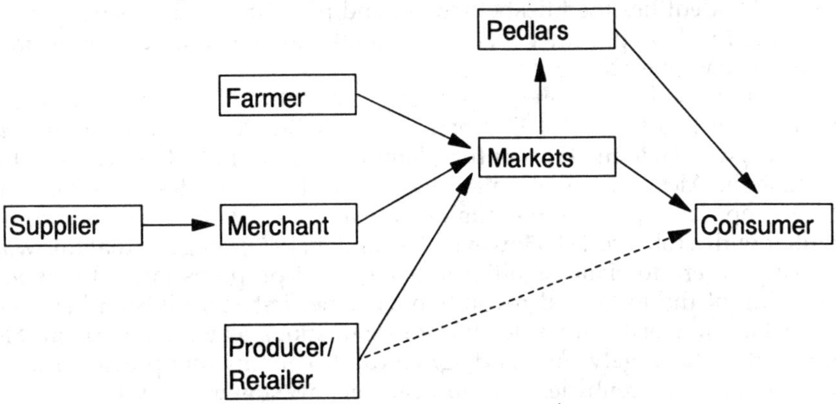

Figure 1. 1 Schematic of main distribution channels before the industrial revolution

The industrial revolution and the mass market

The industrial revolution refers to a period in history when craft manufacture gave way to large-scale production. The replacement of manpower by machinery was the most important cause of this change. Watt's development of a steam engine capable of delivering rotary motion in 1782 was one of a number of landmarks in the 18th century leading the way to both methods of mass production and mass transportation. The clothing trade was dramatically changed with cloth and eventually clothes being made far more cheaply in factories than by the laborious ways of the cottage industry.

The manufacture of steel was important in achieving industrialisation. This in turn needed coal and more coal was required to drive the machinery the steel was used to make. Large communities grew up around local coal-mining and steel-making areas in South Wales, Scotland and the North East of England. The South East became drained of its population as people left the land for the high wages of the new industrial cities. Britain became the manufacturing centre of the world and ports such as Liverpool grew rapidly on the back of export trade.

Between 1750 and 1850 the industrial revolution was focused largely on the manufacture of capital goods. But the techniques of mechanisation were soon applied to producing the consumer goods the new working class were now demanding. To gain acceptance such goods had to be promoted. The age of mass advertising has been traced to the wall posters, made possible by improved printing technology making printing cheaper, and cheaper ways of making paper. By 1880 billposting was a major industry (Hamish Fraser, 1981). Taxation on newspaper advertising restricted the development of the printed page as a means of mass promotion until the 1850s, and even then newspapers were slow to respond to the opportunity. Brand names became a more practical option when trademark law began in 1875.

If mass production and a mass media had made it possible to see a rapid growth in the availability and demand for consumer goods, the nature of the new production method required a change in the method of distribution . No longer was it feasible for maker to meet user in the marketplace. Retailers who did not manufacture were essential if manufactured goods were to be distributed efficiently.

The transport revolution

A piece of the jigsaw that was needed before the picture of industrialised society could be complete was that of transportation. After Roman times the embryonic road system they had created fell into disrepair. The Vikings rejuvenated coastal shipping after they settled in Britain and France, but it was not until the 18th century that any real improvements in inland transportation took place.

Waterways

By 1600 the length of navigable rivers in Britain was estimated to be no more than 700 miles (Rolt, 1973). A number of ingenious methods such as locks and sluices were developed to extend the access afforded by nature. By 1750 the length of navigable waterway had grown to 1,400 miles (Duckham, 1983). The first canals were being built around this time. By 1800 a network of over 2,000 miles was available, largely for the movement of bulky goods such as coal, but soon used for distributing manufactures. By 1830 the network had developed to approximately 4,000 miles long when the innovation of the railway superseded the canal.

Railways

Experiments with horse drawn carriages running over wooden rails were carried out in the 1700s but the development of steel rails and the steam engine ensured the growth of a railway network in the 19th century. At its peak, a century later, railway track extended for over 20,000 miles, a system five times bigger than the canal system and one that offered a faster and cheaper means of transport for both goods and passengers.

The canal system first complemented the railways and indeed was often owned and operated by them. But by 1830 rail engines capable of speeds of 20 mph were available. By the 1880s speeds rose to 40 mph and the fate of inland canals, even those wide enough to accept motorised barges, had been sealed (Barker and Savage, 1974).

Local railways began in London in the 1860s. The Metropolitan railway linking Paddington with Farringdon Road opened in 1863. What is now the London Underground was born but early travellers might have preferred the current crush in today's electric trains to the smoke from the steam engines used when the underground railway first began.

The roads

Few goods can move for an entire journey solely by water or rail. Some element of road transport is inevitably involved. After Roman times the self-sufficient manorial system had little use for well-constructed roads. Some maintenance of roads was traditionally undertaken by the Church and in 1555 individual parishes were given the responsibility. Parishioners had to do the work unpaid and the duty was never a popular one. An alternative system of toll roads, the turnpikes, began to evolve. Separate Acts of Parliament were required for each and between 1750 and 1770 there was an ever-increasing number of these (Albert, 1983). By 1838 22,000 miles of turnpike existed and 106,000 miles of ordinary road (Barker and Savage, 1974).

The turnpikes were often the focus of civil dispute because of the tolls and because local labour still had to be provided free by parishioners. Once the law requiring free labour was repealed, turnpikes fell into disrepair. It was only with the invention of tarmac, used extensively from 1902, that the building and maintenance of a really effective road system became possible, using local and national government funding. Fig 1. 2 presents data on the length of each of the three systems, road, railway and canal from 1750 to 1980. It shows how the coming of the railway coincides with the mass market towards the end of the 19th century. The road system, while extensive, was not usable throughout the year until the beginning of the 20th century.

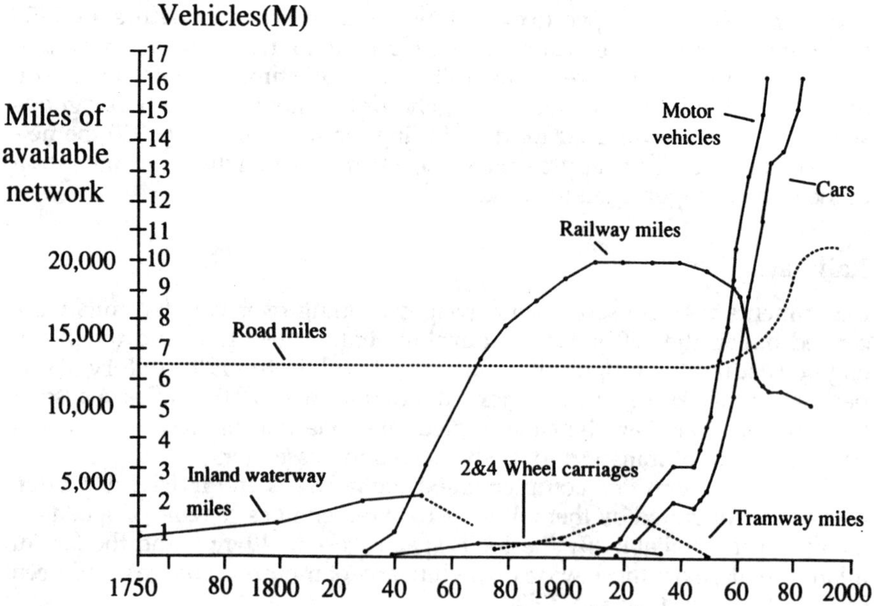

Figure 1. 2 The transport network (*sources:* various, plus author's estimates)

Because of the poor condition of most roads outside of the few major cities, packmules offered the only flexible, if expensive, means of transport in the Middle Ages. But by 1630 regular coach services were operating between major cities. The horse remained the major source of motive power on land well into the 20th century, by which time some 2 million were in use. In 19th-century cities the horse-drawn carriage was the main means of transport for the middle and upper classes; others mainly walked or went by river boat. By the end of the century there were probably 400,000 two- and four-wheel carriages in use. As late as 1891 some 22,000 private carriages were licensed in London. In 1896, 11,000 horse-drawn cabs plied for hire (Hobhouse, 1975). Cheaper public transport in the cities became commonplace in the late 19th century with horse buses but mechanisation, first with the tramways and later the bus and car, added to the speed and reliability of transport. By 1924 some 2,624 miles of tramway had been built, which, in Fig 1. 2, seems insignificant until one realises that they were solely within the major cities.

An even more significant event was the exploitation of the internal combustion engine for cars, lorries and the bus. The running costs of a car were lower than those of a horse but the adoption of the car was slowed by the Red Flag Act of 1865 which limited speeds to 2 mph in town and 4 mph in the country and which required someone to walk in front of the vehicle holding a red flag. Speed limits were raised to 12 mph in 1895 and to 20 mph in 1903. By 1914 horse carriages still outnumbered cars although public transport had been largely motorised. From 1950 the number of motor vehicles increased almost exponentially, but while this also served to change much of the shape of retail business, it was the railways which probably had more to do with the next significant change in the retail part of the distribution system, the advent of the multiples. Before this is discussed, the role of the wholesaler needs to be introduced as a significant modification to the entire system that prevailed prior to the industrial revolution.

The wholesaler

The origin of wholesaling as an activity can be found in the medieval merchants whose role it was to trade large quantities of merchandise between different regions or between different countries. Although merchants were not manufacturers, they formed guilds to regulate and protect their activities. Many became very powerful, some acted as bankers to the rulers of the times, some became rulers themselves. The financing role of the wholesaler was retained into the modern era. A wholesaler would pay a manufacturer or farmer for goods and then allow a retailer credit until the goods were sold (Stacey and Wilson, 1958) acting in effect as the financier for the supply chain. In addition any wholesaler performs a distributive role acting as an intermediary between smaller manufacturers and smaller retailers who could not justify the cost of trading with each other directly.

Jefferys (1954) suggests that wholesalers in the 19th and 20th centuries also replaced much of what had been, traditionally, retail activities such as the grading and packeting of food. Retailing had been a skilled activity. The shopkeeper would need to be knowledgeable about the goods he or she sold to avoid costly mistakes in buying. One reason why these skills were no longer relevant to the retailer was the change in the source of much of the merchandise they sold. At the end of the 19th century Britain accounted for about half of all world trade, being the first country to industrialise and the one major source of manufactured goods. Countries that Britain traded with often paid for their imports of manufactured goods with exports of cheap food. These arrived necessarily in bulk and needed fast and reliable distribution. Retailers such as the Argentine Beef Company came into being at about this time.

Wholesale markets, such as Smithfield for meat, Billingsgate for fish, Leadenhall for poultry and Covent Garden and Smithfield for fruit and vegetables could trace their origins to Roman times (Borer, 1968). As the volumes of imported food grew so these markets increased in size and others were developed in the provinces. Commodity markets were set up to trade tea, wool, fur, metal and grain as Britain developed as an international trading centre.

Merchants, historically, guarded their control over various trades by restricting membership to their professional groups and in particular sought to exclude retailers from wholesale activities (Willan, 1976). This led inevitably to accusations of profiteering. Indeed one of the motivations for the setting up of both the English and Scottish Cooperative Wholesale Societies in 1863 and 1868 respectively is said to be that existing wholesalers were making undue profit (Kinloch and Butt, 1981). The power of wholesalers and the trade associations they formed with manufacturers became an issue in the 20th century. Marks & Spencer, for example, found difficulty in obtaining supplies directly from the manufacturer. In one incident the production manager of what is today a major supplier to M & S was sacked for dealing directly with them (Rees, 1985). The power of the Millinery Distributors Association can be judged by the agreement that manufacturers, who sold to wholesalers, could not sell directly to retailers and vice versa (Stacey and Wilson, 1958). The distinction, however, between a wholesaler and a retailer was not always as clear as these restrictions might imply. Debenhams, for example, acted as both a wholesaler and a retailer from their early days (Corina, 1978) as did Tesco (Corina, 1971) and many other 'retailers' (Alexander, 1970). Some provincial retailers would buy regularly from London stores and, in earlier centuries, hawkers and other street traders would often buy from fixed shop retailers.

During the 20th century the power of the pure wholesaler began to decline. By 1950 only a quarter of wholesaler transactions were with retailers, the rest being with other wholesalers or large agencies such as government departments. Stacey and Wilson (1958) offer various explanations for the wholesaler's loss of control over distribution channels. For perishable merchandise there had been pressure to reduce the time foodstuff spent in the distribution system. For products that might need servicing or repair, direct contact between retailer and manufacturer could be important. But the central answer is likely to be a far simpler one: wholesalers are not necessary in a distribution channel where manufacturer and retailer concentration is high enough to make direct contact economic. Certain wholesalers such as those serving independent grocers exist today because of the low concentration on one side or other of the distribution system. The distribution system varied depending upon the product but from about 1850 to the turn of the

20th century, the dominant overall pattern can be represented by Fig 1. 3 – the wholesaler was very much in control.

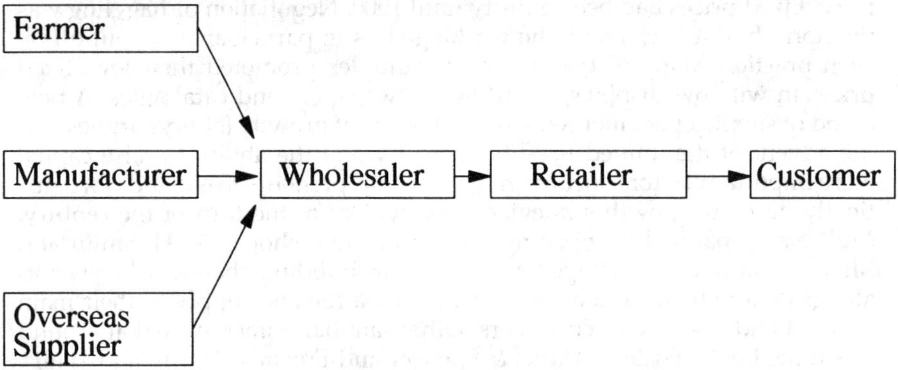

Figure 1. 3 Schematic of dominant distribution channels, 1850–1900

The producer/retailer had all but vanished from the scene and many retailers were isolated from the source of their goods by the powerful wholesale interests. Retailing had become a largely deskilled activity, totally reactive to the distribution system it served. There were many exceptions to this generalisation but the majority of retailers were small businesses buying from large wholesalers. Many retailers still traded from market stalls either in the street or in the market halls constructed in most industrial towns and cities. Street trading was common practice for those without even a stall. Pedlaring was a licensed activity from the 18th century when some 2,000 licences were in use each year, a figure that probably underestimates the number of pedlars quite substantially. The *Census* of 1851 identified 30,000 pedlars while a social historian of the time (Mayhew, 1851) claimed there were 13,600 in London alone. Mayhew put the number of costermongers, or barrow boys, at 30,000 in London. In addition there were 13,600 sellers of chickweed, crockery, second-hand clothes, live animals and coal. Street trading and pedlaring were occupations of last resort but Michael Marks, the founder of Marks & Spencer, started as a pedlar before acquiring a market stall and Jack Cohen, the founder of Tesco, began commercial life as a stall holder.

The rise of the multiple

At the turn of the 20th century there were few large retail businesses. Many were single shops or stalls. The market share of multiple retailers, those with ten or more outlets, was around 5% of all retail sales. But this share rose steadily throughout the century as Fig 1. 4 illustrates. Fig 1. 4 was constructed using a variety of sources of data and by merging different data series. The precise levels of market share may not therefore be exact, but the trend is undeniable, as is the acceleration in the early 1960s of the share of multiple retailers.

Jefferys (1954) suggests a number of features of a multiple retail business that gave it a source of competitive advantage over other retail formats:

economies of scale in buying; and economies of standardisation in selling and in administration. Many leveraged their cost advantage by selling on price. Fixed prices had been a rarity until 1900. Negotiation or haggling was the norm but, it is claimed, the working class in particular were put off by such practice. Many of the emergent multiples promoted their low, fixed prices in window displays, hoardings, newspapers and catalogues. A new breed of shopkeeper emerged with ambitions of growth. Jefferys argues that the advent of the limited liability company and the ability to raise capital were important factors encouraging such entrepreneurs to expand. Two distinctly different growth strategies were evident at the turn of the century. Multiples expanded by opening more and more shops. W. H. Smith and Menzies started as newsagents in the 1850s building chains of businesses alongside a railway system that guaranteed a reliable supply of their main product and a source of customers. Other familiar names started at around this time: Boots, Fosters, Marks & Spencer and Freeman Hardy and Willis. Most appealed to the growing affluence of the working class by emphasising low prices.

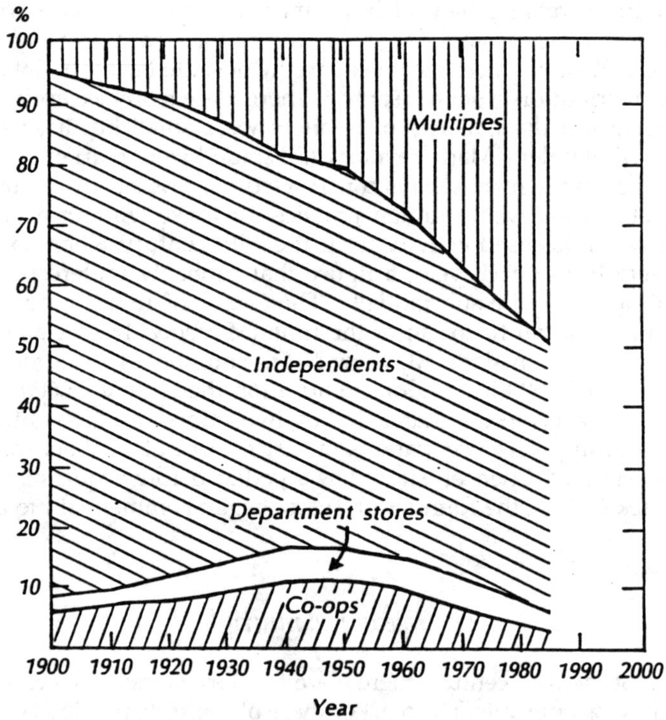

Figure 1. 4 British retail trends (*source:* Davies and Harris, 1990)

An alternative strategy was followed by the department store. Many had once been small drapers but had recognised the potential of adding more and more product lines. Their appeal was to the middle classes, including the new breed of manager who were themselves a product of the industrial revolution. Ferry (1960) credits the Frenchman Aristide Boucicaut with running the first true department store, Bon Marché, in Paris, which opened in

1852, although others soon appeared in most leading cities in the world. But as Fig 1. 4 implies the department store format has never been a dominant force in British retailing. True the distinction between a department store these days and a multiple such as Marks & Spencer is not that obvious. The true department store does its buying at store level by department, each operating as a business within a business.

In America the department store has been more successful, accounting for over a quarter of all retail sales. One reason may well be the different scale of the two countries. In Britain distance is not an issue and duplicating a similar retail format in every sizeable town and servicing it from a central location is not that difficult a task to manage logistically. As will be discussed in the next chapter, the centralised multiple would find it relatively easy to exert its buying power over the other members of the distribution chain but a number of legal changes favoured the growth of multiples in Britain, the most significant being the abolition of Resale Price Maintenance (RPM).

RPM was a system whereby suppliers of a product could fix a minimum or actual selling price. The concept was enshrined in British law in the Restrictive Trade Practices Act of 1956. In 1955 it was estimated that half of all retail sales were subject to RPM (Stacey and Wilson, 1958). In America the Robinson Patman Act of 1936, amended by the Clayton Act, was concerned with preventing anything that might tend to prevent competition (Lewison and Delozier, 1986). In practice this meant that any discounts given to retailers by manufacturers would only be legal if the discount could be justified by an actual saving in cost. Furthermore negotiations on price between manufacturer and retailer had to be done regionally.

Throughout the world similar legislation has existed or still exists. Its effect is to negate the negotiating power of the large retailer. The justification for such legislation is nearly always the same, to ensure the survival of the small independent shopkeepers whose presence might be important to the local community. At the time of writing some elements of RPM persisted in Britain. The Net Book Agreement acted as a constraint over retailers' discounting of book prices. The Publishers Association argued strongly for the Net Book Agreement because of the threat posed to the existence of small, specialist bookstores – not to their own profits of course.

Lobbying by retailers such as Tesco in the 1960s and customer enthusiasm for anything that lowered prices, lead to the virtual abolition of RPM in Britain in 1964 (Corina, 1971).

Social change and economic growth

Retailing exists solely because the customer is willing to spend money. The retail sector will stand to benefit from growth in consumer wealth and in consumer numbers. Fig 1. 5 presents statistics on the rise in total population, real consumer expenditure in general and in shops specifically. It also presents the number employed in total and, specifically, in retail. The data series are not all complete from the 18th century but the rises in population and consumer expenditure are clear enough. What is equally notable is the negligible increase in the number of retail employees, implying that the main cost of supporting a retail business, labour, has been falling.

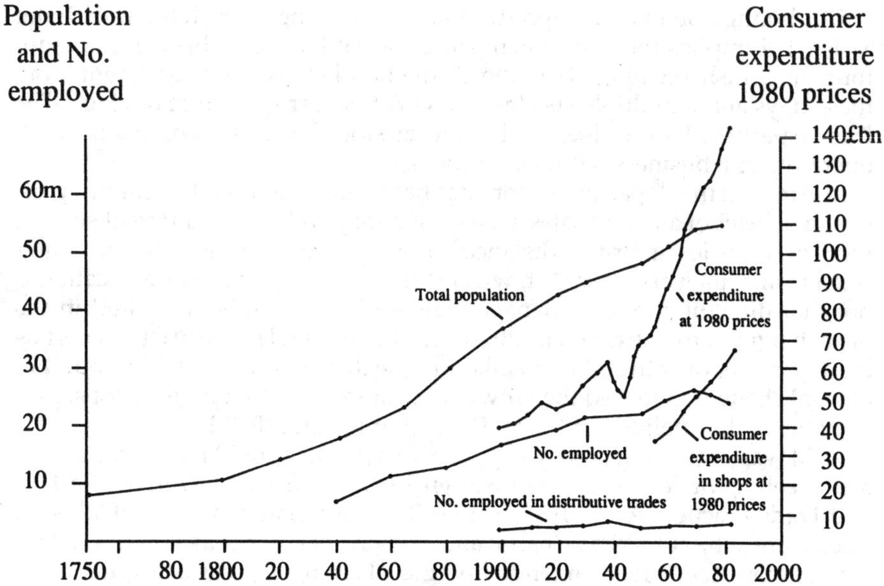

Figure 1. 5 Social change (*sources: Economic Statistics 1900–1983*, Liesner; *Abstract of British Historical Statistics*, 1985, Mitchell, 1962)

The increase in population masks the greater significance of where they lived. Urbanisation forced significant change on the distribution system. The population of Manchester grew by 236% from 1800 to 1850. By 1901, 30 British cities had populations over 100,000 inhabitants. However working for wages in the new industrial cities did not always mean it was easy to use that wealth. Many workers were paid with tokens rather than money and the only place to exchange tokens or 'truck' for goods was in the company-owned store. In 1887 'truck' payments were made illegal but the formal money system was still in its infancy. Although England had established a central bank back in 1694, all banks were free to issue their own, sometimes less than reliable, banknotes until 1884 (Heidensohn, 1979). By the 20th century the money system was better established but consumer credit was still difficult to obtain for the working classes. Some retailers would extend credit, particularly those selling door to door. For others it was the pawnshop, a feature of city life until quite recently (Tebbutt, 1983). Later years brought hire purchase and then credit cards. Buying goods in shops was never easier. Fig 1. 5 would imply a boom in the retail sector this century and a proliferation of retail activity.

Development of retailing

Retailing had become a separate activity that took place in fixed shops. Might it be logical to expect that the number of such shops would increase? As Fig 1. 6 reveals this has not been the case. The graph relies on scaling the number of residential shops recorded by Jefferys (1954) to match the data from the 1911 *Census* on total shop numbers, but it does appear likely that total

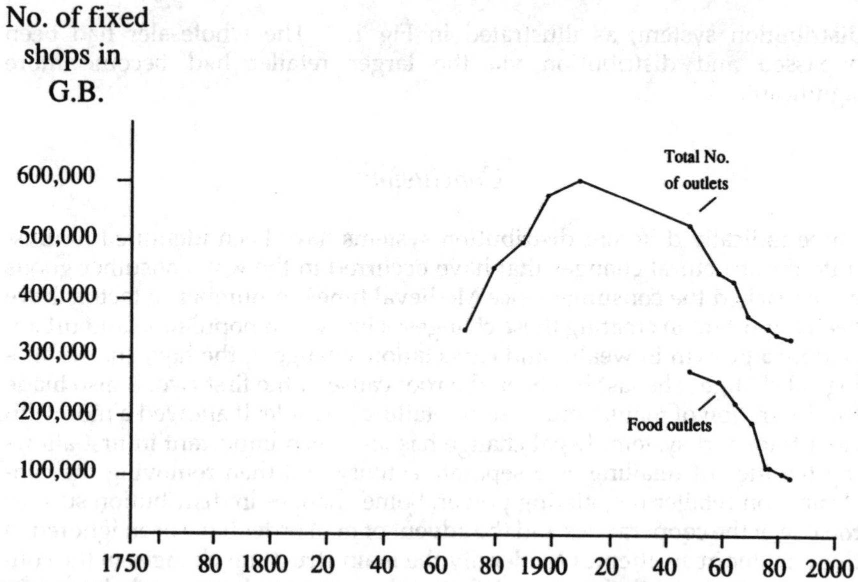

Figure 1. 6 Changes in retail outlet numbers (*sources:* Jefferys, 1954; *Census of Distribution*, 1971; Retail Enquiry, 1976–88)

numbers of fixed shops peaked early this century, thereafter to decline. What was happening was an increase in average shop size as retailers became less specialised and had more to sell. In some countries it is difficult or impossible to build larger shops because of regulation or planning processes that favour the smaller shop, but this was not the case in Britain. This in turn provided retailers with economies of scale and scope. Self-service, introduced relatively late into Britain, ensured that labour costs did not rise. But the driving force behind the move to larger, fixed shops was increased wealth and the change in expectation this created in the mass of the population. Who would now be satisfied with having to shop in the open air moving from one small market stall to another? The ever larger fixed retail outlet became the norm by the 1950s and the owners of many of these businesses now dealt directly with the manufacturer creating another significant change in the

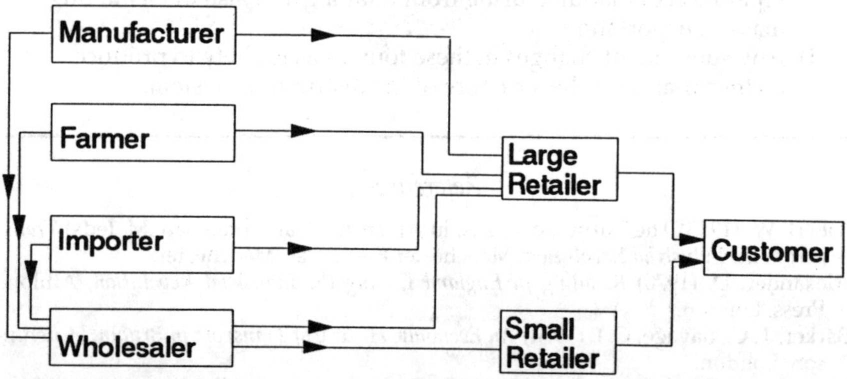

Figure 1. 7 Schematic of dominant distribution channels, 1900 to present day

distribution system, as illustrated in Fig 1.7. The wholesaler had been bypassed and distribution via the larger retailer had become more significant.

Conclusion

Three radically different distribution systems have been identified to illustrate the structural changes that have occurred in the way consumer goods have reached the consumer since Medieval times. A number of factors have been important in creating these changes: a growth in population and urbanisation; a growth in wealth and expectation; change in the law; and technological change. The last has been the root cause of the first two. It also made the separation of manufacture from retailing possible. It allowed a more efficient transport system. Legal change has also been important in first allowing the idea of retailing as a separate activity and then removing the constraints on retailer negotiating power. Some changes in distribution such as the rise of the cooperatives and the advent of mail order have been ignored in this chapter in an attempt to identify the main structural changes in the consumer market and their causes. What such an approach cannot do is explain fully the rise of first manufacturer power and then retailer power within the distribution system shown in Fig 1.7 since the Second World War. Those issues are the starting point for Chapter 2. Before then a case study tracing the historical development of one major retail multiple, Marks & Spencer, is presented to illustrate many of the points raised in Chapter 1 and some further issues that provide a platform for Chapter 2.

Keypoint summary

1) There have been a number of radical changes in the way consumer goods have been distributed since pre-industrial times.
2) Legal, social and economic factors have helped shape the structure of the distribution system.
3) Technology change had also been highly influential in allowing a separation of manufacturing from retailing and also in facilitating mass transportation.
4) Any subsequent changes in these four areas is likely to produce further change in the structure of the distribution system.

References

Albert, W. (1983) The Turnpike Trusts, in Aldcroft, D. and Freeman, M. (eds) *Transport in the Industrial Revolution*, Manchester Free Press, Manchester.

Alexander, D. (1970) *Retailing in England During the Industrial Revolution*, Athlone Press, London.

Barker, T. C., Savage, C. I. (1974) *An Economic History of Transport in Britain*, Hutchinson, London.

Blencowe, R. W., Lower, M. A. (1979) *The Diary of a Georgian Shopkeeper*, Oxford Uni-

versity Press, Oxford.
Borer, C. B. (1968) *England's Markets*, Abelard-Schuman, London.
Brown, J. (1986) *The English Market Town*, Crowood Press, Marlborough.
Corina, M. (1971) *Pile it High Sell it Cheap*, Weidenfeld and Nicolson, London.
Corina, M. (1978) *Fine Silks and Oak Counters*, Hutchinson Benham, London.
Davis, D. (1966) *A History of Shopping*, Routledge and Kegan Paul, London.
Davies, G., Harris, K. (1990) *The Independent Retailer*, Macmillan Education, Basingstoke.
Duckham, B. F. (1983) Canals and River Navigations, in Aldcroft, D. and Freeman, M. (eds) *Transport in the Industrial Revolution*, Manchester Free Press, Manchester.
Ferry, J. W. (1960) *A History of the Department Store*, Macmillan, New York.
Hamish Fraser, W. (1981) *The Coming of the Mass Market, 1850–1914*, Macmillan, London.
Heard, N. T. (1973) *International Fairs*, Dalton, Sudbury.
Heidensohn, K. (1979) *The Book of Money*, Macdonald Educational, London.
Hobhouse, H. (1975) *A History of Regent Street*, Macdonald and James, London.
Jefferys, J. B. (1954) *Retail Trade in Britain 1850–1950*, Cambridge University Press.
Kinloch, J., Butt, J. (1981) *History of the Scottish Cooperative Wholesale Society Limited*, CWS, Manchester.
Lewison, D. M., Delozier, M. W. (1986) *Retailing* (2nd Ed) Charles Merrill, Columbus, Ohio.
Mayhew, H. (1851) London Labour and the London Poor 1851, in Rubinstein, S. (ed) *The Street Trader's Lot, London 1851*, Sylvan Press, 1947.
Rees, G. (1985) *St Michael, A History of Marks and Spencer*, Pan Books, London.
Rolt, L. T. C. (1973) *Navigable Waterways*, Arrow Books, London.
Sorokin, P., Merton, R. (1937) Social time, a methodological and functional analysis, *American Journal of Sociology*, Vol 42, p 615.
Stacey, A. H., Wilson, A. (1958) *The Changing Pattern of Distribution*, Business Publications, London.
Tebbutt, M. (1983) *Making Ends Meet: Pawnbroking and Working Class Credit*, St. Martin's Press, New York.
Willan, T. S. (1976) *The Inland Trade*, Manchester University Press.
Winstanley, M. J. (1983) *The Shopkeepers World 1830–1914*, Manchester University Press.

Case Study: MARKS & SPENCER UK

To illustrate the many changes that have taken place in retailing, a case study is included on the historical development of Marks & Spencer. Their evolution from a single market stall to the beginning of a multinational company is a story of sustained growth. M & S, as they are better known, have been a model for many other retail businesses worldwide, and they will be used as a reference point throughout this book to illustrate many of the points that will be made. The author's view is that this one retailer offers a blueprint for much of the future relationships between manufacturer and retailer. Hence the emphasis given here to one company.

An outline history

Michael Marks emigrated to England from Eastern Europe in around 1882. He worked as a pedlar in the north of England but in 1884 he took a stall in the open market at Leeds. Other stalls followed, all trading under the sign 'Don't ask the price – it's a penny'. Marks later took space in the Leeds covered market hall and by 1890 was operating five of his penny bazaars and a warehouse, all within a short train ride, in a number of northern towns.

In 1894 Marks joined forces with Thomas Spencer, an accountant who worked with one of Marks' suppliers, Dewhirsts. By 1900 the Marks and Spencer partnership had 36 branches including 12 shops as well as the bazaars. The business was centred on Manchester but had already spread south with branches in London.

Michael Marks had died in 1907, just two years after his partner Thomas Spencer. Their partnership had been turned into a private limited company in 1903, with ownership divided between the Marks and Spencer families. Marks' son Simon was born in 1888. In 1915 Simon Marks married the sister of his school friend, Israel Sieff. By 1926 the two brothers-in-law, Simon Marks and Israel Sieff, were established as the Chairman and Vice Chairman of the company. Marks & Spencer became a public limited company in that same year and the two brothers-in-law stayed at the helm of the business until the 1960s.

Some of the company's growth came from acquisition in the early days, for example of the London Penny Bazaar company in 1913. A third of all Marks & Spencer branches were by then in the London area and in 1924 the company moved its headquarters from Manchester to the capital city. The original bazaars were gradually replaced by superstores usually in prime high-street sites. By the 1940s Marks & Spencer had become established as something of a British Institution. The St Michael brand name had been chosen in 1928 for textile products of their own specification to complement the St Margaret label from their main hosiery supplier, Corah. Earlier the business had prospered mainly by selling branded goods but the St Michael 'own-brand' soon came to dominate sales.

M & S had become Britain's leading retailer. Perhaps more notably they had grown to and retained that position over 100 years despite quite dramatic changes in the social and economic structure of their marketplace.

M & S had exported its St Michael products around the world well before they opened their first store abroad, in Canada, in 1972. European initiatives in France and Belgium began in 1975 and the acquisitions of two American chains, one clothing and one food, were announced in 1988. By this time the company owned nearly as many stores outside of Britain as within its home base. Exports, often to locally owned shops, went to some 30 countries, but sales in the home market still accounted for over 90% of turnover.

Marks & Spencer stores

Exhibit 1 graphs the rise in store numbers from the first market stall in 1884 to a chain of 288 in 1991. (Data prior to 1928 is relatively scant and depends largely on the diaries of the owners.) The number of stores has not grown much since the late 1930s but, as Exhibit 2 reveals, the typical store size has tripled over the last 50 years. The sales area available to the company, Exhibit

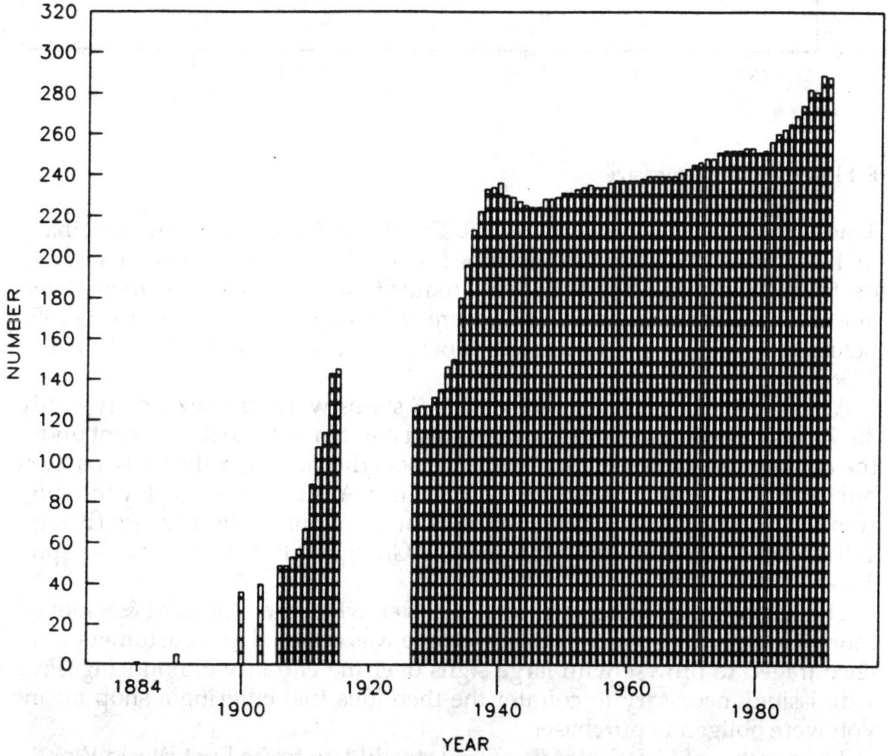

Exhibit 1 Number of stores

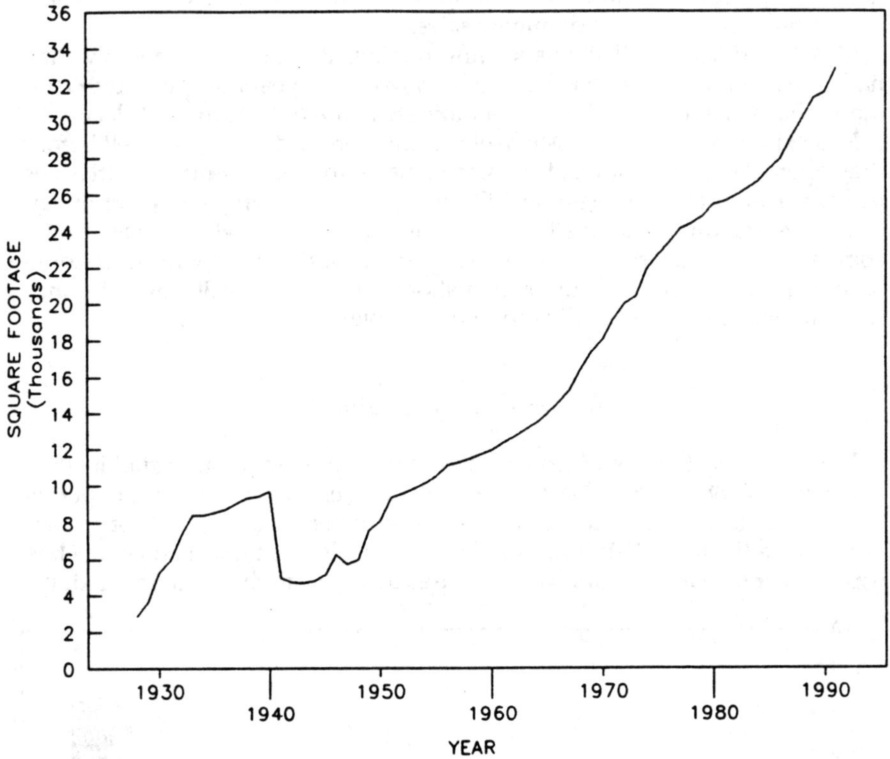

Exhibit 2 Average store size

3, has grown steadily since the 1920s. The 1939/45 war was a severe setback to the company's physical growth. Some 100 stores were damaged, 16 destroyed and many buildings were requisitioned by the government. Even after the war, controls on building were only fully lifted in 1954. It was 1953 before the company had the same footage available to it again as it had in 1938.

At the turn of the century most M & S shops were still bazaars, typically 30–70 feet in length, 6–13 feet in depth and painted red. Stock was kept under the counter or in a nearby lockup. Shoppers did not enter the early bazaars but stood outside to be served over a counter. At the end of the day the shop was shut up by pulling down shutters at the front of the bazaars (Briggs, 1984). One such store still survives in Granger Market, Newcastle upon Tyne.

The term Penny Bazaar was retained even when the typical M & S looked more like a modern shop. Counter service was retained and customers were encouraged to browse with large signs over the entrance announcing 'Free Admission', necessary to counter the then idea that entering a shop meant you were obliged to purchase.

The number of M & S sites increased steadily up to the First World War. In 1911 the company bought the Arcadia Bazaar Company and in 1913 a similar business owned by Estermans. By 1915 there were 145 stores but the number

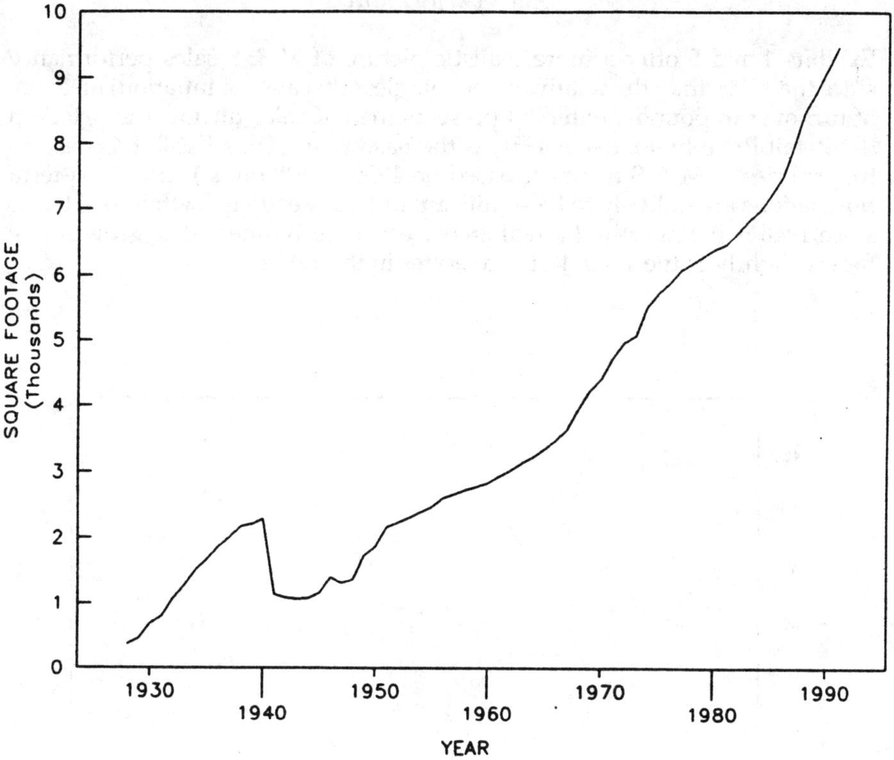

Exhibit 3 Total selling area

declined in the 1920s (Rees, 1969).

In 1926 M & S became a public limited company. The monies raised were spent on an extensive building and rebuilding programme in subsequent years. Between 1931 and 1935 alone 129 stores were built or rebuilt. The style of the new stores was significantly different. They were much larger. The word 'Superstore' was applied to them and the average size rose to 10,000 sq feet of selling space. Many stores were built around a simple cube, building in the potential to expand by adding extra floors or enlarging existing floors.

By the 1980s the potential to expand on existing, exclusively high-street sites had become very limited. The year 1986 saw the first out of town development in the Gateshead Metro Centre. A number of satellite stores began to appear concentrating on a limited product range such as children's wear, furniture and, in 1987, a chain of food-only stores was begun.

A greater emphasis on interior design was discernible in the 1980s. The austere look of the interwar years with its wooden flooring and simple presentation was totally gone. Instead carpeting, instore and window displays, pine-clad pillars and muted ticketing were more reminiscent of a department store.

Sales performance

Exhibits 4 and 5 offer a more realistic picture of M & S sales performance since the 1920s than the relatively meaningless (because of inflation) measure of turnover in pounds. Exhibit 4 presents the UK sales turnover indexed on the Retail Price Index using 1956 as the base year. (Thus Exhibit 4 presents the real rise in M & S turnover based on 1956 as 100 units.) Any short-term fluctuations are unlikely to be significant but the steady growth in real terms since 1946 is noteworthy (a real increase of over 8 times). The growth rate falters slightly in the 1970s but accelerates in the 1980s.

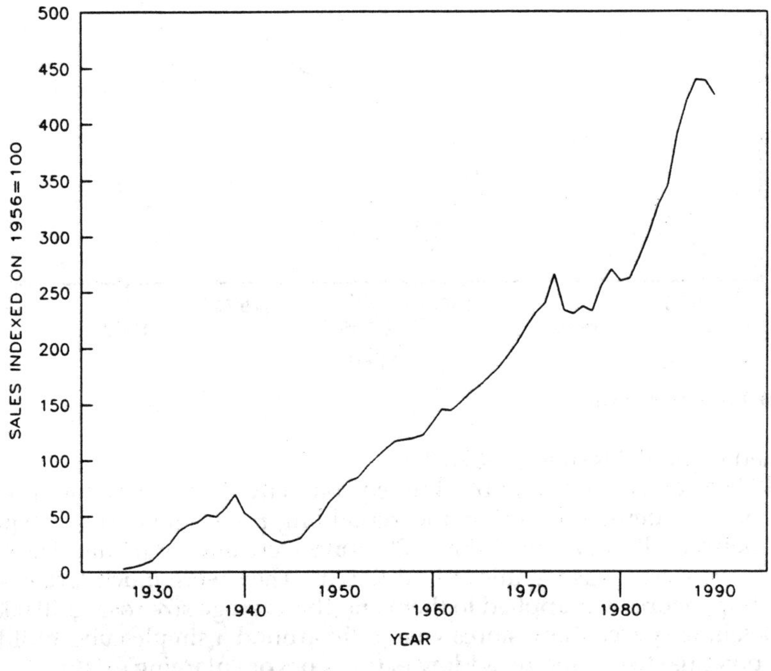

Exhibit 4 Retail turnover growth

Exhibit 5 examines the success of M & S in competing for all other demands on consumer expenditure. Not only has M & S benefited from the inevitable increase in disposable income over the years, it has increased the share that is spent in its premises. This is over a period where the proportion of total consumer expenditure in shops has declined – for example from over 55% to just over 40% from 1955 to 1983. The growth rate in the late 1940s and early 1950s is notable as is a similar increase in penetration rate in the 1980s.

The main asset of a retailer which does not own any manufacturing facility is its floorspace. How well that is made to work is the main determinant of retail success. Exhibit 6 attempts to assess the retailer's management of this asset by assessing the change in sales performance (adjusted for inflation by

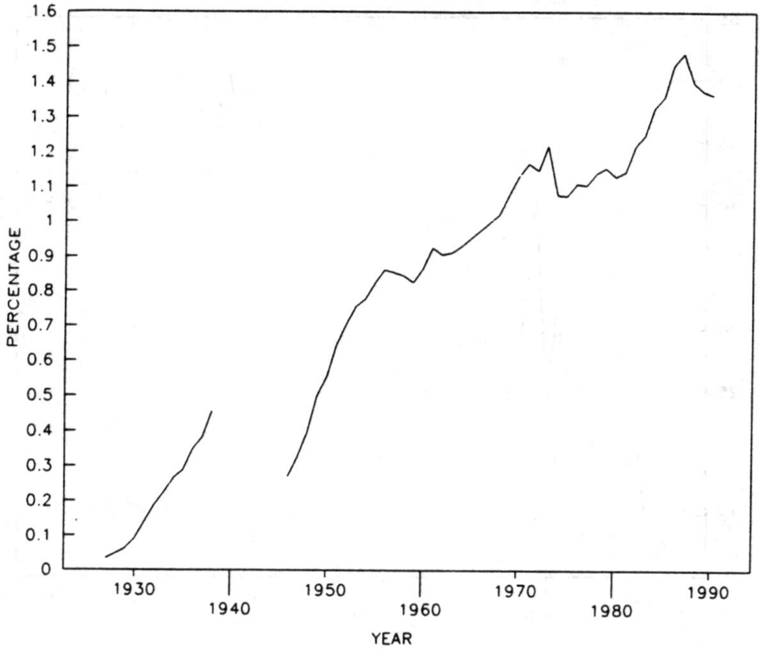

Exhibit 5 M & S sales as a % of consumer expenditure

dividing by the Retail Price Index for each year) for each square foot of selling space. Again short-term fluctuations, particularly in the war years, should be ignored.

The graph implies a steady improvement in real performance up to the 1970s as one explanation for the sustained growth in total sales. In other words M & S did not achieve growth merely by adding extra floorspace. In the 1970s growth in floorspace was a major contributor to overall growth but in the 1980s, sales per square foot starts to rise again and by 1987 has exceeded the levels in real terms that were achieved in the early 1970s. Between 1915, when the company had become a national chain, and 1991 turnover in *real* terms had increased by a factor of 164, more than two orders of magnitude.

Employees

In recent years employee costs in wages and salaries have represented some 9% of turnover. Social security, pensions and welfare costs increase this to over 11%. Exhibit 7 examines the trends in how well the staff resource has been employed since 1951 when data was first gathered expressing staff numbers as full-time equivalents. The graph shows a steady rise in deflated

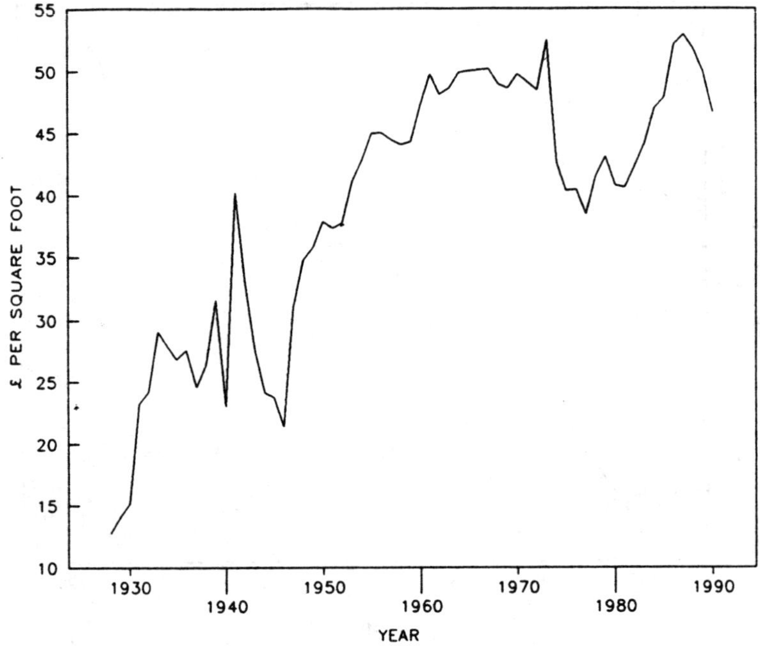

Exhibit 6 Real sales per square foot

sales per employee from the middle 1950s.

Part of this increase must be due to greater productivity and in particular a move to self-service in stores, but the growth from 1960s onwards is in part due to a steady increase in the use of part-time staff, as indicated by Exhibit 8. The graph here presents the ratio of the total number of people employed by M & S to the number of full-time equivalents this represents. The rapid rise in the ratio up until 1975/76 implies a substantial trend to employing more part-time staff, a trend visible across the industry. Sales per full-time equivalent employee peaked in 1973, followed by a fairly steady fall until the recovery in the 1980s.

Management

Human relations is an important concept within M & S, described by one author as 'a Private Welfare State', who also recounted the attempts of a union official to talk to staff (Rees, 1969). No-one turned up and M & S remained as they have always been, non-unionised. Whether the label is philanthropy or 'enlightened self-interest', M & S enjoy a high reputation for their treatment of staff.

The early days of the company were dominated by its founder Michael

Exhibit 7 Real sales per employee

Marks. There is no evidence that his partnership with Thomas Spencer in 1894 added much in the way of innovation. A certain William Chapman, a friend of Spencer's, became involved with the company after Spencer's death in 1905 and became the senior director in 1908, the year after Michael Marks' death. A struggle for control over the business between Simon Marks and Chapman lasted until 1917.

Simon Marks' relationship with Israel Sieff, his brother-in-law and boyhood friend, was clearly important in the development of the company, although it is Marks who emerges from what was written of them and by them as the dominant persona. Israel Sieff wrote of his friend and business associate 'From the beginning he was desperate to show he could succeed' and that he was 'egotistic enough to want his goods to have a distinct quality, second to none' (Seiff, 1970). Sieff joined the board in 1915 and Chapman, out manoeuvred by Marks, retired in 1917. With him went the son of Thomas Spencer who had not apparently played a major role in the business. This left Marks and Sieff, both only 29 years old, in control.

In 1924 Marks visited the United States to learn about the management principles used by American stores. He was impressed by the 'statistical control of stocks in relation to sales' and the 'rapid method of channelling information from the sales counter to the centre' (Sieff, 1970). Concepts such as identifying the relative sales of merchandise for the area they occupied were

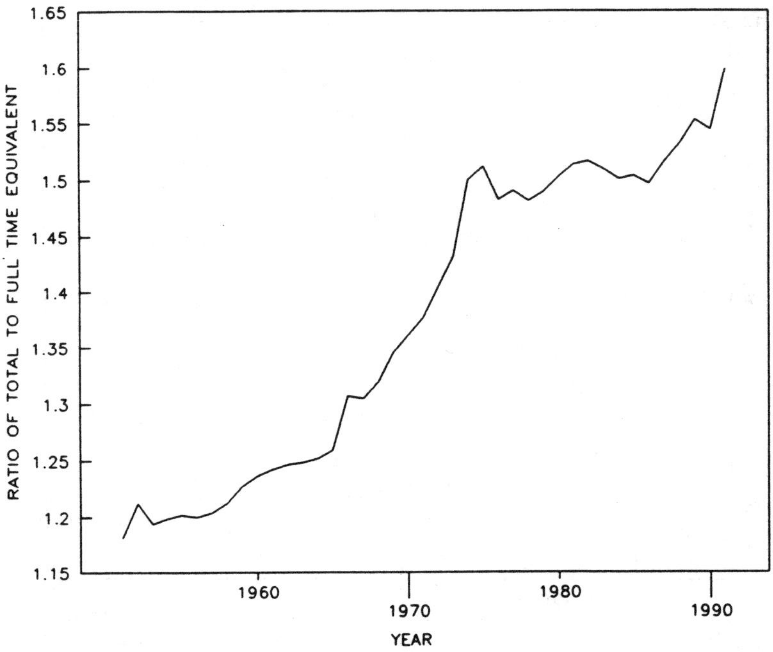

Exhibit 8 The growth in part-time employees

introduced on his return. Israel Sieff graduated in economics and helped found Political and Economic Planning in 1931 at Cambridge University. The respective skills and orientation of each man are evident in the way the company subsequently developed.

Simon Marks died in 1964 to be succeeded as Chairman by Israel Sieff until 1967. Israel's brother Edward held the role until 1972 when Israel's son, Marcus, who joined M & S in 1935, succeed him. In 1984, Derek Rayner, already Lord Rayner, succeeded as Chairman, the first chief executive in modern times not to have been a member of the family dynasty but nevertheless an employee since 1953. In 1988, Richard Greenbury was appointed to the new role of Chief Executive Officer, after 35 years with the company.

Product policy

For all practical purposes M & S sales are solely own brand. The St Michael name was hailed in 1988 as 'The UK's best-selling brand'. Their share of the British clothing market was 16% from selling 20% of UK clothing production. It is this product area that M & S had been most closely associated with. Any challenges to their position or any weakness in it are scrutinised by the business press. Yet M & S had shown a remarkable ability to move in and out of various product areas as Exhibit 9 reveals. Food sales moved from less than 15% of sales in 1957 to over 40% in 1985. Similar fluctuations can be seen in the war years when the company found itself in the catering business, providing hot food for those who could not expect a cooked meal at home. Turnover from catering quadrupled from 1941 to 1942. Catering disappeared in 1961 but returned in the Metro Centre store in the 1980s.

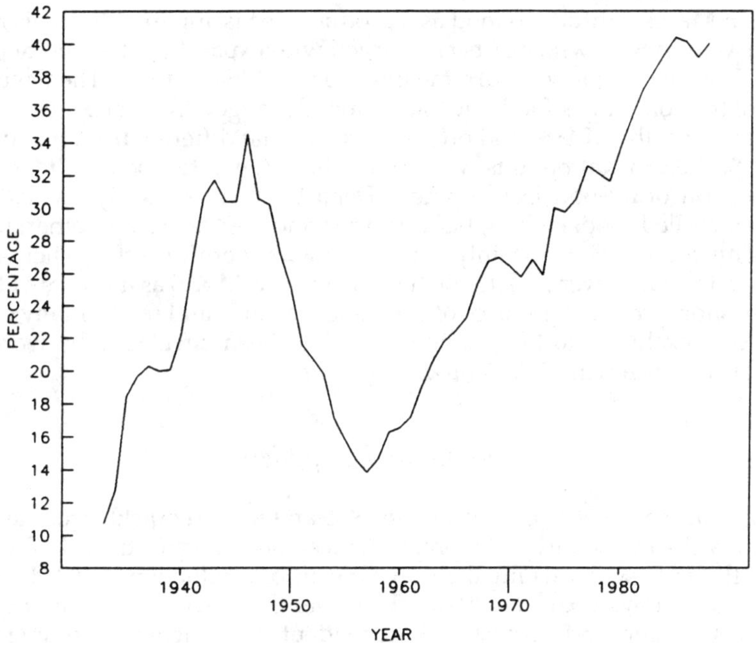

Exhibit 9 Food sales as a % of turnover

In the 1920s the company sold hardware, cutlery, china, toys, stationery and haberdashery and much more. The principle was not to specialise in terms of merchandise but to sell to a price. Up until 1908 the price point had been a penny. The emphasis was on finding goods at an acceptable quality to retail for a penny. The simple pricing policy moved to sixpence for a while but disappeared in the war years. It returned in the interwar years as 'nothing over 5 shillings'.

Although Simon Marks had returned to a clear price point he had also refocused the business: 'Our name used to be associated with cheap goods at limited prices from 1d to 6d. Now it was to be associated with rather more expensive goods, toys, clothing up to 5 shillings per article' (Sieff, 1986). He believed the business could learn from Woolworths who were selling a more compact range of goods in modern, large, well-lit and attractively laid-out stores while M & S's offer was, according to Israel Sieff, 'a confusing jumble of goods of all kinds varying in price from a penny to three pounds'.

In the 1930s the product range was gradually reduced so that by 1939 90% of turnover was in textiles and food, with textiles accounting for three times the volume of any other product category. The reduction in range did not affect total sales.

Volumes in individual lines increased substantially giving M & S considerable purchasing power. This power was used to bypass the wholesalers, who still dominated M & S supplies in 1926, and to deal directly with manufacturers. Some direct purchases had to be made in secret, such was the sensitivity of dealing directly with retailers within the manufacturing sector and especially with a penny bazaar.

Simon Marks' attitude to food as a product area is apparent from his reaction to Marcus Sieff who had been charged with expanding the food department: 'You're not going to turn me into a grocer' (Sieff, 1986). The development of the company's food offer subsequently lagged that in textiles.

In the 1930s the M & S food offer was somewhat different from that of the 1980s. Broken KitKat biscuits was a major line. A greater focus on food saw the creation of a Food Development Department in 1948. By the 1980s a range of chilled foods, wines, biscuits, fruit and vegetables and other, if not speciality foods, then certainly different foods were on offer. Their food prices in the 1980s were relatively high. Few used M & S as a source of their weekly shop – more as a source of convenience foods and treats. Many of the lines were exclusive to M & S, and some had been developed by working with farmers as much as food processors.

Working with suppliers

A textile laboratory was established in 1935 and moved quickly from testing what was already being sold to preparing technical specifications. M & S had a brief flirtation with owning their own means of production in 1937 by buying an interest in a textile convertor. However the practice of specifying raw materials, design and process to independent manufacturers became well established. M & S controlled without owning, due to their large purchasing volumes, leading to the label of a 'manufacturer in disguise'.

A Merchandise Development Department was created in 1936 and a Design Department charged with improving quality and design. In 1947 a Production Engineering Department was formed to assist suppliers in modernising their plant.

M & S worked not only with garment manufacturers and textile manufacturers but they also worked with companies such as ICI who produced synthetic fibres and dyestuffs. This involvement left the company well placed to take advantage of the mass fashion markets in the late 1930s and after the war. The company's target customer was the working-class woman who previously had not expected to be able to afford the design and quality on offer in their stores.

Standards of hygiene and sanitation had been very high in both stores, warehouses and in the operating plants of suppliers in the 1930s. Suppliers were also provided with detailed product specifications and M & S inspectors would assess a supplier's output against both the specification and, where appropriate, sealed samples from approved production.

Two views emerge of the relationship between the company and its suppliers, one of a retailer calling a tune that a supplier must dance to, and the other of a close partnership where the links are, according to Lord Rayner in 1987, 'fundamental to the success of our business'. The relationships with some suppliers dated back to the early days and by 1988 the company could claim to be working with over 900.

Credit

M & S had refused to accept credit cards such as Visa and Access but in 1985 issued their own chargecard. By 1988 2.2 million customers held the M & S card. Also in that year 13.4% of sales were made by using the card. The chargecard was heavily promoted during its launch in 1985. A magazine, free to cardholders, followed together with the innovations of special shopping evenings for cardholders in their local stores. Some 700 were held in 1987/88 alone. Data on cardholders offered the potential for direct mail for the promotion of, for example, a new venture into financial services.

Overseas operations

Marcus Sieff records that the moves by the British Labour Party in 1945 to increase nationalisation prompted M & S to look abroad. Export business had led to the formation of the Marks & Spencer Export Corporation in 1940 but the first corporate move abroad was to South Africa with an exchange of shares with Woolworths (no link to the American and British company of the same name). This shareholding ended in 1971 and interest switched to Canada with a 50% holding in People's Department Stores. An attempt to acquire all the share capital in 1974 ran foul of Canadian foreign investment regulations, limiting M & S to a 55% holding. People's had two subsidiaries, Walkers Stores and D'Allairds. The first became Marks & Spencer in 1976, a year after the next overseas initiative, this time in Europe. The first Paris store opened in 1975. Others followed elsewhere in France, Belgium, Eire and Hong Kong. In 1986 four D'Alliards ladies' fashion stores were opened in New York State. In 1988 the purchase was announced of Brooks Brothers menswear stores operating in the USA and 21 in Japan. With the Brooks Brothers purchase from the Campeau Corporation came exclusive rights to sell food in Campeau's American, 920-strong department store business. Later in 1988 came the announcement of the purchase of Kings Super Markets, a small American foodchain.

Distribution and service

M & S opened their first warehouse in Manchester before 1900 but their own involvement in physical distribution had never been great, preferring instead to contract out to third parties while retaining the right, as with suppliers of merchandise, to specify standards. In food retailing the emphasis on freshness led to changes to using airfreight for many imported lines and to the development of a chilled distribution system to support in particular their range of prepared meals.

By the 1980s much of the company's information system supporting the distribution of merchandise from suppliers to stores had been computerised. The company completed the installation of an EPOS system and a hand-held terminal system for stock control in-store in 1987/88. These changes merely echoed the introduction by Simon Marks in the 1930s of a weekly system of stock checking controlling the production and flow of goods from factory to shops that improved stockholding and availability.

Within their stores the variety chains as a group tended to have fewer staff and a less complex product offer than the department stores. It is doubtful whether M & S ever considered the concept of a floor walker whose role in the traditional department store had been mainly to welcome and direct customers entering the sales floor.

In Britain M & S had decided not to offer changing rooms to customers, preferring to emphasise a no quibble refund policy on returned goods. This policy was modified in the French stores in the 1970s where changing rooms had to be introduced early on and in Britain in the 1980s, first for menswear and subsequently more widely.

Company philosophy

A number of principles have been identified as encapsulating the business philosophy of Simon Marks and Israel Sieff. As articulated by Lord Sieff in 1966, they were as follows:

1) To offer our customers a selective range of high quality, well designed and attractive merchandise at reasonable prices.

2) To encourage our suppliers to use the most modern and efficient techniques of production and quality control dictated by the latest discoveries in science and technology.

3) With the cooperation of our suppliers, to enforce the highest standards of quality control.

4) To plan the expansion of our stores for the better display of a widening range of goods and for the convenience of our customers.

5) To simplify operating procedures so that our business is carried out in the most efficient manner.

6) To foster good human relations with customers, suppliers and staff.

By 1988 these six had become eight similar principles with the addition of a commitment to support British industry unless equivalent products were unavailable and an explicit statement about staff sharing in the success of the company.

Appraising Marks & Spencer's success

The guiding principles certainly describe M & S, but probably do not offer in themselves a blueprint for success. A number of attempts have been made to produce a business appraisal of the company. One of the most thorough is that by Tse in 1985 who linked the company's outstanding achievement to three 'obsessive concerns', which are quality/value for money/human relations.

To explain their success, Tse's book examines M & S using a number of perspectives drawn from academia and business, for example the eight managerial attributes that Peters and Waterman identified in their book *In Search of Excellence*. As articulated by Tse these were as follows:

- A bias towards action.
- Simple form and lean staff.
- Continued contact with customers.
- Productivity improvement via people.
- Operational autonomy to encourage entrepreneurship.
- Simultaneous loose – tight controls.
- Stress on one key business value.
- Emphasis on doing what they know best.

Another perspective Tse drew upon was Michael Porter's view of competitive strategy with its emphasis on competitive advantage, also argued by many writers on corporate strategy as a key to success. The approach stresses the need to emphasise those aspects of a business that usefully differentiate that business from its competition. Quality management became a focus of attention for academics in the 1980s concentrating on Japanese practice. As Tse points out, quality had been the focus of M & S since the 1930s. On people management Tse likens the M & S approach to the Theory Z approach of William Ouchi, typified by having employees of long standing, flexible management, participative or even collective decision making and with a broad concern for the welfare of employees.

One other perspective that might be useful in explaining the relative success of M & S is that of control. The company controls its sources of supply, closely monitors its marketplace through a Customer Service Department (handling 2,500 letters, parcels and phone calls each week) and monitors its own sales, and longer-term trends, through its Economic Planning Department.

Simplification of the business and concentrating on a limited range of distinctive competencies is another theme in modern management thinking. M & S's business has been simplified at least twice, once by Simon Marks who rationalised the product range in the 1930s, and once again in the 1950s when paperwork and bureaucracy were weeded out by concentrating on essential communication and estimation rather than on precise measurement.

References

Briggs, A. (1984) *Marks and Spencer 1884–1984. A Centenary History*, Octopus Books, London.

Rees, G. (1969) *St Michael: A History of Marks and Spencer*, Weidenfeld and Nicolson, London.

Sieff, I. (1970) *The Memoirs of Israel Sieff*, Weidenfeld and Nicolson, London.

Sieff, M. (1986) *Don't Ask the Price. The Memoirs of the President of Marks and Spencer*, Weidenfeld and Nicolson, London.

Tse, K. K. (1985) *Marks and Spencer. Anatomy of Britain's Most Efficiently Managed Company*, Pergamon Press, Oxford.

Other sources

Annual Reports, Marks & Spencer plc, London.

Archives of Marks & Spencer.

Retail Prices Indices 1914–1986, Department of Employment, HMSO, London.

2

THE RISE OF MANUFACTURER POWER

The purpose of this chapter is to investigate the origins and source of manufacturer power within the supply chain for consumer products. In Chapter 1 it was argued that the industrial revolution was the root cause of a separation of retailing from manufacturing. But because the retail trade was a fragmented collection of largely independent businesses and most manufacturers were also relatively small, wholesalers could exercise their power in the supply chain as the necessary intermediary between manufacturer, farmer or overseas supplier and the retailer. Resale Price Maintenance (RPM) aided the wholesaler, and subsequently the manufacturer, in controlling the retail sector. Such words as 'power' have been used thus far without any attempt to define what they really mean in the context of a marketing channel. It is useful at this stage to refer to academic research into the area for some clarity on what these concepts mean.

Academic research into manufacturer/retailer relationships

Academics have approached the issue of manufacturer/retailer relationships in a number of ways. Generally their conceptual framework has been one of 'distribution channels' in their totality, where issues in the distribution of industrial and consumer goods and even services are investigated as one, in the belief that, theoretically at least, it matters little what is distributed and what types of businesses and customers are involved. Manufacturer/retailer relationships have therefore been viewed by academic researchers as one aspect of a more general issue. Within this research are a large number of different perspectives, each designed to provide an understanding of why distribution channels form and behave in the way they do. The practitioner is generally less concerned with the why and more concerned with *what* to do in a given circumstance. Where the two interests overlap is in the desire to *understand* distribution channels. The academic may reject the pragmatic approach of the practitioner because of its absence of rigour and the practitioner reject the academic's approach because theory can appear too far removed from what actually happens. Nevertheless, at the very least, academic research can provide insights into practice and structures or frameworks that enable the practitioner to be more analytical about the issues facing business. Theory may be incomplete but at least it provides a starting point for better practice. For example we may not be able to understand perfectly why conflict occurs between members of a distribution channel and therefore predict when it will happen, but we may be able to identify likely causes of conflict and likely solutions to it.

So what have academics contributed thus far to our understanding of distribution channels? Gattorna (1978) provided a wide ranging review of the academic literature and suggested that there were a number of distinct perspectives therein, each of which provides an incomplete insight into distribution channels:

(i) The micro-economist, aiming to apply economic theory to the individual firm, gives us the idea of firms undertaking all of their own distribution for so long as the cost of getting it done outside is higher. Otherwise the business sheds such activities (vertical disintegration).

(ii) The institutional perspective points out that the existence of intermediaries can reduce the total number of transactions in a market and create benefits to customers by holding stocks of product. There may be a relationship between the number of levels of intermediary needed and the physical size of the lot of goods transferred; the smaller the lot, the larger the number of levels needed to achieve savings in transportation costs.

(iii) The approach of functional analysis, from the likes of Mallen (1973), suggests that different functions such as marketing are allocated to different channel members in such a way that provides the greatest benefit to the consumer *or* to the channel member with the most power. The overall goal is to achieve the lowest possible channel cost. Another functionalist, Bucklin (1966), sought to describe the role of each channel member in terms of five types of activity: physically moving goods; storing them; producing them; searching for a buyer or seller; influencing the buyer. One useful consequence of such an analysis is to see the consumer as possibly undertaking many of these activities. Few shoppers now expect home delivery for other than household durables, the shopper performs the physical movement. Encouraging bulk purchase may reduce the distribution system's need for storage. Self assembly furniture involves the buyer in production. Alternatively the distribution system could be changed to remove some of the shopper's role. Ready-prepared meals and restaurants remove the production role of cooking.

Gattorna singles out one other functionalist, Alderson, as introducing the concept of 'sorting', a role undertaken by wholesalers and retailers who sort out the offers of suppliers to build an assortment more useful to the customer.

(iv) Systems theory views the distribution channel as a series of objects and relationships, a single entity rather than a collection of discrete institutions.

(v) The behaviourial approach is allied to that of systems by examining the relationships between channel members. A number of concepts exist in this literature which, while rarely defined precisely, are still useful in developing understanding. Power, generally accepted as the ability to control the strategy of other channel members, is seen as a function of relative dependence. The dependent member of a channel is often the least powerful and the more susceptible to conceding to the wishes of other channel members. Power is difficult to measure absolutely, although perception of power can be assessed.

Gattorna suggested that conflict and cooperation are opposites in the context of channel operation. Conflict has its origins in situations where the actions of one channel member are inconsistent with the goals of another member, but it is a latent force, provoked by a particular incident or issue. Conflict is assumed to be, but is not necessarily, harmful. It can be dysfunctional and lead to inefficiency in the channel but it can also be constructive if the system contains mechanisms to resolve the conflict. Conflict at least means that a relationship exists and if the exit costs from the relationship are high, then critical areas of conflict must ultimately be resolved. Cooperation will occur when companies are better off with a solution to any problem than they are without one. If the exit costs from a relationship are low then the problem may not be resolved, the channel relationship just ends as one or other member withdraws.

Gattorna quotes Stern's work on leadership to infer that some centralised power is a prerequisite for 'orderly' behaviour in a channel. The leader is often the member with the greatest power, although the authority of one such member of the channel may not be accepted by others.

In this author's opinion the behaviourial approach to analysing distribution channels is the most useful to the practitioner and it is one that is referred to throughout this book, particularly the concept of 'power' and the nature of relationships between companies. How and why power has shifted in the supply chain for consumer goods is a central issue. The rise of the brand was the basis for the gradual evolution of manufacturer power.

The rise of the brand

In the latter half of the 19th century many producer/retailers divided their two functions into separate activities, but, as the following examples illustrate, the origins of many modern brands do not necessarily stem from a neat division into two activities by such businesses.

Alfred Bird opened his first shop in Birmingham in 1837, describing himself as an 'experimental chemist' (Foley, 1972). Bird's wife had an allergy to eggs, it seems, but was partial to custard. Neither could she tolerate yeast-based products. In 1843 Bird perfected a yeast substitute that was later to be called baking powder. Bird's Custard Powder soon followed. By 1850 the two products had achieved national distribution aided by some relatively modest advertising. In 1880 the first pictorial advertisements began to appear. Bird's son introduced packaging machinery into what was still combined retail and manufacturing premises in 1879, the year when his father died. The son began to appoint sales agents to replace his own selling activities – a move that was the foundation of a national salesforce. More significantly Birds became a brand manufacturer rather than a retailer, because the company decided it could expand far better by selling to other retailers rather than by opening other shops.

Another chemist, Jesse Boot, also began with a single shop, this time in

Nottingham in 1877. He too recognised the value of advertising and sent a bellringer touring the streets of the town promoting the fact that he sold soft soap at 4½ pence for two pounds weight, compared to prices of 4 pence a pound elsewhere (Boots, 1977). Boot's approach to business was to combine manufacturing and retailing operations, a strategy that persists to this day. He bought other branded products and retailed on price, giving discounts for volume. The original retail site became a centre for wholesale, retail and mail order. In 1885 a manufacturing division was begun. By 1933 the one-thousandth retail branch of Boots had opened but the manufacturing side had grown too. Boots today make brands that are sold by other retailers and use other manufacturers to make some of their own-brand goods. Their 1989 annual report listed brands such as Neurofen, Strepsils, Optrex, Sweetex, Farley and Ostermilk. Their No. 7 range of cosmetics is not sold in Britain by other retailers but is retailed in Finland, for example, by the S0K group. Boots also retails under its own name in the same way as many other retailers of own-label products.

Meshe David Osinsky was born in Kurkel in the Russian province of Kovno in 1885. In 1900 he emigrated to England and settled in Leeds to begin life as an unlicensed pedlar (Sigsworth, 1990). Meshe Osinky became first Maurice, and then Montague, Burton. A shop was opened, perhaps with the help of a loan from the landlord, a greengrocer, in Chesterfield. The business was solely retail, selling on price to the working classes. Another shop followed in Mansfield and then a factory in Leeds and another in Sheffield. By 1914 the company had 14 retail outlets and was selling goods it made in its own factories to other retailers. The number of factories and shops grew steadily, if at times uncertainly during the interwar recession and Burtons remained a manufacturer/retailer combine. By the 1970s Burtons was a major high-street presence with names including Burton, Top Man, Top Shop and Dorothy Perkins but the profitability of the tailoring division had faltered. By the 1980s Burtons had shed most of its production capacity. The brands they retailed were made for them not by them.

One last example of diversity in the evolution of branding is the story of Heinz. Henry Heinz was the entrepreneurial son of a brickmaker from Allegheny in the USA. The son grew horse-radish, bottled it and sold it to grocers and bakers. In 1875 Heinz moved to nearby Pittsburgh to produce three 'varieties' horse-radish, celery sauce and pickles (Potter 1959). Despite some major business problems the manufacturing business prospered. The most famous variety, Ketchup, was introduced in 1876. Gradually the business grew to the international force it is today. Heinz was never a retailer and had begun directly as a food processor.

These four examples illustrate the diverse origins of today's brands. The idea that some producer/retailers became pure retailers and others manufacturers is too simplistic a model of the complex process that occurred in the latter half of the 19th century. What is clear is that a number of entrepreneurs developed products, some of which were highly innovative but others more developments from what had always been available either from producer/retailers or by making them oneself. Mechanisation led to reduced cost of production but the key to growth for those manufacturers *without* retail premises was to ensure mass demand and distribution for *their* products, rather than those available from other manufacturers, wholesalers or retailers. De Chernatony (1989) claims that the early system of small manufacturers supplying local retailers served to produce variable quality. Wholesalers provided an answer to this problem by commissioning products to their specification in the late 19th century. But manufacturers became concerned about their reliance on wholesalers and sought to sell directly to retailers to ensure outlets for their increasing production capacities. The ability to offer low prices, because of large-scale manufacture, must have been one key needed to open the new channel, direct from manufacturer to retailer but the other two keys were the physical ability to sell economically directly to retailers and the creation of consumer demand for the product provided by the manufacturer, rather than the generic product itself.

Manufacturers needed to brand to distinguish their products and build a consumer franchise.

Branding

In 1878 it became possible in Britain to protect the name of one's product by registration. Case law evolved to discourage attempts to circumvent the use of a similar name or packaging by those unscrupulous enough to produce a near copy. This is known as passing off, the wrong committed by someone attempting to present their goods as if they were those of another. Branding became a legally protected activity. RPM was often applied to brands, giving them even greater protection. By 1938 an estimated 30% of consumer expenditure went on products subject to RPM (Edwards, 1966).

So what is branding and the significance of the brand? Jones (1986) quotes Kaldor's (1950) view that product branding by manufacturers and its associated advertising represented a way for manufacturers to speak over the heads of the retailer and to the ultimate buyer to achieve channel control. The same description is ascribed by Murphy (1987) to no less than H. G. Wells. Branding is closely associated with the product's design, labelling and particularly its name. Gardner and Levy (1955) argued in their seminal paper that a brand name is more than just a 'symbol employed to differentiate' and saw it as 'a complex symbol that represents a variety of ideas and attributes'. This complexity is seen as akin to a personality, an analogy repeated by King (1973) who suggested that products as mundane as toilet tissue could be made into brands with their own personalities.

Jones (1986) sees value to the customer/consumer of the brand because it represents a 'guarantee of homogeneity and quality' but he argues that purchasers receive more than just these functional benefits as they also obtain something less tangible for their money that is 'substantially psychic' a notion repeated by Kim (1990) to whom a brand is 'disembodied, abstract, ephemeral'. These intangible benefits are difficult to define, but Ryan (1989) suggests that one such is the feeling that the customer is 'doing the right thing' by buying the product, particularly in the eyes of one's peers.

Baker (1984) offers a definition of a brand that reflects as much the benefits to the marketer as to the user: 'a set of characteristics which clearly and readily differentiates it from all other products'. The ability of the brand name and the branding process to differentiate one manufacturer's offer from another, in a positive way, is a common theme among writers who have attempted to encapsulate the essence of branding (Kotler, 1988; de Chernatony and McWilliam, 1989; Ryan, 1989; Doyle, 1990; Murphy, 1990). Words just as frequently associated with brand or branding are 'quality' or 'quality guarantee' (Jones, 1986; Blackett, 1989; de Chernatony and McWilliam, 1989; McWilliam, 1989; Murphy, 1990). These two attributes, differentiation and quality, that a successful brand embraces, offer benefits to both supplier and consumer. Through differentiation the supplier is able to claim a unique offer that the consumer would need to consider on other than price. Through the inference of quality, the supplier is able to reassure the purchaser about his or her decision to buy. The consumer rewards the provider by buying more often and/or by paying a premium and is rewarded in turn by the psychic benefits the brand uniquely symbolises, particularly in front of his or her peers.

Branding is seen as such an important aspect of product management that brand names can be valued for sale (Murphy, 1990; or for licence, Perrier, 1989). Differences in accounting practice between countries mean that while brand values can often be capitalised as goodwill in the balance sheet, in many countries the value oddly enough has to be depreciated, over 40 years in the USA but over as few as 5 in Japan. However a brand name enjoys a separate financial existence from any physical product. When Cadbury Schweppes sold Premier Brands to its management, the right to use the Cadbury brand name on certain products was part of the deal, even though Cadbury Schweppes relied upon the same name themselves. The brand name Benson & Hedges is used by two cigarette companies. But just putting a name to a product and advertising it is no guarantee of successful branding. Davies (1992) proposed four tests for the existence of a brand, Fig 2. 1, that can be used to assess whether branding or merely naming has occurred.

Test 1 Differentiation Does the supposed brand name differentiate the product positively from other, similar products in the marketplace in the minds of customer and consumer?

Test 2 Premium price Does the supposed brand command a higher price in the marketplace than a similar product sold as a commodity, because of the supposed brand's image for quality and/or reliability?

Test 3 Separate existence Can the supposed brand be valued, used, sold or licensed separately from the business or product currently owning the brand name?

Test 4 Psychic value Does the supposed brand offer benefits to the customer at a symbolic or sensory level?

Figure 2. 1 Four tests for the existence of a brand

Structural bases for power

Branding represents one source of manufacturer power because it creates a demand at the end of the supply chain, the so-called demand/pull effect, that retailers feel obliged to meet to ensure shoppers patronise their stores. This is particularly effective when relatively large manufacturers are selling highly branded items via relatively small retailers who are in no position to do other than stock such lines and agree to the manufacturer's terms. But when retailer concentration levels rise, as they have in Britain, and such large retailers concentrate their purchasing at head office rather than buy at store level, retailer negotiating power is increased (Davies *et al.*, 1985). The manufacturer now needs the retailer as much as the retailer once needed the manufacturer. The power that the manufacturer once employed through branding has become balanced by the retailer's ability to control access to the customer.

Grant (1987) compared the market capitalisation of retailers and manufacturers in five British retail sectors in 1985 to demonstrate how in four of the five the largest retailers and the largest manufacturers were similar in size. In the fifth sector, furniture, retailers tended to be far larger, a position exacerbated, if you were a manufacturer, because retailers in this one sector collectively outspent the manufacturers on advertising, implying that the manufacturers might have lost the potential advantages to them of a demand/pull

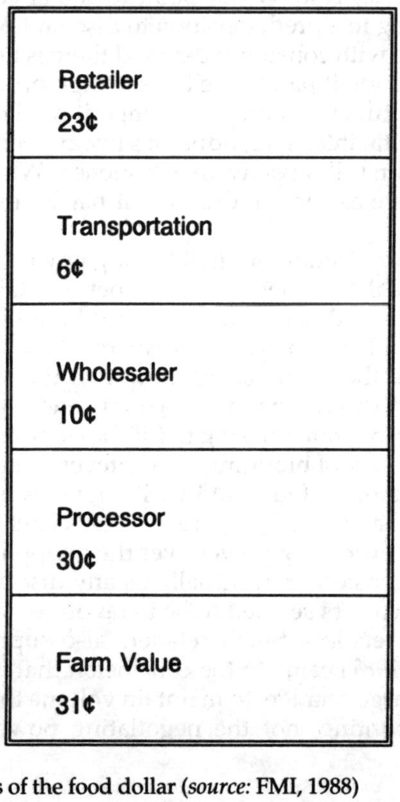

Figure 2. 2 Components of the food dollar (*source:* FMI, 1988)

strategy (Fulop, 1986). Shoppers for furniture could well become more 'loyal' to the store than to the manufacturer.

Such economic power can be used to reallocate profit within the supply chain. Fig 2. 2 illustrates the food supply chain in the USA. For every dollar the consumer spends on food, on average the farming sector gets 31 cents, the manufacturer/processor sector 30 cents, the wholesale sector 10 cents, the transportation sector 6 cents and the retailer 23 cents. Each sector will be keen to hold on to as much of its share of the customer's dollar as possible. Shifts in power between the various sectors can result in one channel member conceding some of its share of the value-added in the supply chain to another. In Britain the level of concentration in food retailing has increased steadily. This may be linked to a reduction in the relative profitability of the manufacturing sector.

The ability to purchase large quantities is not in itself a guarantee of an ability to obtain preferential discounts. In the USA Robinson Patman legislation limits the potential for discounts to those that can be justified by a cost saving due to the size of the transaction. No similar legislation exists in Britain where retailers are relatively free to negotiate any level of discount, or other concessions, to levels that could be regarded as discriminatory in the USA.

The legislative framework for competition between members of the same supply chain is an important factor but this is again only one consideration. Grant (1987) and Davies *et al.* (1985) point to the effect of overcapacity in manufacturing leading to a predisposition to discount. Where supply potential is more in balance with consumer demand there is little or no incentive to discount to guarantee retail patronage but the high profitability of food processing in the 1970s attracted increased competition. Porter (1980) points to the propensity of capital intensive industries towards price cutting if the volumes needed to sustain full capacity are threatened. While food processing is not as capital intensive as some industries, it has become more so over the years.

To summarise, concentration of retail buying power means a large manufacturer has to ensure the retailer stocks its lines to retain market share. One way of ensuring this is to develop and sustain a brand image strong enough to ensure shoppers will only patronise retailers who carry that brand. Large retailers can leverage their purchasing power in the absence of legislation designed to constrain discriminatory discounts and are more likely to succeed if manufacturers are not working to full capacity and particularly when the product, through lack of branding or whatever, is not unique.

In the 1980s in Britain, the Office of Fair Trading investigated the competitive situation in the supply of groceries. Their conclusion was that large retailers may well be exercising power over their suppliers, but that this was in the interest of the customer eventually as any discounts were passed on (OFT, 1985). Manufacturers seemed to be in favour of legislation to curb the power of the larger retailers. Small retailers also supported such an idea. Interestingly Grant (1987) came to the conclusion that it was manufacturers giving discounts to large retailers to maintain volume that was the root cause of preferential discounting, not the negotiating power of the centralised multiples.

The concept of power

Rosenbloom (1990) describes a marketing channel as an 'interorganizational social system' arguing that behaviour within a channel may not be governed totally by economic variables. Thus members of the channel may possess economic power and the legal environment may allow them to use it but they may still choose not to. Conversely channel members may hold power despite the economic and legal structures.

The ideas of French and Raven (1959) are frequently cited to provide a framework for analysing power in any social system. They postulated five bases for the perception in one party that another could or did hold power over them. Power in turn can be defined in a number of ways but most writers accept a meaning involving the ability of one party to control the actions of another (Gaski, 1988). (For a review of various concepts of power, see Hogarth-Scott and Parkinson, 1989 and Rosenbloom, 1990.)

Coercion

French and Raven identified the coercive basis for power as the expectation by one party that the second party will be able to punish for failure to accede to the latter's wishes. For example a supplier may refuse to continue to supply a retailer who sold their premium brand at a substantial discount, thus denying the retailer profit from sales and potentially the patronage of those who are loyal to this premium brand. A retailer may similarly de-list a supplier who does not agree to the retailers' demands (Davies *et al.* 1985). Both manufacturer and retailer have the ability to deny their services to the other and such sanctions are used or threatened frequently enough. The extent of power this gives depends largely on the effect that carrying out the threat can produce. In markets where products are undifferentiated, where retailers carry a broad product range and the retail sector is concentrated, most suppliers are far too small to make credible their threats to de-list. For example even the largest of British food manufacturers might account for only 5% of a supermarket chain's turnover, while the likes of Sainsbury and Tesco might account for 15% of the manufacturer's sales. Smaller manufacturers are worse placed. Only where such retailers might lose patronage can the manufacturer rely upon coercive power. In the supply of fresh produce the situation may be far worse. Farmers are far from well placed to negotiate for high prices as produce tends to be indifferentiated – one lettuce being much like another to the shopper.

Views differ on the value of using coercive power. Etgar (1978) found that where manufacturers used economic reward or coercion they achieved a higher degree of control over the channel than when they used other bases for power. Beier and Stern (1969) argued that the use of non-coercive power made for better relationships and Lusch (1976) concluded that the use of coercive power led to conflict. The author once worked for the confectionary business of the Mars Group. They agreed to supply Marks & Spencer with a variant of one of their leading lines, Opal Fruits. As M & S sold only own-label products, Mars could not sell them their branded product. However, Mars found they could not agree to the methods M & S technologists insisted upon, arguing that what was demanded was unnecessary and costly. M & S in turn felt they could not agree to accept Mars' own methods. The impass could not be resolved. In this instance the attempt to use coercive power caused both partners to lose, Mars the revenue they could not otherwise obtain by supplying M & S, M & S the potential extra revenue from carrying another line. (Eventually M & S sourced a similar product from another manufacturer.)

Legitimate power

French and Raven (1959) argued that one party might accept that the other had a legitimate right to influence them. The concept seems to imply a hierachy, where one party can order the other around, but legitimate power can be less authoritarian. Most franchises involve the franchisee agreeing to run a business as laid down by the franchisor. Many franchise agreements contain penalties should the franchisee default. Other franchisees would be keen to ensure that standards were maintained by all, adding further to the view that sanctions by the franchisor would be a legitimate use of power. Franchising is discussed in greater detail later in this book as a way a manufacturer can obtain control over the distribution channel, but the potential powers of franchisors can also be constrained by law. Car manufacturers have traditionally sold via agencies that are constrained to retail only that manufacturer's brands. Under proposed EC legislation, manufacturers will no longer be able to insist on a sole agency and car retailers will be free to enter into similar agreements with other suppliers. This change in legislation will create an interesting situation in Europe. Car production is over capacity and retailer concentration is rising. How long therefore before we see the first own-label car?

Referent power

When one member of the distribution channel is seen to be very much to the fore, by virtue of a good reputation for quality for example, other members of the channel might be willing to defer to them. The very insistence on certain methods of quality control by such retailers as M & S means that suppliers to them gain a reputation for quality. Retailers can be keen to stock certain brands to indicate a position in the market place to their customers. A Manchester department store, Lewis's, decided it needed to reposition itself away from an image that had become too closely associated with sales, discounts and middle to low price-point merchandise (Begg, 1986). Part of its strategy was to convince suppliers of premium brands to supply to them. Rosenbloom (1990) recounts a similar story involving Levi Jeans and J. C. Penney.

A number of manufacturers offer assistance to retailers on where products should be displayed in store (Fannin, 1988). Retailers will sometimes allow sales representatives to re-merchandise a display on condition the new display is more productive than the old. This example could also be taken to be an example of the fourth perceived basis for power, expert power.

Expert power

Manufacturers often offer sales training or sales-training aids to retailers to develop product knowledge and selling skills. The understanding of the marketplace a manufacturer gains through its own research can often be useful to the retailer. For example the levels of stock in the pipeline might be too high or too low given the predicted sales levels in the marketplace. If the retailer accepts that the supplier has certain expertise or knowledge that makes for better decision-making about how to exploit the market, then the retailer is likely to defer to the manufacturer and, in effect, do as the manufacturer requests. The expertise of one party is the basis for power, but a less subtle approach is to use reward.

Reward power

If the retailer expects financial reward by deferring to the manufacturer, then the expectation of reward can become the basis for manufacturer power. There can be few examples of marketing channels where this does not apply because of the commercial basis for the relationship. However, rewards can also be offered for specific actions by the retailer – extra discount for increased display area for example. Unfortunately 'rewards' can also become concessions the manufacturer has to agree to rather than rewards it gives to the retailer. In effect it is the retailer who is rewarding the manufacturer, not the other way round. There is one other facet of reward power, the reward a supplier could provide to the individual retail buyer rather than to his or her employer, in the way of gifts or outright bribery. What constitutes legitimate entertainment of a buyer is an issue raised in the interviews following this chapter.

Who has the power?

Fig 2. 3 attempts to summarise the issue of power within the distribution channel. Where power is equal the arrows linking the members are drawn horizontally. Where one channel member holds power over another, the

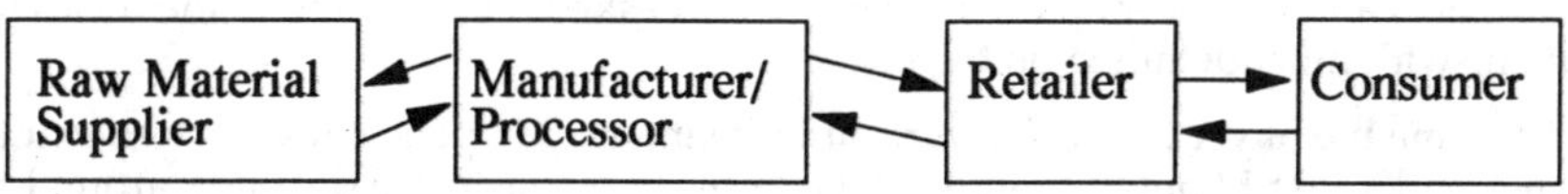

Power and Exchange under Manufacturer Domination

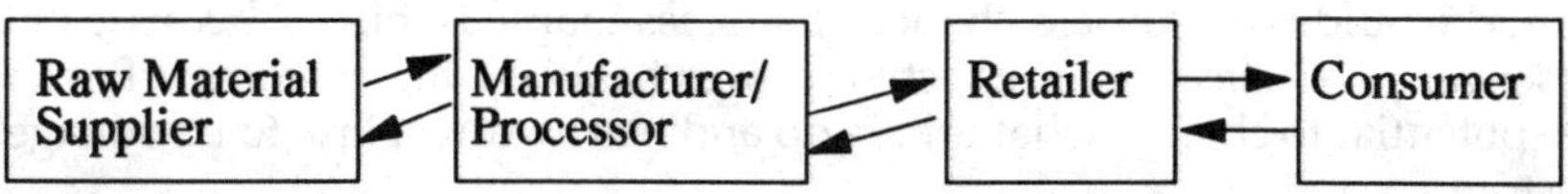

Power and Exchange under Potential Retailer Domination

Figure 2. 3 Power in the distribution of consumer goods

direction of the arrows indicates the direction of power. The discussion thus far has centred on the relationship between manufacturer and retailer. There are other players in the distribution system: suppliers to manufacturers, wholesalers, transport and logistic companies and the customer and consumer.

Fig 2. 3 assumes a distribution channel of just four players for simplicity's sake but similar points can be made for different or more complex systems. The first part of Fig 2. 3 would represent much of the power pattern in the distribution of fast-moving consumer goods where the manufacturer has successfully branded its products. In Britain product areas such as confectionary, petfood, newspapers, breakfast cereals and detergents would seem to be relevant examples. The diagram assumes that few if any suppliers in such sectors hold power over the manufacturer. As many raw materials are natural products, times of shortage will mean supplier power. But normally the exchange between supplier and manufacturers, indicated by the two arrows, is within an environment where the manufacturer holds most bases for power. In other sectors, one example might be car manufacture, the component supplier might be in a position of power due to unique technology or expertise but, as a generalisation, power seems to be vested more with the manufacturer than with the supplier. Where the manufacturer has a unique or highly branded product, the retailer is a small scale buyer and the manufacturer is perceived to hold power, the exchange relationship will see the manufacturer negotiating from a position of strength.

In both parts of Fig 2. 3 the retailer-to-consumer exchange is represented as favouring neither party. In a self-service environment, the customer/consumer has little potential to use his or her only basis for power over the retailer, that of patronage. Few retailers would be affected by the loss of an individual customer. Few retailers could be made to change their business by the actions of a single customer. The customer may be deemed to be powerful by the retailer who then tries to judge what the customer wants, but consider the difference in the power structure between retailer and customer and retailer and manufacturer in the following, fictitious, examples:

> I was delighted with the shirt I purchased from a branch of Debenhams, but for one thing, the lack of detailing around the pocket. The shirt had Debenhams own name on the label and I knew the store manager well. I asked him for another identical shirt but one with more detailing on the pocket.

> I became the buyer for men's shirts at Debenhams. My personal view was that the own-brand shirts I bought would sell better if there was more detailing around the pocket. The supplier, with whom I spend over £5 million a year, is due to see me today when I will suggest making the change I believe is necessary.

What would be the likely outcome of each example? Most probably I as 'customer' would have far less chance of success than I as 'buyer' because of the absence, in practice, of an effective power basis for the customer. Power is the potential to change what others do and has no direct link to patronage or custom.

Where retailers are interacting with the customer, the customer can often exert power over the retailer in negotiation. The basis for power is likely to be coercive, the threat to go elsewhere for that new fitted kitchen unless the retailer concedes on price. Under RPM a retailer would be better placed to refuse to negotiate; but without RPM and in a time of recession, shoppers seem more prepared to ignore price marking and haggle (Davies, 1992).

In the second part of Fig 2. 3, the retailer is depicted as holding power over the manufacturer. The balance of power is generally accepted to have moved from that depicted in the first part of the diagram and towards that represented in the second. But manufacturers can still choose to, or can attempt to use, the notion of power to control the channel and maximise their own share of the profit to be made. Fig 2. 4 presents a checklist that can be used as a starting point to assess the potential of any manufacturer's product to use

The product sold

- Is the product unique and widely purchased?
- If not does the product qualify as a brand using the four tests of branding: differentiation; premium price; separate existence; psychic value?
- If not can the product be branded at least as successfully as any existing brands?
- Finally are enough shoppers loyal to the product/brand to the point where the retailer would lose significant patronage if the product were not stocked?

Capacity and investment structure

- Is there pressure to maintain and expand sales volume because of excess production capacity?
- Is there spare capacity among competitors selling similar products or is there a shortage of capacity?

Market structure

- Is retailer concentration higher or lower than manufacturer concentration (in the product sector)?
- Is retailer buying centralised in the major retail businesses?
- If manufacturer and retailer concentration levels are high is it necessary to use any existing wholesalers?

Legal structure

- Is there effective legislation against discriminatory discounting that would ensure no manufacturer can use discounting to ensure a retailer's patronage?
- Is there effective legislation supporting RPM so that retailers do not compete overly on price?

Power perception

- Can either retailer or manufacturer rely on coercion, particularly the threat not to supply or not to stock, to ensure compliance?
- Is there a formal or informal agreement with the retailer over stocking and display that ensures retailer compliance?
- Does the retailer's image benefit from stocking the product or from its association with the supplier?
- Does the retailer rely on the manufacturer's expertise?
- What rewards does the retailer receive for compliance and are these bigger and better than those available from competitors?

Figure 2. 4 A checklist for the potential for manufacturer power

power in the distribution channel as an effective strategy. The interviews which follow this chapter include the views of practitioners on relationships between buyers and sellers.

Is branding enough?

So one way of achieving channel power, or at least countering that of the retailer, is to develop a brand image, to acquire market expertise, a reputation for exclusiveness or quality and to support the retail outlet selling the brand. This approach to channel management has served many manufacturers well but is branding such a simple formula to apply? A successful brand not only has to meet the criteria suggested earlier to qualify for the branding race but the brand has also to be more successful than those that other manufacturers are trying to establish. Establishing a brand is no easy matter. In existing markets, that is to say markets where there is a history of similar products being sold, the leading brand is often the brand that was launched first and as often as not fifty or more years ago (*The Economist*, 1988).

Defending an existing position is easier than building a new position. Small wonder that whole companies are being purchased, not just for their tangible assets but for the established brand names they control. The high cost of launching new brands has been cited as a major reason for the acquisitions and 'mega-mergers' of the last decade (Craig, 1985). To establish a new brand name normally involves communicating the intangible imagery inherent in branding directly to the customer/consumer via media advertising. Ries and Trout (1981) pointed to the difficulty of gaining the attention of the public in what has become an over-communicated age. Their book's subtitle, *The Battle for Your Mind*, aptly illustrates the challenge facing the would-be brander. Even if the brand can be established, it must grow market share to ensure retailers give the brand preference over other competing lines. If the brand is to be profitable for the manufacturer, it must aim to achieve dominance in its sector as profitability seems highly dependent upon relative market share (Buzzell and Gale, 1987). Business units achieving market shares of below 10% tend to provide a return on investment of around 12% while those achieving a share of over 50% tend to provide a return of 40% to the company. Branding may not be the best and is unlikely to be the only strategy the manufacturer should select. Branding in isolation can succeed with highly innovative products no matter how powerful the retail sector. The successful marketer may be better advised to look further than his or her consumer research that aims to provide an understanding of consumer purchase behaviour, and towards an understanding of how the retailer buys, the topic considered in Chapter 3. But first some interviews with those involved day to day with the interface between suppliers and retailers to illustrate both the power of branding but also what to do as a supplier if brand power is not strong enough.

Keypoint Summary

1) Power is one of the concepts that has been researched by academics interested in the broad area of 'marketing channels', particularly those who approach the area by examining relationships between firms.
2) A brand is a complex concept. Branding is one major source of manufacturer power but one that is being counterbalanced by rising retailer concentration.
3) Legal structure is a significant determinant of the retailer's ability to use its purchasing power.
4) The nature of the relationship between manufacturer and retailer is important to understand.

References

Baker, M. J. (1984) *Macmillan Dictionary of Marketing and Advertising*, Macmillan, London.

Begg, J. (1986) The New Lewis's, The Retailing Event Conference, London, Hay MSL.

Beier, F. J., Stern, L. W. (1969) Power in the Channel of Distribution, in Stern, L. W. (ed) *Distribution Channels*, Houghton Mifflin, New York.

Blackett, T. (1989) The Nature of Brands, in Murphy, J. (ed.) *Brand Valuation*, Hutchinson, London, p 1.

Boots (1977) *Centenary Booklet*, Boots, Nottingham.

Bucklin, L. P. (1966) *A Theory of Distribution Channel Structure*, Institute of Business and Economic Research, University of California.

Buzzell, R. D., Gale, B. T. (1987) *The PIMS Principles*, Free Press, New York, p 9.

Craig, R. (1985) The Mighty Urge to Merger: Big Name Buyers Bag Brands, *Advertising Age*, Vol 56, No 84, p 38.

Davies, K., Gilligan, C., Sutton, C. (1985) Structural Change in Grocery Retailing : the implications for competition, *International Journal of Physical Distribution and Materials Management*, Vol 15, No 2, p 3.

Davies, G. (1992) Retailing, in Catterill, P. (ed) *Contemporary Britain*, Blackwell, Oxford.

de Chernatony, L. (1989) The impact of the changed balance of power from manufacturer to retailer in the UK packaged groceries market, in Pellegrini, L. and Reddy, S. K. (eds) *Retail and Marketing Channels*, Routledge, London and New York.

de Chernatony, L., McWilliam, G. (1989) The Varying Nature of Brands as Assets, *International Journal of Advertising*, Vol 8, p 339.

Doyle, P. (1990) Building Successful Brands: the Strategic Options, *Journal of Consumer Marketing*, Vol 17, No 2, p 5.

The Economist (1988) The Year of the Brand, 24 Dec. p 101.

Edwards, C. D. (1966) *Trade Regulations Overseas*, Oceana Publications, New York.

Etgar, M. (1978) Selection of an Effective Channel Control Mix, *Journal of Marketing*, July, p 53.

Fannin, R. (1988) Planograms: Friend or Foe?, *Marketing and Media Decisions*, May, p 48.

FMI (1988) *Products as a Key Cost*, Food Marketing Institute, Washington, DC.

Foley, J. (1972) *The Food Makers. A History of General Foods Ltd*, General Foods, Banbury.

French, J. R. P., Raven, B. (1959) The Bases of Social Power, in Cartwright, D. (ed)

Studies in Social Power, University of Michigan Press, East Lansing, Mich.
Fulop, C. (1986) *Retailer Advertising and Retail Competition in the UK*, Advertising Association, London.
Gardner, B. B., Levy, S. J. (1955) The Product and the Brand, *Harvard Business Review*, Mar/Apr, p 33.
Gaski, J. F. (1988) Towards a Generally accepted Conceptually Coherent Channel Power Lexicon, *AMA Educators Conference Proceedings*, p 256.
Gattorna, J. (1978) Channels of Distribution Conceptualisations: A state-of-the-Art Review, *European Journal of Marketing*, Vol 12, No 7, p 470.
Grant, R. M. (1987) Manufacturer–Retailer Relations: the Shifting Balance of Power, in Johnson, G. (ed) *Business Strategy and Retailing*, Wiley, Chichester.
Hogarth-Scott, S., Parkinson, S. T. (1989) Conflict and Cooperation in the Development of Retail Marketing, *Proceedings of 22nd MEG Conference*, Vol 1, July, p 151.
Jones, J. P. (1986) *What's in a Name?*, Gower, Aldershot.
Kaldor, N. (1950) The Economic Aspects of Advertising, *Review of Economic Studies*, No 18.
Kim, P. (1990) A Perspective on Brands, *Journal of Consumer Marketing*, Vol 7, No 4, p 63.
King, S. (1973) *Developing New Brands*, Pitman, London, p 3.
Kotler, P. (1988) *Marketing Management* (6th Ed) Prentice-Hall, Englewood Cliffs, NJ, p 463.
Lusch, R. F. (1976) Sources of Power: Their impact on Intrachannel Conflict, *Journal of Marketing Research*, Nov, p 382.
McWilliam, G. (1989) Managing the Brand Manager, in Murphy J. (ed) *Brand Valuation*, Hutchinson, London, p 154.
Mallen, B. E. (1973) Functional Spin-Off: A Key to Anticipating Change in Distribution Structure, *Journal of Marketing*, Vol 37, p 18.
Murphy, J .M. (1987) (ed) *Brand Strategy: A Key Marketing Tool*, Macmillan, Basingstoke.
Murphy, J. M. (1990) *Brand Strategy*, Director Books, Cambridge, p 65.
Office of Fair Trading (1985) *Competition and Retailing*, London.
Perrier, R. (1989) Valuation and Licensing, in Murphy, J. (ed) *Brand Valuation*, Hutchinson, London.
Porter, M. (1980) *Competitive Strategy*, Free Press, New York.
Potter, S. (1959) *The Magic Number. The Story of 57*, Max Reinhardt, London.
Ries, A., Trout, J. (1981, 1986) *Positioning: The Battle for Your Mind* (1st and 2nd edns), McGraw-Hill, New York.
Rosenbloom, B. (1990) *Marketing Channels* (4th ed) Dryden Press, Orlando, Fla.
Ryan, C. (1989) *Brand Building: The Retailer's Secret Weapon, Adding Value to Retail Offerings*, ESOMAR, Edinburgh, April.
Sigsworth, E. M. (1990) *Montague Burton. The Tailor of Taste*, Manchester University Press.

Case Study: INTERVIEWS ABOUT THE RELATIONSHIPS BETWEEN BUYERS AND SELLERS

Interview 1 was with a Buying Controller working for a large British retailer. His background included 13 years experience with his current employer. His role at the time of the interview was concerned with the buying and marketing of products within the broad area of music and video.

The two questions put to the Buying Controller were these:

1) As a buyer, are you treated as a 'customer'?
2) What do you understand by the idea of 'relationships' with your suppliers?

This is a summary of the interview:

In general, the company culture is to build relationships with suppliers, and we employ people of that mind. We try not to work to the idea of dictating to suppliers, because whilst this may yield short-term gains, medium-term and longer-term benefits can be achieved by building relationships and by each party understanding each other better. Our margin growth in recent times, both gross and net, has been remarkable and is a tribute to the way we go about our business.

We use not to know what was selling in stores, or what profit it could yield. However, EPOS (electronic point of sales), and latterly DPP (direct product profitability) has significantly changed our base of knowledge and therefore the way we work. We know what is selling; we know the true stock position; we know the net profit on each line – this has to impact not only on tactical and strategic decision-making, but also on supplier relationships. 'Knowledge' is a powerful tool, and it can be used to positive benefit for both suppliers and of course the retailer.

The policy towards sharing sales data with suppliers may vary between buying groups, depending on the needs of the business. However providing sales, and forecasts based on sales, can yield margin gain for the retailer, because suppliers can plan production more cost-effectively.

Having better sales data gives us a position of power which we must be careful not to abuse. We should, for example, be careful not to pressurise smaller suppliers for short-term gain which may actually force a supplier out of business – that would not be in the customers' interest, let alone ours. Sales data can be used to true positive benefit by helping smaller suppliers, particularly if they operate in a complicated market (logistics, market dynamics, etc.) and the retailer can expect a degree of benefit as well. The challenge is to maximise the benefit without dangerously affecting the supplier's profitability.

The difficulties start when one deals with suppliers of similar power or, indeed, with suppliers of power greater than the retailer. For example, when the brand is strong – even dominant – the supplier may feel he does not need the individual retailer. An Elton John CD can only be bought from EMI, and if we don't buy it, another retailer certainly will, and the customer will simply go wherever it is stocked. It would do us significant damage not to stock a popular CD, and the supplier knows it.

Having better sales data gives us some influence in such relationships, but it hardly restores the balance. Our challenge is to demonstrate what we as a retailer can offer that supplier in terms of marketing support, so that the supplier may wish to support us in a similar way. For example, we may be able to offer access to a particular target market, increase the market size for that product (in simplistic terms – very simplistic – a supplier may not care about how the market is split up between retailers, but they do care about increasing the overall size of the market).

Our relationship with one large supplier has changed significantly of late. Until relatively recently, our business has been suffering due to a breakdown in communications, a lack of understanding on both sides, and a fundamental lack of trust. For example, we had been promised goods when there was no chance of supply: we had steadfastly refused to provide sales data, seemingly out of spite.

A personnel change at the company provided an opportunity for a fresh start. We got together, informally at first, and started to build from scratch. We looked at what needed to be done. Honesty was the first thing, and this openness needed to filter through to the teams on both sides. We made a conscious effort to get to know each other better by meeting outside of the work environment. Corporate entertainment is often given a bad press. In this instance there is no question that it yielded positive profit benefit to both parties.

An earlier example of positive benefit through building relationships came as a direct result of initiatives taken by the supplier. This company has 'enjoyed' a distant relationship with us, rarely spending time telling us what they were trying to do with their brands, and this disadvantaged their products compared to competitors. I still remember the first meeting after their change of policy. The opening line from the newly appointed Trade Marketing Manager was 'I've come to understand *your* business better'. I could have fallen off my chair! Barriers came down almost immediately, and the performance of their brands with us improved and, more to the point, our total business in that market increased as well.

They even offered to prepare a space allocation for one of our displays. I was suspicious at first, but we let them go. Rather than have all their brands in the best positions, own label was in the dominant location – a sign that they recognised the dynamics of our business. It put our business on a new footing which then went from strength to strength.

Interview 2 was with a Director of a company importing small leather goods and handbags from the Far East for sale to a wide range of retail businesses. His background included sales and marketing in stationery and education products as well as his current product field, over a career spanning 34 years.

A number of questions were put to him including the following:

1) What changes have there been in the role of a salesperson selling to retailers?
2) How do you form relationships with retailers and how do you manage conflict?
3) What do the terms power, cooperation and control mean in these business relationships?

This is a summary of the interview:

Thirty years ago the old-time salesperson still sold from samples out of a suitcase. Times changed and salespeople were taught professional selling skills – how to talk about the advantages of a product and its benefits. In recent years salespeople have changed to selling concepts. My people won't call on a retailer until they have visited a branch, analysed their product range and identified where the buyer is missing an opportunity that we can help with. You don't then sell the product, or try to get a buyer to drop a line they already carry because yours is cheaper. That only provokes a downward price spiral. Our way is to show the buyer how he or, increasingly, she, can develop the market and increase market share and profit. Price is mentioned last, not first.

Buyers have changed as well. Fifteen years ago buyers made their own decisions, now they collect product and submit it to a committee who decide. The reaction is less immediate.

I like to get as close as I can on a personal as well as a business basis. If a buyer is ill, she gets flowers or a card and something on a birthday. Regular, casual entertainment is a waste of time; if you are going to entertain, do something that will be remembered. Over the year the cost is the same.

Most of my customers are friends. I've helped many build up their business over the years, although that is less easy these days as buyers move on more rapidly. On the other hand, if I hear a buyer has changed, then I know there's an opportunity for us if the retailer is not a customer.

I try anything to avoid conflict. If I know a delivery is going to be late, I tell them. I'll fly product in if I have to, even though my margin is lower, rather than risk a problem. When you have a good relationship, you have a responsibility. You have to be conscious of that trust and not try to pass off rubbish. Buyers often won't take decisions because of a fear of failure. I tell them that if the product doesn't sell then they don't have to take the stock, it's at my risk. Conflict has never done me any good. On price, I position the product at a price point and I know what margin they need. On some products I may have to make less but overall I will make a profit.

The retailer has the power, but I wouldn't think of opening my own outlets because of what that might do to the other relationships. On cooperation there is less in today's market from the buyer to us than the other way. So I never offer a line I'm not happy with so that I can always sell it somewhere else. Promises are broken more often these days. In the Far East your word is still important but that's not now the case here.

The manufacturer is just a cruncher of metal. The supply chain is led by the retailer and ourselves. I work on the offer with the buyer. Value for money and design are the most important issues; some retailers have a particular image of themselves. The biggest service issue is to advise on product range and market trends, what is selling well elsewhere, what new materials are available. We need to hold stock. The worst thing is if they achieve extra sales and we cannot supply. I have to be in business to provide a service, to ticket goods if needed or hold back-up stock, be prepared to do a special deal to achieve extra sales. If I didn't provide the service, the retailer would be better going direct to the manufacturer. We are responsible for controlling the supply chain so that our customers don't get involved in the detail.

A number of issues are raised in these two interviews that are addressed in the coming chapters of this book. Some immediate points to make are the benefits as seen by the retail buyer and product marketer of forming relationships. However such relationships can only be valid if the retailer's supplier is willing to understand the retailer's business. Chapter 3 is concerned with just this issue.

3

THE RETAIL BUYING PROCESS

The purpose of this chapter is to identify how and even why retailers buy and to begin to identify how suppliers might respond. Much is known about consumer buyer behaviour and the study of industrial buyer behaviour has become well established. Less appears to have been written about retailer buying, perhaps because, as two authors claimed, it is difficult to generalise about retailing buying (Parkinson and Baker, 1986). Two factors may explain this apparent lack of interest: first, that much of retail buying used to be fragmented, and it used to take place at store level with the retail manager or his or her subordinates making most, if not all, of the decisions. Second, that retailer buying was, and still is in many instances, a wholly reactive rather than proactive process. If it sells, buy more; if it doesn't, hold a sale – but times have changed.

Davies *et al.* (1985) cite two trade sources on the decline in the number of retail buying points that accounted for 80% of British grocery turnover, from 750 in 1970 to 220 in 1983, while in the multiple sector the decline quoted between 1970 and 1980 in total was from 202 to 49. Both statistics reflect the centralisation and concentration in grocery retailing. Grant, in his 1988 sample, surveyed the manufacturers serving the Argyll retail group. The number of accounts served by the 51 suppliers in his study had fallen from 9,815 in 1977 to 4,951 in 1987, despite the fact that many of the suppliers had grown their sales volume or acquired other suppliers. George Davies (1989), the driving force behind the Next group of largely fashion retailers, sheds some light on change in the second factor in differentiating between two different approaches to retail buying: 'The difference between a retailer and a shopkeeper is someone who actually understands the consumer and develops his product from the design and the yarn through to the marketing and sale of the finished garment, while a shopkeeper enters the process 80% down the line'.

The Next organisation espoused the 'retailer' approach, while many businesses still react to the manufacturer's product offer by selecting, rather than proactively deciding, what the customer wants and organising matters to deliver the appropriate product.

Retailer buying is certainly structurally different from other forms of industrial buying where what is bought is used to build or make something different. A retailer sells exactly what is bought, albeit in smaller quantity. But a retailer is *also* trying to create a 'product' from what is bought for resale. This product is a distinctive service offer to the shopper, something that can be described as the retailer's position in the market. George Davies again: 'the most important thing you can do as a retailer is create a strong identity on the High Street; so that the public retains an image of the shop and recognises it immediately they see it.'

McVey (1960) placed the more proactive retailer into its consumer context when he described retailers as coming to be seen as the 'agent of the shopper' in contrast to their being the outlet for the manufacturer. Shoppers, he suggested, rely on the retailer to negotiate and select on their behalf. While this view of retailers and retailing is somewhat altruistic, the underlying concept fits with Davies' view of the buying function in Next. An edited range of merchandise is selected with a coherent picture in mind of how the shopper is supposed to perceive the total retail offer. The retailer selects the merchandise to create something, a total look or experience or lifestyle, that the shopper would otherwise need to create for themselves by shopping around. Similar concepts can be seen in other similar fashion retailers such as the Limited.

Later in this book ways of identifying the retailer's position in the marketplace are discussed as an essential piece of background knowledge the supplier needs about its retail customer. The supplier needs to know whether the retailer is aiming overtly or not for a clear market position. Many retailers appear to have no clear market position and, if the retailer competes through location rather than image, then this may be no disadvantage in practical terms. But most retailers do have an image, for better or for worse.

The position the retailer holds in the marketplace is but one of the factors that will influence the retail buyer and the buying process itself. A number of models of buying have been developed, based on earlier research, that provide frameworks for identifying issues in the buying process.

Models of buyer behaviour

At the core of any buying process are a set of decisions being made that depend upon the novelty of the purchase. Is it a new product, or a new supplier, a modification to a previous purchasing task or a reorder from an existing supplier? The buying process consists of a number of stages that extend from the initial stimulus to purchase through to the review of the supplier's and its product's performance. These two elements, the class of purchase and the phases in the purchase process, have been used by Robinson *et al.* (1967) to identify the significant events in *any* buying situation. Fig 3. 1 takes their framework and suggests how it might be applied to a retail organisation.

The straight rebuy is by far the least complex type of purchase, so much so that many manufacturers and retailers have routinised such purchases using electronic data interchange (EDI), which is discussed in more detail in Chapter 7. The opportunities for another firm to become a supplier when such a relationship persists could well be low. However the retailer's focus is often very much on the later items in the list of buy phases, particularly the performance of the product itself and any sustained reduction in benefit to the retailer will eventually trigger the search for a substitute or prompt a renegotiation with the existing supplier.

A number of factors might cause the retailer to want to modify the

Phases in the Purchase Process (Buy Phases) ↓	Types of Purchase (Buy Classes): New Task	Modified Rebuy	Straight Rebuy
Identification of Need	✓	?	X
Product Criteria Required	✓	✓	X
Supplier Search	✓	?	X
Selection of Supplier	✓	?	?
Order Specification	✓	✓	✓
Performance Review	✓	✓	✓

Figure 3. 1 Buy class and buy phase illustration

purchases of an existing line. Chanil (1991) reported on a survey of buyers working for American discount retailers. One question dealt with the problems buyers had with sellers, any or all which could prompt a modified rebuy, a search for an alternative supplier. Fig 3. 2 lists the percentages of buyers citing each individual problem.

	%
Late deliveries	83
Lack of communication	52
Lack of promotional support	36
Billing disagreements	33
Frequent personnel changes	31
Rapidly changing terms/allowances	31
Dealing with manufacturer's reps	26
Poor quality control	24

Figure 3. 2 Survey of American discount buyers' problems with suppliers

Such surveys may not reflect more than the opinion of an unrepresentative sample of all retail buyers but the prominence of the two related issues of poor delivery and communication certainly looks significant. One retailer in the survey advised suppliers to 'be more realistic with delivery dates'.

Reliable delivery is a frequently mentioned issue in the appraisal of new suppliers or new products. Buyers in multiples and in cash and carries gave insurance against 'supply shortage' as the second most important reason for stocking more than one brand (McGoldrick and Douglas, 1983). While maximising customer demand was the most important reason of those tested, supply shortage seemed significantly more important than a desire to play one supplier off against another. Reliable delivery was cited as being of importance in the selection of a new supplier. Delivery may be more important in sectors such as grocery but even in fashion where lead times can be very long, the ability to offer short delivery times and to make reliable delivery promises seems to be increasingly important (Davies, 1989). Delivery was second only to quality in a large survey of purchasing managers generally (Dowst, 1987). The retailer's problem is quite simply this: if the product is not in stock, the customer is unable to buy and may buy elsewhere rather than defer the purchase or select an alternative. Emmelhainz et al (1991) and Swindley (1992) showed that retail buyers are likely to be appraised primarily on turnover, whether they purchase food or apparel – another reason why delivery failure is likely to be a sensitive issue and one that can initiate a search for a new supplier.

The search for a new supplier or a new product is classified as a new task. The significance is that the process is likely to be extended and the number of people involved to be increased. Various studies have been published of retail buying criteria in the selection of a new source (Doyle and Weinberg, 1973; McGoldick and Douglas, 1983; Shipley, 1985; Nilsson and Host, 1987; Banting and Blenkhorn, 1988; Wagner *et al.*, 1989). Nilsson and Host (1987) provide a review of many earlier studies of factors deemed relevant to retail buying. They identified 389 criteria mentioned in such work illustrating the profusion and perhaps the confusion of factors that may affect the buyer's decision making. Fig 3. 3 lists the major categories that Nilsson and Host decided best represented earlier work. As they themselves acknowledged, the mere presence of factors in previous work does not prove that they are important; neither is the relative frequency with which they are mentioned any guide to relative importance.

Profitability and sales (overall profit and sales volume)
Financial terms (margins, allowances, advertising support)
Assortment (relationship to existing lines, supply of own brand)
Consumer evaluation (value, physical and psychological characteristics)
Supplier marketing (launch campaign, continued support)
Supplier characteristics (reputation, services, reliability)
Competitive considerations (advantages over other retailers)
Distribution factors (transport, ability to adapt to store needs)
Sales presentation (quality of presentation, data)
Tactical consideration (shorter-term issues)

Figure 3. 3 Categories of decision criteria (after Nilsson and Host, 1987)

For the practitioner trying to obtain a pragmatic insight into the purchasing process for his or her own products, matters are, in reality, even worse.

Much of the research into criteria used by buyers is context specific and is a measure of opinion rather than a predictor of action. Just because a buyer says a criterion is important is no reliable guide to the actual decisions that the same buyer makes in the future or even will have made in the past. Furthermore, criteria in selecting a product may be different from those used in rejection. Finally the context for the decision process can be a dominant factor. As a simple example, the criteria used to select groceries will be different from those used to select fashion, but the criteria used by one buyer of groceries in one retailer might also be different from those used by another buyer in even the same organisation, let alone in another, perhaps because of the buyer's personality, the pressures on the buyer that day or different perceptions of company policy or personal objectives. To help make sense of the multitude of factors that might influence or determine any buying decision and how these factors might interrelate, a number of attempts have been made to produce diagrams or models listing all likely factors and suggesting linkages between them.

Process models

Webster and Wind (1972) proposed a general model of organisational buying that can be used to study any buying process. They argued that buying can be likened to problem solving, the problem being one that can only be resolved through the activity of buying. They suggested that the business environment and the organisation the buying takes place within exercise influences over the buying process. In retailing one obvious result of environmental factors is the retailer's expectation of consumer demand, which is a function in turn of consumer confidence and the economic environment. Legal and cultural factors can be equally important: a change in VAT rates has an immediate effect on demand; fear of holes in the ozone layer prompts rejection of products containing chlorofluorohydrocarbons; and changing attitudes to animal welfare produce changes in the nature of demand for fur coats. Webster and Wind point to the effect these environmental influences can have on the availability and demand for goods and the pressures the retailer might feel from not only its customers but also other influential groups including trade unions, pressure groups and the media.

The retail organisation as a whole is potentially affected by a range of environmental factors but the organisation itself provides another context for decision-making. The communication system within the retail business can dominate buying. Many retailers now benefit from daily information on the rate of sale of individual product lines. The information comes directly from their electronic point of sale. As will be discussed in Chapter 7, the information can be used either to replenish on the basis of one sold is one ordered from the supplier, or the basis that one sold may not be providing an adequate return and a different signal eventually reaches the supplier. Totally different response options can be expected from retailers who do not know how much has been sold until they count stock, perhaps at the end of a week or even a month or longer.

Organisational culture can dominate not so much how communication happens but also what is communicated. To produce a coherent retail image is far from easy. In retailing middle- to up-market fashion for example, merchandise must coordinate, an identical shade must be achieved in the same colour, but perhaps in different materials in the separates section. Small wonder that many retailers are or have been closely associated with a single, perhaps dominant individual whose personality might be imposed on the company to ensure coherence in merchandise policy (for example, Roddick and Body Shop, Laura Ashley, Conran and Habitat, Davies with Next, Ratner and Ratners). How many retail firms might depend upon the direction of such individuals for their ethos and fortune? Products might be selected more for their compatibility with the vision of its leader than for their apparent profit potential as freestanding lines. How, or even whether, a clear vision is communicated is likely to be an issue shaping buyer behaviour.

In organisations, many buying decisions are made by a group rather than by individuals. How the group process works, who holds authority and for what are all factors to be considered by the seller. As are the reward system and the criteria used to decide what a 'successful' purchase decision really means.

It has long been recognised that organisational buying is not totally rational – not that too many irrational decisions get made, but that the motives governing buyer behaviour are not always task orientated. The buyer might be motivated in part by a desire for status. He or she might feel threatened by the presence of a strong marketing department who may question or even try to dominate buying decisions. The individual's personality, experience and background may well be relevant factors. In total, there may be as many as forty or fifty factors that could be usefully included in any appraisal of a retailer's buying process (Webster and Wind, 1972).

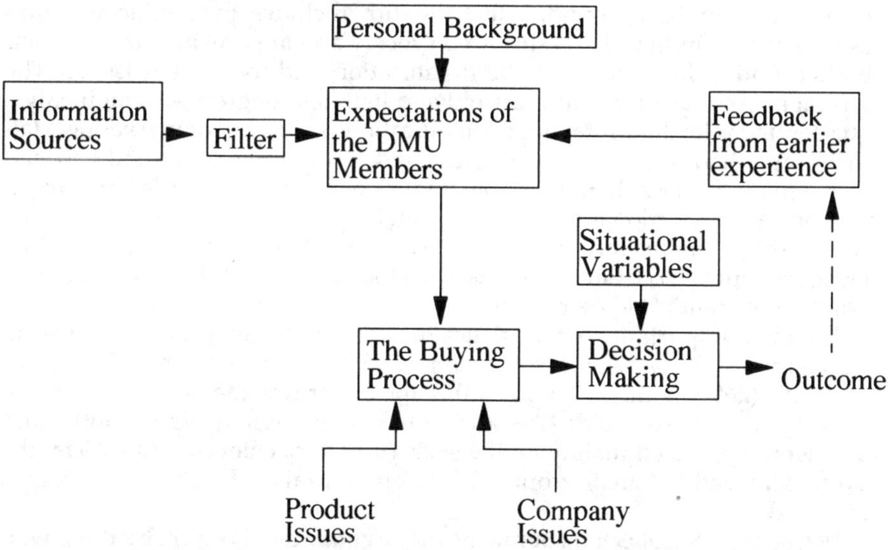

Figure 3. 4 A simplified model of retail buyer behaviour (after Sheth, 1973)

Sheth (1973) provided a less complex model of buyer behaviour which can be used to examine how some of the major groups of influences and processes interact in buying. Sheth's model was derived more in the context of industrial rather than retail buying but the principles can be readily transferred as illustrated in Fig 3. 4, which is a simplified version of Sheth's original model adapted to retailing. Environmental issues are largely ignored and the model focuses on the interrelationships between different elements of the process, whereas Webster and Wind's model concentrated on listing all possible elements. Central to the model in Fig 3. 4 are the expectations of members of the Decision Making Unit, those individuals who, collectively, have some degree of influence over the purchase. These in turn are created by the information each receives from the marketplace, often distorted by a filter mechanism that each of us brings to bear on the data we are exposed to. The buyer's acceptance of information from one source may be greater than from another, which is deemed less credible or reliable. The personal factors that shape the predispositions of the Decision Making Unit members include their educational backgrounds. For example, a technologist who has to advise on product quality will not only have different skills but also probably a different orientation towards business, directed perhaps more towards the scientific world, at times, than the commercial one (Twiss, 1974).

The boxes in Fig 3. 4 can be used as a framework in this way to discuss retailer buying. The next sections in this chapter focus on the personal background of retail buyers, their attitudes and the nature of the Decision Making Unit. Later chapters pick up on other elements in Fig 3. 4.

Personal characteristics of the retail buyer

Sheth argued that a number of factors influence a buyer's expectations, including their background, which in turn includes their education and experience. Swindley (1992) surveyed grocery and apparel buyers as to their background, relationships in the organisation and job-related issues. The typical buyer was under 40 years old and half held degrees although only a quarter had relevant professional qualifications in buying or marketing. Half the sample had been with their company less than five years and half had been buyers for less than the same amount of time. Two thirds had experience in other functional areas within retailing. Reflecting the British retail scene, 80% of merchandise by value was bought centrally, i.e. not at store level, and only 22% from wholesalers. Of the sample, 74% bought both manufacturer's brands and own label.

The most important characteristics they saw in being a retail buyer were negotiation skills (42%), market awareness (35%), and commercial and financial skills (26%). Some 71% agreed that the buyer was the main influence on what their company sold; 47% saw own-label increasing significantly; and 48% were appraised mainly by the sales turnover achieved and 44% by the profit achieved. A small group, 17%, were appraised by the gross margin achieved.

Warner (1988) collected comments made about retail buyers by those who deal with them, including the following:

- They are ruthlessly professional.
- They are selfish, egotistical and tough.
- The combination of brains and brawn is lethal.

- They are arrogant, rude and use personal abuse.
- Some major accounts have the attitude that they have an absolute god-given right to make excessive demands on suppliers.

A picture emerges of the stereotypical retail buyer as young, well qualified, clearly targeted, focused on negotiation, looking to increase own-brand, dealing directly with manufacturers – and giving them a hard time!

Dickenson (1967) identified seven different types of retail buyer, suggesting a single stereotype may be misleading (or even that the British retail buyers of today represents a different breed):

- The Loyal Buyer (buys from the same source).
- The Opportunistic Buyer (selects suppliers who further their long term interests).
- The Best Deal Buyer (selects suppliers who offer the best deal at the time).
- The Creative Buyer (specifies to the supplier the type of product required).
- The Advertising Buyer (attempts to obtain advertising support in every deal).
- The Chiseller (constantly negotiates price concessions)
- The Nut and Bolts Buyer (selects for the best value).

The Decision-Making Unit

Webster and Wind highlighted the need to realise that the industrial or commercial buyer is often working as part of a team, the buying centre or Decision Making Unit (DMU). The more novel or complex the buying decision, the larger the DMU will become. Within the DMU a number of roles may be identifiable. Sometimes there will be more than one individual with the same or similar role and sometimes an individual will have more than one role. The significance of the DMU is that the supplier may need to influence or satisfy all the different roles, not just that of the buyer. Traditionally the DMU is said to involve five roles:

1) The *user* is the role for whom the product is purchased. In retailing this role is not as obvious as for example in manufacturing, where a production manager might use the equipment being purchased, but the user role can be taken to refer to store personnel or even the shopper. A problem for many suppliers today is that retailers often forbid them from contacting store personnel directly. Store personnel may still be responsible for specifying reorder quantities and their opinions may also influence members of the DMU. One option in influencing them is to advertise to them via the trade press or to rely upon the interest evoked from consumer marketing.
2) The *influencer* is often a specialist role, perhaps the technologist or merchandiser who is concerned with a particular aspect of product performance. The role of the technologist is considered further in Chapter 6, but both technologist and merchandiser will have their own agenda as well as criteria a product needs to meet.
3) The *deciders* are responsible for making the sourcing decision. They may not be involved in the detail of the buying process but their sanction is necessary for any new buy or modified rebuy. They are often

senior to the buyer and difficult for the supplier to contact.

4) The *buyer* is the individual charged with day-to-day buying activities. He or she may or may not be able to adopt the role of decider. Swindley (1992) found that 80% of his sample had sole responsibility for selecting products from a given range, but only 44% had sole responsibility for deciding which product areas were carried. Some 91% had sole or shared responsibility for proposing which product areas were carried.

5) The *gatekeeper* plays an unusual role in any organisation as the channel through which information on a particular issue, a product or market, for example, is assumed to flow. Gatekeepers are acknowledged as having specialist knowledge and can be deferred to, probably because of experience. A gatekeeper may well be a senior buyer to whom junior buyers go for informal advice on suppliers, for example.

Tse (1985) provides an illustration of the DMU in one organisation, Marks & Spencer, by analysing four roles in that company's buying team for textile products. *Selectors* are responsible for market appraisal, identifying styles compatible with M & S's position in the market, obtaining samples from suppliers and liaison with stores. *Merchandisers* are responsible for forecasting; and for ensuring raw material supplies, agreeing range, colour and sizes, negotiating price, determining packaging and presentation and sales testing. The precise division into the two roles of selector and merchandiser is unusual in retailing but it reflects a division into marketing and buying aspects of the buying function that is seen in many retailers, with marketing tending to report to buying. Briggs (1984, p 71) described the merchandising role in M & S as to 'translate the business of the Buying Department into sales'. *Technologists* in M & S assess material properties, advise on production matters, determine technical specifications and monitor suppliers' production methods. Much of this is done in conjunction with *quality controllers* who also have specific responsibilities including testing for wearing and washing properties, determining suppliers' quality control systems and sampling quality themselves. This group form the informal core of the buying committee, effectively the main part of the DMU, but without some of the influencer and perhaps the decider roles. Typically a review of a product area is held under a chairperson – a senior manager, often a director. The role of the full-time members of the DMU is then to present their ideas for ratification by the group.

Who makes the actual decision in any buying committee can nevertheless be difficult to determine, when perhaps a 'vociferous group member can influence or even dominate the deliberations' (McGoldrick, 1990). How important a buying committee rather than an individual buyer is in making individual decisions in retailing as a whole is unclear. McGoldrick and Douglas (1983) found only a minority (albeit a substantial minority) of grocery retailers used them to select snack foods but Swindley's (1992) survey suggests that few buyers can make decisions on their own, leading to the view that informal committees exist even if the formality of a buying committee may not be used. In Chanil's (1991) survey only 20% of suppliers believed that buying committees were involved in decision-making for their products, while the buyer and merchandising manager were seen as being involved by 93% and 87%, respectively, in selection. It is tempting to suggest from these statistics that sellers may be underestimating the significance of buying committees, particularly in their policy-making role. From the author's own observation, the clearer the market position the retailer is aiming for, the more involved the senior management seem to be in selection, so as to ensure coherence of product offer and compatibility with the desired market position. Suppliers need to grasp the essence of how such judgements are made.

Buyer/seller models

One of the weaknesses of the models proposed by Sheth and Webster and Wind is that they are focused solely on the buying firm. The environment is considered to be the general business environment, including all suppliers. The relationships between individual companies are not a central part of either model. Hakansson (1982) is one of a number of researchers who sees the social aspects of buyer/seller relationships as central to an understanding of the buying process. Fig 3. 5 illustrates the main elements of such a perspective. Hakansson discusses three different perspectives on buyer/seller interaction: the notion that buyers are passive and sellers active; the notion that most purchases are discrete, one-off events; and, finally, that interactions are part of a relationship. The last of the three represents much of what many manufacturers are trying to achieve in their trade marketing and a social system model of retail buying provides a useful framework to understand the main elements in such an approach.

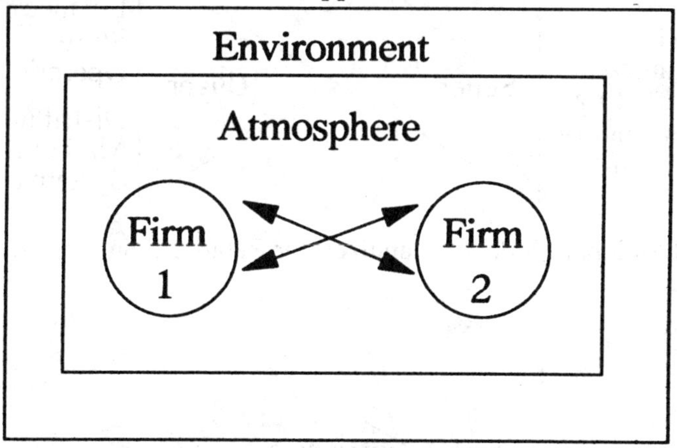

Figure 3. 5 A social system of buyer/seller interaction (after Hakansson, 1982)

Hakansson sees the interaction process as a series of episodes. The first is a product exchange, the second an information exchange, the third a financial exchange and the fourth a social exchange. These exchanges do not necessarily happen in that order but the important point is the number of exchanges that occur between two firms dealing with each other. The aim for the seller is the 'routinisation of exchange episodes' – in other words, to make all exchanges run smoothly, not just those between the salesperson and the buyer. Bonoma and Johnston (1978) recommend analysing business-to-business marketing at the level of the exchange between the two businesses, the so-called dyadic approach, where interactions within the buying firm and between the buyer and other sellers take second place to exchanges between one buyer and one seller. Thus factors like the personal relationships between individuals and their perceptions of each other's firms are important.

Writers on marketing such as Bagozzi (1975) believe that too little emphasis is placed on the exchange process which he sees as at the heart of marketing, defining marketing in turn as 'the discipline of exchange behaviour'. Dwyer *et al.* (1987) concur, emphasising that any exchange is 'not a discrete event, more part of a relationship'. They use the analogy of marriage, defined as a restrictive trade agreement, where the initial exchanges and the formal agreement are just part of a longer-term relationship. Dwyer *et al.* propose five stages in their model of relationship development: awareness, exploration, expansion, commitment and dissolution. Arndt (1979) coined the phrase 'domesticated market' to describe the outcome of such a relationship where the two organisations work as one to exploit the end market and not each other. The idea of forming a relationship between two firms presupposes that the effort is worth while. The size and importance of the transaction will have an important effect on the predisposition of the retailer to become more closely involved with any one supplier and the size of the retailer will determine whether the manufacturer deems it economic to invest the necessary time and effort.

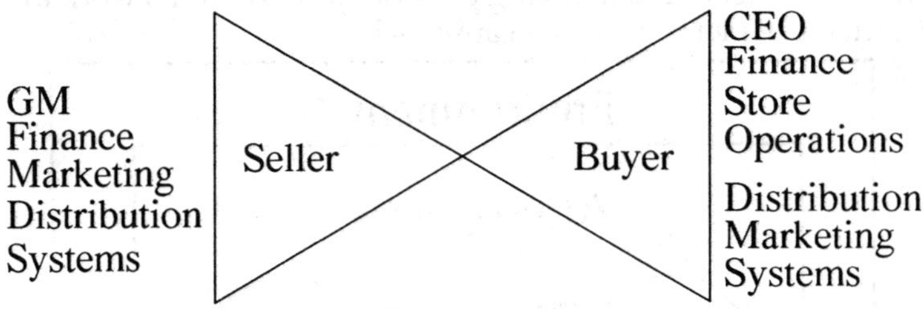

Traditional Model of Manufacturer/Retailer Relationship

Evolving Model of Manufacturer/Retailer Relationship

Figure 3. 6 Alternative models of manufacturer / retailer relationships

In such a close relationship between two organisations, there is no point trying to focus just on two individuals who are the main points of contact, the retail buyer and the supplier's salesperson. What is needed is a radical restructuring of the relationship between two firms from one where the focal point for the interaction *was* two people, the salesperson and the buyer, to one where interactions and relationships are developed between a number of key employees. Fig 3. 6 presents one manufacturer's view of how they see the relationships between themselves and individual, large retailers evolving.

With the traditional focus on the relationship between salesperson and buyer most communication is channelled through these two individuals. In reality a good deal of communication takes place between other functions in both organisations such as accounts and distribution. However it must be questioned as to how much ownership these individuals have of the relationship. In the evolving model, contact is regular and routine not only between the different marketing and buying functions but also between senior management. A general manager from the manufacturer meets regularly with the chief executive of the retailer to discuss the policies that might be needed to maximise the benefit both companies expect from the marketplace. Financial managers meet to see how cash flow can be improved by better cooperation and how capital investment decisions should be made by the manufacturer in the light of retailer plans. Such comments smack of the altruism referred to earlier in this book that might be presumed in both sides for such an idea to work, but a later chapter and the interviews before this chapter, it is hoped, show that such ideas can be used in practice. The evolving model makes it clear that relationships between both organisations have to be genuinely close.

Buying groups

The ideas discussed thus far are more relevant to the large retail company and to product categories where individual suppliers form a substantial part of such retailers' business. The concept of relational marketing can be used as a principle to guide the design of any selling/buying interface, but the idea of building substantial interorganisational linkages is not going to be relevant for a large manufacturer in dealing directly with many small retailers. However manufacturers can probably benefit from building closer relationships with wholesalers and retail buying groups. Hardy and Magrath (1987) suggest that buying groups tend to flourish in industries marked by fragmentation among suppliers. In America buying groups exist for wholesalers as well as retailers. Even professionals such as doctors, veterinarians and lawyers have their own voluntary purchasing organisations. In one survey, 44% of independent pharmacists were members of a buying group or co-operative (Glaser, 1992). The advantages of joining a buying group include the discounts that can be obtained from the collective volumes purchased and the reduction in time spent dealing with suppliers directly. The buying group is acting very much as a traditional wholesaler in this role. One further benefit is own-label – something the smaller retailer might find uneconomic to develop is possible via a buying group.

But buying in groups can have its drawbacks. Membership may limit choice and commit the retailer to adopt procedures more akin to those one might expect in franchise. Tensions can exist between larger and smaller members of the group. Nevertheless Hardy and Magrath identified a number of groups that have evolved through five stages of growth from the formation of a group that exists solely due to its buying power to one that offers order handling, warehousing, merchandising, own label, store identity and support services such as product development and training. Buying groups are a way independent retailers can respond to the power of the multiple retailer without losing the independence they might lose by joining a franchise.

In Britain voluntary associations or chains, sometimes also known as symbol groups, are defined as an association between one or more wholesalers contracted to supply a chain of independent retailers. The retailer agrees to take a certain amount of goods each week and in exchange receives a discount. About 50 such organizations exist, offering products ranging from electrical goods to frozen food and from healthfood to shoes (Newman Books, 1987). Some such as Spar are relatively complex organisations, in this case involving a number of wholesalers worldwide.

The problem for the manufacturer dealing with voluntary groups or traditional wholesalers and cash and carries is the absence of direct contact with the retailer but the one advantage of the voluntary group is the strength of the agreement the retailer might make to take certain lines and volume. The wholesaler might offer a discount, that depends upon volume, to the retailer to try to ensure patronage but the voluntary chain might provide a more reliable way of influencing a number of independents.

The case study following this chapter is of a small retail fashion chain. Their relationship with their suppliers are traditional – manufacturer and retailer each have their distinct roles and contact and cooperation are limited. Even though the retailer represents a major outlet for one particular manufacturer, there was no close relationship.

One point of interest is the reason given for de-listing a supplier. Quite simply the merchandise did not sell. Compare this with the (all too complex?) lists from the research cited earlier in this chapter.

Keypoint Summary

1) Today's retail buyer is a young professional wielding considerable power.
2) How decisions are made by retail buyers is context specific and seen as complex. However the process can be analysed as a series of interrelated processes and influences.
3) Recent research suggests analysing retail buying/trade marketing as a 'relationship'. Suppliers may need to change their approach in trade marketing from selling towards building relationships.

References

Arndt, J. (1979) Towards a Concept of Domesticated Markets, *Journal of Marketing*, Vol 43, Fall, p 69.

Bagozzi, R. P. (1975) Marketing as Exchange, *Journal of Marketing*, Vol 39, October, p 32.

Banting, P. M., Blenkhorn, D. L. (1988) The Mind of the Retail Buyer, *Management Decision*, Vol 26, No 6 p 29.

Bonoma, T., Johnston, W. (1978) The Social Psychology of Industrial Buying and Selling, *Industrial Marketing Management*, Vol 7, July, p 213.

Briggs, A. (1984) *Marks and Spencer 1884–1984*, Octopus Books, London, p 71.

Chanil, D. (1991) Reaching Further, Climbing Higher, *Discount Merchandiser*, Vol 31, No 7, July, p 22.

Davies, G. (1989) *What NEXT?*, Century, London.

Davies, K., Gilligan, C., Sutton, C. (1985) Structural Changes in Grocery Retailing: The Implications for Competition, *International Journal of Physical Distribution and Materials Management*, Vol 15, No 2, p 3.

Dickenson, R. A. (1967) Buyer Decision Making, Institute of Business and Economic Research, Berkeley, Calif., in Kotler, P. (ed) *Marketing Management* (7th Ed), Prentice-Hall, Englewood Cliffs, NJ.

Dowst, S. (1987) Wanted, Suppliers Adept at Turning Corners, *Purchasing*, Jan 29, p 73.

Doyle, P., Weinberg, C. B. (1973) Effective New Product Decisions For Supermarkets, *Operational Research Quarterly*, Vol 24, No 1, p 45.

Dwyer, F. R., Schurr, P. H., Oh, S. (1987) Developing Buyer–Seller Relationships, *Journal of Marketing*, Vol 51, April, p 11.

Emmelhainz, M. A., Stock, J. R., Emmelhainz, L. W. (1991) Consumer Response to Retail Stock Outs, *Journal of Retailing*, Vol 67, No 2, p 138.

Glaser, M. (1992) Buying Groups: What Have You Done For Me Lately?, *Drug Topics*, Vol 136, No 11, p 48.

Grant, A. (1988) The Death of the Sales Force?, *Admap*, April, p 37.

Hakansson, H. (1982) *International Marketing and Purchasing of Industrial Goods*, Wiley, Chichester.

Hardy, K. G., Magrath, A. J. (1987) Buying Groups: Clout for Small Businesses, *Harvard Business Review*, Sept/Oct, p 16.

McGoldrick, P. J. (1990) *Retail Marketing*, McGraw-Hill, London.

McGoldrick, P. J., Douglas, R. A. (1983) Factors Influencing the Choice of a Supplier by Grocery Distributors, *European Journal of Marketing*, Vol 17, No 5, p 13.

McVey, P. (1960) Are Channels of Distribution what the Textbooks say?, *Journal of Marketing*, Jan, p 61.

Newman Books (1987) *Retail Directory 1987*, London.

Nilsson, J., Host, V. (1987) *Reseller Assortment Decision Criteria*, Aarhus University Press, Aarhus.

Parkinson, M. J., Baker, S. T. (1986) *Organisational Buying Behaviour*, Macmillan, Basingstoke.

Robinson, P. J., Faris, C. W., Wind, Y. (1967) *Industrial Buying and Creative Marketing*, Allyn and Bacon, Boston, Mass.

Sheth, J. N. (1973) A Model of Industrial Buyer Behaviour, *Journal of Marketing*, Vol 37, October, p 50.

Shipley, D. D. (1985) Reseller's Supplier Selection Criteria for Different Consumer Products, *European Journal of Marketing*, Vol 19, No 7, p 26.

Swindley, D. (1992) The Role of the Buyer in UK Multiple Retailing, *International Journal of Retail Distribution Management*, Vol 20, No 2, p 3.

Tse, K. K. (1985) *Marks and Spencer: Anatomy of Britain's Most Efficiently Managed Company*, Pergamon, London.

Twiss, B. (1974) *Managing Technological Innovation*, Longman, London, p 8.
Wagner, J., Ettenson, R., Parrish, J. (1989) Vendor Selection Among Retail Buyers: An Analysis by Merchandise Division, *Journal of Retailing*, Vol 65, No 1, Spring, p 58.
Warner, L. (1988) The Powers that Buy, *Marketing*, 23 June, p 26.
Webster, F. E., Wind, Y. (1972) A General Model for Understanding Organisational Buying Behaviour, *Journal of Marketing*, Vol 36, April, p 12.

Case Study: EMMA SOMERSET

Women's fashions

Women's fashions in Britain are sold primarily by speciality shops, variety chain stores such as BhS and Littlewoods, department stores and by mail order. If anything the speciality shops increased their market share in the 1980s (Exhibit 1).

	1982	1984	1986	1988
Women's, girls', children's and infants' shops	33.1	36.5	37.6	37.8
Mixed retailers	38.2	35.2	35.2	31.7

Exhibit 1 Percentage of sector sales (*source: Business Monitor*, SDA25, *Retailing*)

However, sales of ladieswear at £8.4 billion had shown a decline in real terms in the late 1980s (KeyNote, 1991). Gross margins averaging 45% had been whittled down to net margins of below 4%. The heavy spending group aged 15 – 24 were declining in numbers but the 35–54-year-old group was increasing. Many of this age group earned their own money and this was the group that spent proportionally more on dresses.

Large multiples such as Marks & Spencer, the Burton groups' Principles and Evans, Laura Ashley, Next, Richards, Country Casuals and Jaeger competed with a large number of independents for this market. The independents and some department stores provided the outlet for the large number of small manufacturers. Import penetration was generally high in ladieswear. Many continental manufacturers such as Escada, Laurel, Mondi, Triumph and Hucke had established their reputations in the market. Finally a number of manufacturers had begun to open their own shops.

Many smaller manufacturers sold via commission agents. Few agents seemed to see their role as needing a long-term view of building relationships or the reputation of the names they represented. There was no incentive to retain the exclusivity of a brand within a local area to one retailer (something the retailer would value) – rather the opposite as the more accounts that were opened the greater the agent's chance of earning commission.

Some manufacturers could provide a threat to the independent retailer. The retailer could develop sales of the manufacturer's lines only to see the manufacturer open their own outlet or concession once the market had been developed. At the same time retailers could be fickle in their patronage of a manufacturer, buying one year and de-listing the next.

Each year manufacturers displayed their wares at a number of fashion shows in Europe and North America.

Emma Somerset

A teacher of home economics and her wholesaler husband opened their first ladieswear shop in Manchester in 1968. By 1992 the business had grown to a turnover of approximately £4.5 million employing 100 people. The company traded from nine outlets, eight of them in the North of England and one in London. Three different names were used over the shop fronts: Emma Somerset, French Dressing and Betty Barclay. Originally the intention had been to open two separate shops in each town the business located within, French Dressing being targeted at a younger age group than Emma Somerset. Two stores were called Betty Barclay, the brand name of a German manufacturer, for whom the company had become one of their largest British outlets.

The overall positioning of the seven core shops was to 'specialise in special occasion clothes'. While most ages and type of women might be attracted to such an offer, the core customer would be relatively well-off, the working woman who looked for quality brand names and who was prepared to pay prices above those in most chain stores. Apart from Betty Barclay a number of other Continental brand names were stocked, such as Gina Bacconi, Fiorito, Christina Santandrea, Louis Féraud, Jessica McClintock and Fink. Some bridal wear and cocktail dresses were sourced from Britain and the company had begun to put its own labels on to a number of lines. The two Betty Barclay Shops specialised in sportswear coordinates.

In any one year there would be a nucleus of about 45 different suppliers. Each year some new ones would be introduced to provide variety and to replace those whose products had not sold. Not selling well was by far the most common reason for discontinuing supply. Even the relationship with Betty Barclay, that had developed to the point where the company used the German company's name on two of their stores was very much in line with the way the company conducted their business with their other suppliers.

Manufacturer and retailer each held distinct roles. The manufacturers put together their collections each year that needed to reflect changes in fashion and offer something the retailer believed would sell. The director of Emma Somerset responsible for buying saw her role as selecting from the various collections on behalf of her customers. She did not see herself as a designer, looking for a supplier to make for her. Judging what would sell was all important, as once an order had been placed the retailer could not receive a refund on unsold goods. Supplier and retailer acted as separate businesses, rather than as members of the same supply chain. There was some exchange of information on market trends and manufacturer support for any advertising featuring their brands, but that was all.

Both retailer and supplier held a kind of power over the other, but none of the relationships were formal enough for the concept to be totally relevant. Because they controlled the brand and created the initial offer the manufacturer could be regarded as leading the relationship – but the retailer could claim the same position as it too created its own offer and had developed relationships with its regular customers. In few ways could the relationship be regarded as a partnership, even though the two roles complemented each other – they remained two opposite businesses each with different talents.

Note

The relationships between many smaller retailers and their suppliers will be similar to that illustrated by this case study. As will be discussed in Chapters 9 and 10, having two distinct roles and little in the way of a clear relationship may be perfectly logical as the costs of doing so are high. However in this instance is it really in the manufacturer's interests to treat with the retailer so much at arm's length? How well did the supplier understand the retailer's business?

Reference

KeyNote (1991) *Women's Fashions*, KeyNote Publications, Hampton, Middx.

4

UNDERSTANDING A RETAIL BUSINESS

A simplified model of retail buying was used in Chapter 3 to identify the main influences on, and the processes within, the buying activity in a retail business. Retailer buying is characterised among industrial and commercial buying because the buyer is purchasing for resale. The retail buying role is then a complex blend of purchasing and marketing. The retail business as a whole is endeavouring to attract customers to its stores and to extract as much as it can, in financial terms, by doing so. It was argued in Chapters 2 and 3 that the retailer is trying to create a market position as well as retailing a range of specific and individual products and/or services. This implies that behind the fast-moving, rather reactive face that most retailers like to exhibit to their suppliers, there is a longer-term, strategic view of the business that shapes shorter-term decision-making. In the buying model presented in Fig 3. 4 this was shown by 'company factors' influencing the buying process. So within retail businesses, how do their long-term objectives, cultures and strategies impact upon the buying process? The purpose of this chapter is to identify a number of factors that could be important in the strategic management of a retail business and, as a consequence, determine the framework for its relationships with its suppliers. Understanding these factors is likely to be essential for the supplier in any attempt to adopt the more integrated model of supplier/buyer interaction proposed towards the end of Chapter 3.

But do many retailers have a strategy? Gilligan and Sutton (1987) quote two earlier authors as suggesting that retailers tend to be tactical rather than strategic in their thinking. To be 'fast on one's feet' is more important than having a long-term vision of the future for business. Indeed a long-term plan could well be a constraint on a business that needs to react swiftly to short-term trends. That said, retailers are increasingly involved in decision-making that is inherently long-term. Capital investment in ever larger stores, distribution systems and electronic point of sale are examples of long term commitments that imply that retailers do, or will have to, use concepts of strategic rather than tactical planning. Gilligan and Sutton's own survey of 34 grocery and DIY chains indicated that long-term planning is still somewhat embryonic in British retailing. Only 7 firms claimed to use a planning period of more than 5 years. This compared with a somewhat longer-term view taken by American retailers in a survey reported by Feinberg *et al.* (1983) but the British study indicated that many retailers had only recently introduced strategic planning. Even in America, the planning horizons of retailers tended to be far shorter than those of manufacturers.

Suppliers to retail businesses must then expect a shorter term perspective than they are used to within their own organisations. The whole culture of the retailer's business could well be different. Assuming that the norms of the one can or should apply to the other, just because they are both concerned with the supply of the same product to the eventual consumer, guarantees misunderstanding and conflict.

Financial aspects of retailer planning

How retailers plan will vary from business to business but two parallel processes should be evident within any business plan: a financial plan and a strategic plan. The first is likely to be more tangible than the second. The overall financial goal will normally be to achieve better results than last year, where 'better' will mean higher turnover, higher net margin and greater return on capital employed. Costs will be controlled by budgeting and individual business areas will be targeted on both turnover and notional profit. In terms of its financial management, a multiple retail business can be regarded as a matrix – Fig 4. 1.

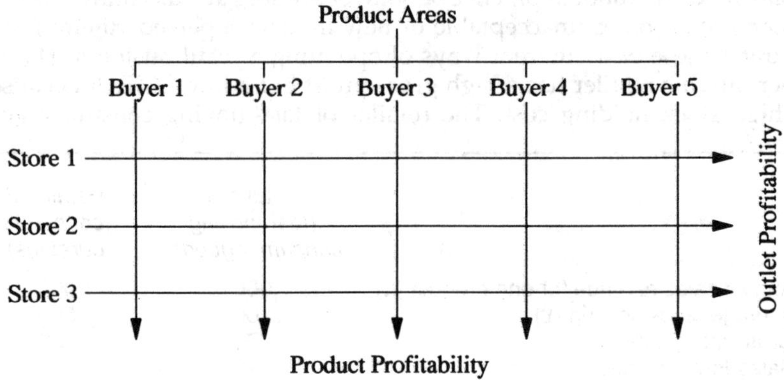

Figure 4. 1 Profit accountability in multiple retailing

Each buyer is responsible for the profitability of a product range. Each store manager is responsible for the profitability of an individual store. Fig 4. 1 is a somewhat idealistic model of what happens in practice. The problem facing a retail business is the allocation of costs to two different types of profit centre. Ideally each buyer should know what the full costs associated with buying and retailing any product are. Ideally each store manager should be able to control all the costs that can be allocated to a store's budget. A number of advances have been made in allocating appropriate costs to individual product lines and these will be discussed later in this chapter. Because of the problems of calculating a true profit for each and every product, however, most buyers appear not to be appraised on true product profitability, but more a surrogate for it, such as a combination of gross margin and turnover (Swindley, 1992). There is a lack of hard information about whether the use of surrogates for true profit can produce sub-optimisation of total profit. One supplier to retailers once complained to the author that his merchandise had been rejected by a large retailer because the gross margin he proposed the retailer make was considered to be too high. The buyer was not so worried about value for money for the shopper but that the gross margin was higher than the one she had to work to. If this was the case, then the retailer might have missed an opportunity for revenue and profit by insisting upon a lower gross margin target. Nevertheless gross margin, and particularly gross margin expressed as a percentage of average inventory investment, is frequently recommended in retailing textbooks as a way of controlling retail performance, as it represents a 'return on investment relationship' (Davidson *et al.*, 1988).

Gross margin return on inventory investment (GMROI) *can* provide a partial picture of a product's contribution to the overall business, but an unclear one. An acceptable GMROI can be obtained in a number of ways, depending upon the nature of the merchandise and the philosophy of the retailer. Low margins can be acceptable if stockturn (the rate of sale of the goods compared to their stockholding) is high. Most grocery and routine DIY products and much of the personal-care product sector suit a low margin/high turnover approach. Products such as furniture, and many consumer durables, tend to have a higher margin and lower rate of sale. Indeed many display models cannot in practice be sold, or are sold at a discount, once their appearance becomes unacceptable or new models supersede them. Fig 4. 2 illustrates these two different ways of operating a retail business. The consumer durable retailer has a high gross profit but a low GMROI because of the high stock holding cost. The retailer of fast-moving consumer goods

	Retailer 1 (fast-moving consumer goods)	*Retailer 2 (consumer durables)*
Annual sales revenue for one product (£)	1,000	1,000
Average stock holding (£)	100	500
Gross margin (%)	20	50
Sales-to-stock ratio	10	2
Stockturn (weeks)	5.2	26
Gross profit (£)	200	500
GMROI (%)	200	100

Figure 4. 2 GMROI calculation for different retailer types

achieves a lower gross margin but a higher GMROI. Both can increase their GMROI by lowering the stock holding cost. One method of doing so is to pay for stock only after it has been sold or find some other way of ensuring that the supplier funds the stock holding costs. This does little to change the total profitability of the product to the marketing channel as a whole. Alternatively the gross margin can be raised by increasing the selling price or negotiating a lower selling price from the supplier.

The problem here is that GMROI is no more than a performance indicator that might be useful in identifying problem products within a similar range. It gives no clear indication of the true value of the line to the retailer. For example any retailer with a stockturn of 26 weeks is likely to be carrying too much stock rather than carrying stock that should be paid for by someone else. Products with low gross margins can be profitable to the retailer if they sell quickly and the cost of selling them is also low. The problem with Retailer 1 in Fig 4. 2 is that the product may not be making any profit, because the low gross margin could be more than absorbed by the costs of retailing it. Thus retailers of high turnover, low margin products tend to use methods other than GMROI even when comparing similar products.

One technique that has been attracting attention is recent years is direct product profitability (DPP), since its inception in the 1960s, (*The Economist*, 1982). The idea is still at an early stage of adoption. In one study by Andrew and Maier (1989), 86% of retailers did not use the concept, 31% of non-users giving 'difficulty in gathering data' as the main reason. Obtaining appropriate data is certainly a problem. In essence, DPP involves constructing a profit and loss account for each stock item. A product variant, such as a special-offer pack or a smaller size, needs its own separate calculation. The gross margin for each stock item is adjusted for any financial incentives offered by the supplier such as discount or credit. The costs incurred by each item are then deducted for the item's share of display, storage, warehousing, transport, labour and head office costs. One method is to charge the line a notional 'rent' for the shelf space it occupies, with the rental charge being calculated by dividing the retailer's total operating costs by the total shelving space it has; but this ignores any differences in handling or spoilage costs.

Calculating a true DPP is a complex task and is only part of the answer to the merchandiser's problem of how to allocate space between products that have similar DPPs because of differences in consumer reactions. Fig 4. 3 identifies the four options a retailer has once it calculates a DPP. One of the issues for a retailer is that a product with a low DPP may still be essential to

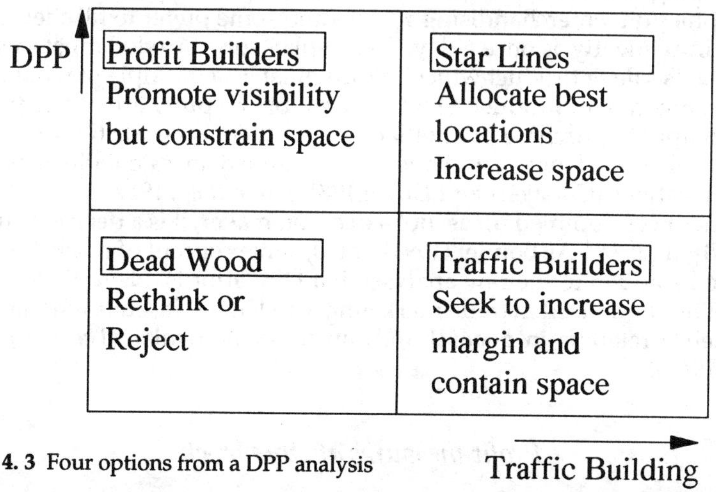

Figure 4. 3 Four options from a DPP analysis

its business success if the product generates a low customer flow (despite being unprofitable). One retailer for example once used a DPP analysis to determine that it made little apparent contribution from retailing petfood. However, when it tried to delete the product area it found it lost customers.

The presence of the product, rather than its margin, was the source of profit to the retailer.

The ideal product for any retailer has a high DPP *and* is capable of attracting custom, a Star Line. Products to be considered for deletion are those with a low DPP and with no apparent benefit from attracting custom. One task for the manufacturer is to convince retailers that its products are, or potentially are, Star Lines. The key issue here is *where* the product will be displayed in the store, even down to where on a run of shelving it appears. Dyer (1980) found that goods displayed at the entrance to the first aisle in an outlet increased normal sales by an average of 363%. Gagnon and Osterhaus (1985) identified other 'hot spots' and found that floor displays worked to increase sales in pharmacies. Scarborough and Zimmerer (1984) suggest a decline in the value of space to a retailer from the front to the back of a single sales floor in the ratio 4:3:2:1 for each quarter of total floorspace. Lewison and Delozier (1986) point to a similar effect on the value of different sales floors in a multi-floor shop. Where the ground floor is 'worth' many times more than the top floor in a department store perhaps different rental values can be used in different parts of the store and on different rows of shelving. The objective of the manufacturer is to ensure that its products are merchandised in appropriate 'hot spots'. It is no surprise that suppliers have been to the fore in promoting the use of DPP analysis, arguing always that their premium brands be given the largest display in the best location. Some of the computerised systems for DPP have associated software that produce a lifelike representation of the shelf layout suggested by the DPP analysis (*The Grocer*, 1987). Thus in one analysis the retailer can decide on both the business and aesthetic logics of space allocation.

Space allocation can also be affected by stocking problems. For example a retailer will be reluctant to allocate space such that the number of products in each packing case does not match the display space. Retailers vary in their philosophies on remerchandising shelves and some prefer to fill shelves perhaps as infrequently as once a day. The display space needed must therefore hold a day's sale of product which in turn must be a multiple of what is contained in one case of product. Finally the shopper's purchase of one product may prompt the purchase of another. So-called cross-elasticities of demand between associated products have been included in calculations of retail space allocations (Corstjens and Doyle 1981 Rinne *et al.*, 1987).

DPP has been summed up as 'not a decision maker; it is a decision support tool' (Whyte, 1988). As Boudet (1991) noted, some concept of market position needs to be added to the raw analysis that DPP affords. Nevertheless it is a tool that has been used in trade marketing – by United Biscuits among others to influence retailers in general and buyers in particular (*The Independent Grocer*, 1988).

Profit measures at store level

For the independent retailer or those who still purchase at store level the foregoing section will apply to the store manager in his or her role as a buyer. In Britain store management working for multiple retailers now have limited purchasing responsibility. Planograms descend from head office for those selling from shelf-dominated stores much as the tablets of stone from the mountain in biblical times. It is often an offence punishable by dismissal not to merchandise shelving in other than the prescribed way. Retailers of less uniform products, such as catalogue shop retailers Argos and some fashion stores, send out photographs of displays to ensure uniformity of design and presentation. It is possible to adjust shelf space allocation to take account of local trading conditions (Johnson, 1989), but this is still a relatively recent idea for those multiple retailers who have spent the last decade or so in centralising their businesses. By way of contrast, retailers of fashion often change the presentation of merchandise locally and regularly. Their creative flair in presentation can be an important element in achieving sales as it is difficult to devise a 'look' that can be imposed to the level of defining what garment is displayed where. That said, the trend to increased emphasis on design in the 1980s led to store designs that did achieve more centralised control as the fixtures and fittings in a completely fitted store could no longer be moved around at will by store personnel and individual fixtures could only be used for a limited number of product types.

These days the emphasis in most retail chain stores is not so much about entrepreneurial flair enhancing trade, but in adhering to a formula defined elsewhere, and in controlling costs. There is a saying in retailing, 'control your costs and the profits look after themselves' – and much debate on

	Budget (£000s)	*Actual (£000s)*
Sales revenue		
Product Class 1	600	621
Product Class 2	400	370
Product Class 3	150	155
Total revenue	1,150	1,146
Non-controllable costs		
Rent	425	425
Rates	66	66
Head office costs	100	97
Total non-controllable cost	591	588
Controllable costs		
Labour	340	345
Light and heat	40	39
Telephone	10	16
Postage	5	6
Local advertising	7	5
Repairs	11	9
Total controllable cost	413	420
Contribution	146	138

Figure 4. 4 Simplified example of retail store accounts

whether stores are profit or cost centres. Most are not treated as pure profit centres because they have little flexibility to change the fundamentals of their business and the management emphasis is very much on budgetary control. Fig 4. 4 presents a simplified version of an actual operating statement or branch account.

The store manager is expected to work within a number of 'controllable' budgets. Labour costs tend to be the key budget area but energy costs can also be significant. Not shown on this example are shrinkage costs, a euphemism for everything that should have been sold but wasn't, because of spoilage, breakage or theft. A separate control document is used to record the merchandise that entered the store. Stock is counted regularly and an annual check conducted by head office is usual. What should have been sold is reconciled with what has been sold together with any shift in stock levels. Many store managers have the authority to mark down, that is discount, merchandise outside of an official sale, but this is also noted in the calculation and 'mark downs' are often budgeted for. The reconciliation between the two measures of sales reveals any unaccounted shortages. Much of any discrepancy is likely to be due to the theft. An estimated 1–2% of retail turnover is stolen; half is put down to customers, half to staff. Few thefts are detected but retailers have a number of methods to use as deterrents (Elder, 1989), although only half of retailers seem to receive regular information about losses due to theft (Touche Ross, 1989). Shrinkage, and particularly theft, represents a serious and growing problem for retailers. Anything manufacturers can do, particularly those supplying articles more desirable to the thief, to make theft more difficult could be welcomed by retailers.

Labour costs

Labour costs in the example in Fig 4. 4 represent a high percentage of turnover. The Institute of Fiscal Studies (1982) calculated a range of labour costs from just under 10% of turnover in food, alcohol and confectionary retailing to just over 18% in clothing and footwear. Labour costs can be reduced by increasing the level of self-service, by keeping wages low and by substituting the more flexible resource of part-time staff for full time employees. In the early 1980s the number of hours worked in retailing in Britain by full-time employees fell to equal the rising level of hours worked by part-timers (Sparks, 1987). The notion is simple enough: part-timers generally cost less per hour because they do not attract certain employment overheads and they can, up to a point, be scheduled to work when retail stores are busy, on Saturdays, at lunchtime and in the early evening.

One problem a greater reliance on part-timers may cause, within the context of a general reduction in the total numbers employed in retailing despite rising sales (see Fig 1. 5), is a decline in service. Competence, responsiveness and reliability are all traits that determine the perception customers hold of a service business (Parasuraman *et al.*, 1985). Retailers relying upon part-time staff may have problems training and retaining staff with an adequate level of expertise. In those sectors where service is important, access to training packages could also be important and manufacturers can and do find opportunities to influence retail staff by providing training to retailers. Strong links are made in some sectors, upmarket furniture and apparel for example, between individual manufacturers and retail sales people, to ensure that the latter do have the knowledge necessary to respond to customer questions. Sales people are given factory tours, talks by designers and technologists and often as not reductions on their own purchases. Relational marketing has been mentioned thus far more in the context of head office staff, but in some sectors the key relationships are still between manufacturer and retail sales people. In other sectors, such as cosmetics, the retail sales people are often the employees of the manufacturer working in what can better be regarded as a concession within the retailer's premises, but more of this later.

Space as an asset

Occupancy costs account for some 13–15% of a typical retailer's sales (Reynolds, 1989). During the early 1990s when revenue slumped in many retail sectors, occupancy costs rose to as much as 25% of turnover for retailers who leased their premises rather than owned them. The problem was that many leases allowed for rental increases but not for decreases. Few UK retailers enjoy the kind of lease that appears relatively commonplace in North America where rental is proportional to turnover.

By 1990, it became clear that there was too much retail shop space at too high a price available despite the rise in retail sales and there was a dramatic reduction in new openings in 1991/92. Earlier, during the 1960s and 1970s, a process of renewal had begun which saw the introduction of city-centre shopping centres, often replacing the traditional high street. During the

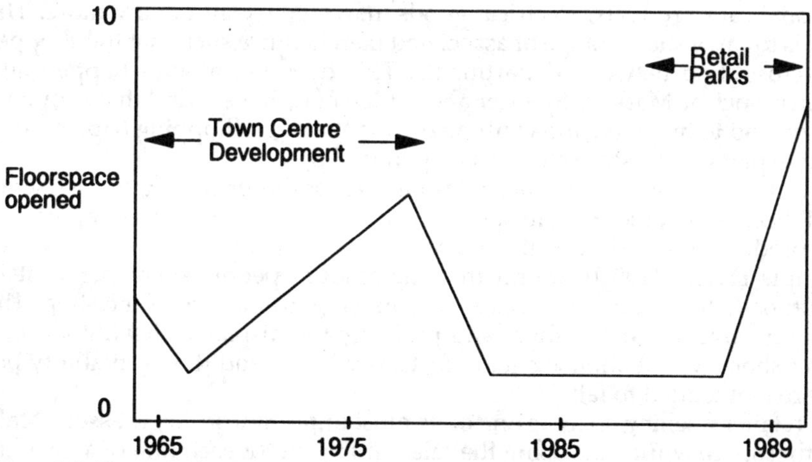

Figure 4. 5 Phases in the increase of retail floor space (*source:* Hillier Parker)

1980s a different process, the suburbanisation of retailing, became the dominant theme. Retail parks were developed on the edge of or out of town. Food superstores, DIY and other 'sheds' were built with good road access to an increasingly mobile population and again on the edge of town. The out-of-town shopping mall became a significant feature of British retailing and concern was raised as to whether the move away from the city centre would produce a 'doughnut effect', leaving the city centre relatively destitute as commercial activity moved away (NEDO, 1988), as had been seen in American cities such as Atlanta.

Ease of access for the car-borne shopper was one reason for retailers' seeking stores on the edge of town. But retailers were also seeking to obtain larger stores. As Fig 1. 5 demonstrated the number of retail outlets has been declining while the volume of retail sales has been increasing. To accommodate this effect the average size of a shop has been increasing, as can be seen for Marks and Spencer in the first case study. There is evidence that larger shops are more economical to run because of the economy of scale effect (NEDO, 1979; Lusch and Moon, 1984). Labour costs appear to be the key, particularly in a self-service environment, as labour can be used more economically in a larger, well-organised outlet. However there may also be significant economies of scope, the savings being possible by increasing the number of product areas on sale in the same outlet which encourages the shopper to spend more each visit. The retail specialist, the butcher, the baker, the candlestick maker, has given way to the grocery superstore. If you increase the depth of merchandise (increase the number of similar lines) you do increase the chance that any one shopper will make a selection. There is a limit to this effect, however, as most shoppers are prepared to switch between brands or styles to some extent, and too much merchandise can even be off-putting. If you increase the breadth of merchandise (increase the number of dissimilar lines) you increase the chance of other, perhaps associated purchases being made and reduce the chance that no purchase at all will be made.

Grocery superstores developed away from a role of just selling groceries and introduced fresh meat, then fresh vegetables and fruit, then fish and now personal care products, electrical goods, newsagency and many more. The trick is to carry such a range of associated merchandise such that the shopper will cross-shop between departments. This does not always happen and retailers such as Marks & Spencer and Littlewoods have found that shoppers do not tend to buy food and clothing during the same shopping trip, treating the two parts of the store almost as separate shops.

It is likely that many product areas have an optimum selling space (Good, 1984) because people seem to spend a certain amount each shopping trip on any product area and the retailer's costs increase with the size of space. For example Davies (1991b) found that the amount people spent per visit to healthfood shops did not increase very much with the size of the shop. The optimum size for such a shop, and probably the display of healthfood in a larger shop, was about 600 square feet. Any larger and the profitability per square foot tended to fall.

A retailer's selling space is one of its most important strategic assets. Making that space work, increasing the sales and profit for each unit of area, is an important aspect of retailing. Manufacturers need to be aware of the approaches used by their retail clients in space management: what are the criteria being used and how do these impact on product selection? Many retailers calculate sales or profit per square foot for individual products or groups of products. Others use sales or profit per running foot of shelving. Some use cubic feet of space as their basis for comparison.

The temptation for the retailer is to cram as much merchandise into the available sales area as possible – because this might increase the chance of a customer selecting something. However, stock density on the sales floor also affects the image that the store projects. A high stock density can imply budget price and a low stock density exclusiveness.

Financial performance criteria

Fig 4. 6 summarises the main financial performance criteria in retailing. In most businesses, return (profit) on capital employed (the worth of the business or the money invested in it) is the key financial performance criterion. This one ratio is the product of two others: profit on sales (net margin) and sales on capital employed. Both of these have contributing ratios.

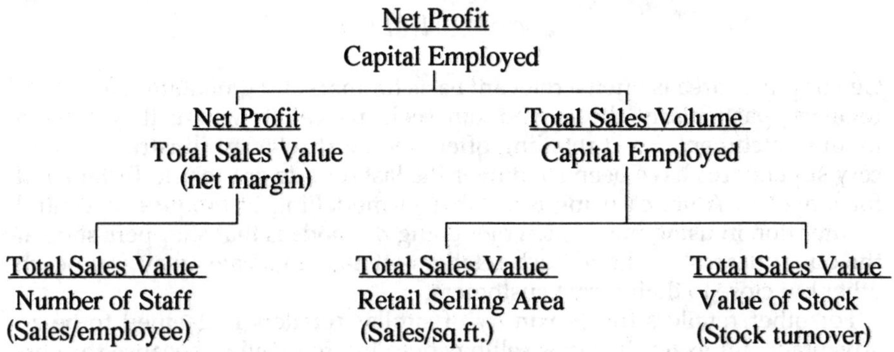

Figure 4. 6 Main financial performance measures in retailing

GMROI is sometimes used as a surrogate for the more precise measures shown here because of the difficulty of calculation. The various ratios form the main financial influences that impinge upon the buying process. Suppliers would be well advised to identify how their offerings might improve the performance measures used by their retail clients and to calculate the levels being met by such clients to suggest why their products can improve upon them.

Strategic planning and market position

Parallel to the financial planning side of a retail business will be a strategic plan, more qualitative in nature and often more difficult to identify. As a starting point for strategic planning, Porter (1985) recommends four broad methods of industry segmentation, that is the division of an entire sector into sizeable chunks so that a business can identify which segment to enter and compete within. The four methods are by:

1) product type;
2) by geographical area;
3) by distribution channel; and
4) by customer type.

Retailers are themselves distribution channels and, at first sight, the retailer has little choice on this dimension, but retailers can choose to enter other distribution channels, such as when Next purchased Gratton's mail order business and launched the *Next Directory*. Customer type is discussed later as a means of market segmentation rather than industry segmentation. The type of customer is difficult to predetermine in operating a retail business as most shops offer open access to the public. Sometimes product type (menswear, ladieswear, childrenswear) or location (town centre, suburban, corner shop) will go a long way towards determining a broad customer type but only in mail order or direct mail retailing is it really possible to control the customer type. Product type and partly geographical area are more relevant ways of dividing the retail sector into its main sub-markets. As has been mentioned already in this chapter, retailers have tended to broaden their product ranges but discrete product sectors still exist, even though the boundaries between them are becoming increasingly blurred.

Location strategy

Geographical area is often a relevant basis for market segmentation for many retailers, particularly those who can seek a location where they have a unique catchment. Food retailing offers the most relevant illustration. Grocery superstores have been sited over the last decade or more in Britain and for longer in America using a number of modelling techniques. A central assumption in using many such modelling methods is that shoppers shop at the outlet nearest to them. Such retailers attempt to locate away from each other but close to their target customers.

For other retailers the proximity of similar retailers is deemed to be an advantage, for example shops selling shoes locate together because the customer might feel the need to undertake a good deal of comparison shopping before deciding. Further issues include the presence or otherwise of an anchor or magnet store in a shopping centre. A retailer such as Marks & Spencer can attract shoppers to a centre to the benefit of other retailers trading nearby. In a shopping centre the numbers of people passing can be another indicator of the potential value of the site. The topic of retail location is therefore quite involved and a number of techniques can be used to enhance the often subjective judgement of the retailer (Davies and Rogers, 1984). The significance to the manufacturer is probably more to their physical distribution activities, because of a need to understand the spatial organisation of retail business, rather than to the trade marketer. Some of the distribution aspects of location are considered in more depth in a later chapter.

In a crowded island such as Britain where distances between retail centres can be small within urban sprawls such as London, Birmingham and Manchester, an analysis of retail potential based solely on the location perspective of the economic geographer can be misleading. Measuring the distance between a retail outlet and the home of the shopper can be particularly misleading, given the changing role of the main shopper, the now inappropriately labelled 'housewife'. She is now likely to have a job, outside of the home probably has the use of a car, has more money but less time to spend shopping and would tend to regard any shopping centre between home and work as being a potential place to shop. The image of a retail centre and that of individual shops is likely to be a significant factor. Attempts have been made to improve the predictivity of models for retail patronage by including a measure of attractiveness or image (Stanley and Sewall, 1976, 1978; Moore,

1988).

Mention of image as a significant element in retail strategy takes us below the level of industry segmentation in strategic analysis. The channel is defined, the product is defined, the geographical aspects of competition are probably clear. The issue now is *how* to compete within the segment that this broad brush segmentation of the market into largely product-based specialisms leaves us.

Positioning or segmentation?

The process of strategic marketing is often assumed to follow these stages (Kotler, 1991):

- Decide which market to compete within.
- Segment the customer base.
- Position a product against an attractive segment.

Porter (1980) proposes that a company's market position has to be sustained by one or more of three bases for competitive advantage, lowest cost, (cost leadership), to be preferred by one customer group (segmentation) or to be preferred by all customers for a proportion of their purchases (differentiation). Davies and Brooks (1989) argued that the nature of retailing, typified by an ease of access by most of the population to any store and the prevailing dominance of product specialisation defining sub-markets, makes it difficult for a retailer to adopt an approach based upon market segmentation. Instead they proposed that retailers should select a differentiated market position and then profile the customer base who are *more likely* to use that type of outlet, to assist their marketing. At the time of writing their book, the Next organisation was often cited as an example of successful market segmentation in retailing but Davies and Brooks argued that it was no such example, rather a successful exploitation of a gap in the market, defined by considering the market as all those fashion retailers competing within it. George Davies' own book on the development of Next, published a year later, confirms this view (Davies, 1989). The original target market for Next was 'someone whose taste level lay somewhere between Jaeger and Marks'. Who this someone was and what market segment they represented, was considered somewhat later in the development of the Next concept.

Nevertheless retailers and retail analysts persist in assuming that segmentation along traditional demographic or lifestyle lines is a useful method (*The Observer*, 1986; *Outlook*, 1988; Evans, 1989; *Retail*, 1989). One flaw in such logic is that the assumption is made that no other retailer appeals to the same segment. In manufacturing it is possible to focus on a particular group of customers by ensuring that advertisements only appear in media used by the target group and that the product is only available via distributors specialising in that same group. It is difficult enough in manufacturing to use market segmentation effectively; in retailing it is well nigh impossible if the retailer trades in the high street. Customers are free to enter any shop and are not obliged to make a purchase when they do so. When two retailers offer the same or a similar proposition to the customer, then the expenditure that would have gone uniquely to one shop is divided among two. Part of Next's problem in the late 1980's was that many other retailers copied the Next formula. The gap between Jaeger and Marks & Spencer began to fill with competitors and even Marks & Spencer repositioned itself to benefit from the market that Next had developed. The gap itself in effect disappeared.

The same situation is apparent in grocery retailing. The superstore is a well tested retail format that is attractive to shoppers and economical and flexible to operate for the retailer. The problem is that the format has been adopted by nearly all the leading grocery retailers, reducing the differentiation in the marketplace (Davies, 1989a).

Retail positioning

Davies and Brooks (1989) propose two types of market position for a retail business that can be profitable: positive differentiation, that is being clearly differentiated from other retailers in the sector; or by being closest to the average shopper's view of the ideal retailer. Davies (1992) identified how certain attributes form a collective view of what the 'ideal' retailer is, while other attributes could be used to segment the marketplace. Schematically this can be represented as Fig 4. 7. At the core of a retailer's offer are the generic attributes that a retailer requires to perform its economic function.

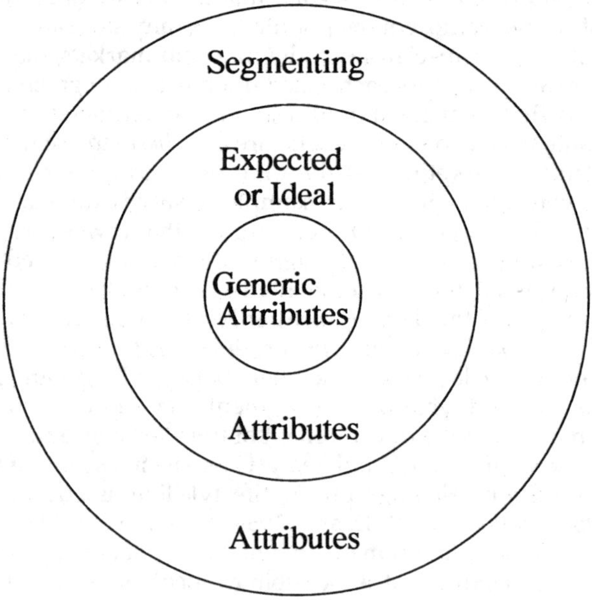

Figure 4. 7 Schematic of retailer image and positioning

These are the utility of place, the availability of products, an assortment of products and basic service. However shoppers have come to expect more from retailers than just these generic attributes. For example, in food retailing these include being perceived to be clean, hygienic, having fresh foods, fast till service and offering value for money. Such attributes are rated highly by *all* shoppers. If the retailer cannot meet these expectations the shopper will tend not to patronise the outlet unless some other important factor provides a counter-balance, such as *very* low prices or because there is *no* other similar retailer around. Collectively the generic and expected or ideal attributes form what Levitt (1980) referred to as the 'table stakes' that any player must realistically possess to compete in a market.

Being seen to have such attributes, that is to be 'positioned against' such ideal attributes, is the most obvious way for a retailer to compete. Fig 4. 8 illustrates how shoppers saw the nine leading food retailers competing in 1990 (Davies, 1992).

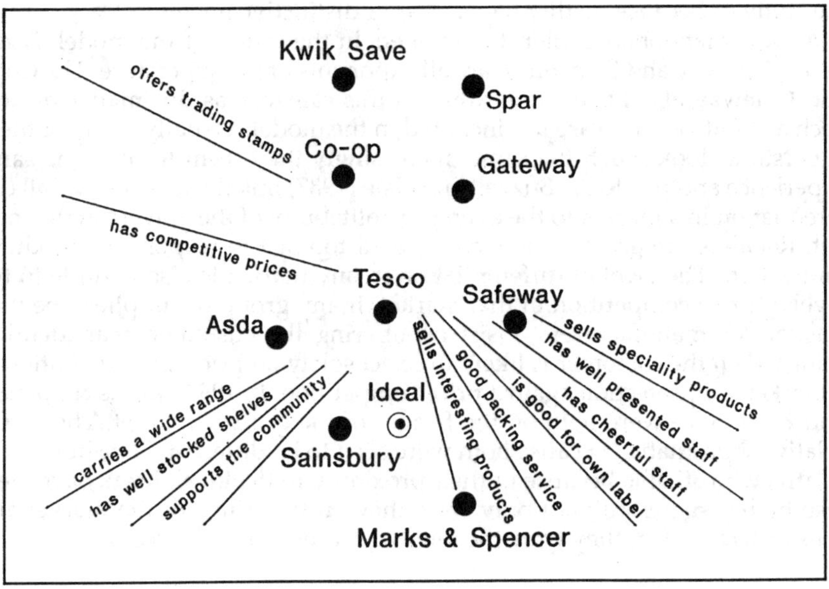

Figure 4. 8 Market map of food retailers overlayed with segmenting attributes

The market research technique used to construct Fig 4. 8 is called multidimensional scaling or image mapping. The process used involves identifying the ideal attributes which are assumed to be represented by the single reference point of the ideal (that contains all the ideal attributes). The vectors are a selection of what are termed segmenting attributes, so called because only a minority of shoppers see them as ideal. The theory is that shoppers will try to patronise those retailers who are associated with the segmenting attributes they desire. The segmenting attributes also explain much of the market structure, the relative positioning of the nine competing retailers. The main question put to the respondents in the market research used to identify which retailers go where on the map is whether respondents see two retailers as similar or different. Those rated as similar in the market research will be positioned close together in the subsequent computer-produced model (Fig 4. 8). Those seen as different will be placed far apart. Thus in 1990 Marks & Spencer were seen as a very different food retailer particularly compared to

Kwik Save. Sainsbury were seen as closest to the ideal and M & S close to a number of segmenting attributes, such as 'sells interesting products', 'speciality products' and being 'good for own label', while also being associated with a number of staff related attributes such as 'well-presented staff', 'cheerful staff' and 'good packing service'. Sainsbury shared this position to some extent, as did Safeway.

Competitive prices distinguished those to the left of the model, particularly Kwik Save. Indeed the computer model does not quite demonstrate the close association of Kwik Save with this particular factor as much as the original market research data implied. Spar and Gateway were not associated with any of the segmenting attributes in the study, either because those attributes that might have been associated with the two were not included in the study or because neither had a clear or distinctive image.

As was mentioned earlier, the retailers in the centre of the model, Asda, Tesco, Safeway and Sainsbury, are all exponents of the superstore. The Coop and Gateway also have some stores in this category as do smaller players such as Waitrose who are not included in the model. Visually many of these superstores look much the same. Increasingly they seem to offer the same experience and products. Buzzell and Gale (1987) link the level of overall differentiation in a market to the average profitability of the players in the market. Retailers are great copiers and are all too fast to respond to another's innovation. The level of differentiation in any market is also a guide to the level of price competition in that market. If any group of suppliers, be they retailers or manufacturers, insist on offering the customer near identical things, then the customer is likely to select solely on price. Differentiation in a market is a protection against price competition. In 1990, Marks & Spencer and Kwik Save were both on the fringes of the grocery market. They were relatively profitable, because both were seen to be different. Sainsbury were relatively profitable because of their proximity to the ideal. Kwik Save were also highly successful; not only were they on the fringe of the market and thus differentiated, they were the lowest cost retailer in the sector.

Cost leadership as a strategy

In any one retail sector there can be only one cost leader – the retailer with the lowest cost base for a given amount of turnover. Until the advent of other discounters, Aldi and Netto, Kwik Save was relatively unopposed in the British market. Argyll's Lo-cost and others provided some competition, but Kwik Save's market position, reinforced by heavy advertising, was particularly strong. Their formula according to Sparks *et al.* (1988) included:

- a limited product range (2,000 lines compared to five times that in many superstores);
- small high-street outlets (away from the superstores and nearer to the lower income groups);
- having only brands on sale (opportunistically purchased in bulk); and
- very low labour cost (made possible by a simple, no frills approach).

In retailing there is evidence that advertising with a clear price-promoting theme builds customer flow (Davies, 1991a, b), but that other forms of retailer advertising expenditure designed to enhance image may be wasted, an issue that is returned to later. Price-led advertising can therefore be very effective for the one lowest cost retailer in every sector, if they choose to use that cost advantage to sell on price. The number of retailers with a distinct cost advantage is relatively limited. Retailers such as B & Q and Boots in Britain, Carrefour in France, Sears and A & P in America could enjoy scale economies because of their large relative size. MFI in Britain have scale economies in kitchen and bedroom furniture, being the leading retailer in both sectors on volume. Migros hold a dominant position in grocery in Switzerland. Argos, the catalogue shop, enjoy a number of cost benefits. Because shoppers have often decided what to buy before they visit the outlet, Argos do not need prime sites. Shoppers will seek them out. Because Argos' display is limited, shrinkage is low. Staff levels are also low. Argos now have a competitor, Index from Littlewoods, and it will be interesting to see what their impact will be as Littlewoods enjoy scale economies to match those at Argos from its other retail activities.

The lowest cost position in the market is the easiest for the manufacturer to recognise, but the most difficult to come to terms with. The retailer will appear to be demanding nothing but discounts. But the issue for the manufacturer is easy enough to resolve. If the manufacturer aims to be the lowest cost provider, then a special relationship with the lowest cost retailer makes sense. The combination guarantees the lowest cost channel to the consumer if the transaction costs between the two can be minimised.

Differentiation as the key?

Porter (1980) described competitive strategy as 'positioning a business to maximize the value of the capabilities that distinguish it from its competitors'. Lees and Worthington (1989) recommended that retailers should aim for a differentiated position in the consumer's mind. Retailers can isolate themselves from direct competition through location or by selling only truly distinctive products, a strategy that is difficult to sustain. They can develop a unique image in the marketplace or develop a retail format that has lower costs than their competitors. As all these four main options for retailers are difficult to sustain, most retailers will use a bit of each in their strategy to develop a unique position in the customer's mind.

Each retailer has, as Martineau (1958) noted, its own 'personality', its own position in the marketplace. Retailer personalities are as distinctive as those of their customers, although the retail personality is multifaceted and complex even by comparison with that of the individual shopper. Yet insights can be gained into the retail personality, and the motivations of the retail business, in the same way as insights can be gained into the personality and motivations of the consumer. In the same way as what the consumer will buy and select is influenced by his or her own self-image, so the retailer's decisions on products will be influenced by its perceived or desired market image. It is likely from the writer's own experience that the retailer will not know exactly how the public perceive their market position and that retailers often have totally different views on where they are seen from the reality of the customers' perspective.

The retailer's suppliers need to understand both the retailer's perceptions of its market position and the actual position its customers deem it to hold. Only then can the supplier's offer be tailored to the retailer's real motivations. And this is a vital point particularly for suppliers of brands. If differentiation is important, then retailers do and will seek to offer different products to the shopper as part of their differentiation strategy. Unless the supplier limits its products to certain retailers, by giving some kind of area franchise, the product offer needs to be different from each retailer. The same brands in the same presentation does nothing to make the retailer *distinctive* in its marketplace. If the manufacturer cannot or will not supply a version of its products that is distinctive and which enhances the retailer's market position, then the retailer will seek even harder to obtain a price or cost advantage over those who will sell the same products in the same way as the only way of gaining an advantage over them. The issue for the brand manufacturer is how much they can tailor their product and its presentation to the retailer's market position without damaging the coherence of the brand image itself. That said, if trade marketing is to mean anything more than trade selling, then meeting the aspirations of the retailer must be central to the role of a trade marketer.

Creating and sustaining a retail image

It is worth considering how a retail image is formed. A retail image might be taken to equate to a brand image, and indeed many writers and retailers see retailers as 'brands' (D'Arcy *et al.*, 1989; Ryan, 1989). Murphy (1990) quotes a director of Tesco as explaining that 'the shop itself, its locations, its atmosphere, the service it offers and the range of goods and prices can become the brand'.

Davies and Brooks (1989) concluded that three elements of a retailer's offer dominate the creation of a retailer's image:

- The product offer itself and in particular the price points.
- The symbolism of the store design including display and atmospherics.
- The people factor of the staff and other shoppers. This view reflects the empirical work of Mazursky and Jacoby (1986) who saw three slightly different clues that consumers extracted from the retailer's premises and communication:

  quality of service;
  quality of merchandise;
  pleasantness of shopping.

Note that advertising, other than as a way of communicating such factors, is not seen as instrumental in forming image.

Shostak (1977) has claimed that service companies need to emphasise tangible aspects of their business in advertising to market their intangible offer, while product companies need to emphasise intangibles to build added value onto their tangible products. Davies and Brooks (1989) argued that trying to *create* an image for a retailer via advertising is self-defeating unless the image is already evident in the store. The image can be communicated via advertising, but if the store does not live up to the communication, the shopper is unlikely to be convinced. The disappointed shopper will walk out before buying. A relatively high walkout rate, the ratio of people not buying to those entering the store, is a sign of one image being expected by shoppers, probably due to advertising, and another being present in the store. Gronroos (1980) quite rightly likens the customer's development of their perception of a service to a detective picking up clues, none of which may provide a clear picture but when taken together can be used to draw a conclusion.

Much of retail advertising, particularly that from the multiple sector, is about discounts and other price-led messages (Davies, 1991b). Some of this communication is co-funded by the manufacturers of the products featured in the adverts. While it is likely that such advertising can produce a direct response from the public, there may even be a longer-term, less desirable impact on the retailer's image. The word 'cheap' in the English language encompasses two concepts, low price and poor quality. Too much overt price-cutting advertising from a store with a utilitarian design will create a cheap image, unless the retailer is selling leading brands. Hence one dilemma facing the brand manufacturer when considering supplying a discount retailer is whether it should risk its brands as being seen in a 'cheap' retail environment.

Rather than spend heavily on advertising, Davies (1991a, b) recommends that retailers should look to build their image inside the store and communicate it both there and via public relations rather than advertising. The examples of Next, Marks & Spencer, Body Shop, John Lewis and Waitrose, whose images are both strong but unassociated with advertising, can be cited to query whether advertising, so essential in building the image of most manufacturer's brands, is particularly relevant to the formation of a retailer's image. Once again manufacturers would be in error in assuming that what is important to them is equally so to the retailers they supply.

Academic research into retail image, including Martineau's article in 1958, has often explained the way a retail image is used by the shopper with the idea of 'congruence'. A shopper, it is said, will patronise the store whose image is most congruent with the image the shopper holds of him or herself. This leads to the idea of shoppers changing their choice of store as and when their self-image changes. For example a woman shopping for her children might select a store with a low-to-middle price range for day-to-day wear and shop more up-market for an outfit for herself for a special occasion. Someone who has just discovered he or she is running an overdraft may become more price sensitive. Someone else who is feeling low might decide to buy something, even on credit, to cheer him or herself up. The same person could seek many different stores as a result as the mind set changes. Another dilemma facing a retailer is whether to try to appeal to the same person in all moods or be focused on one type of purchase experience. This author would argue that it is preferable to promote a clear image for a purchase experience rather than the more broad, diffuse and ultimately unfocused image of too broad an appeal. Being something to everyone risks being nothing to anyone. Inside the store this means an environment that is designed to symbolise the experience or mood that the retailer represents. Red might imply fast-moving, discounts, excitement; blue and green might imply freshness; low ceilings might imply more exclusive merchandise;

regimented aisles might symbolise routine purchase (Omura, 1982).

The products on display cannot span the whole range from exclusive to budget unless the store is divided into clearly separate departments, which in turn risks losing coherence for the business as a whole. The products must be those the customer would expect the retailer to retail or be capable of retailing. A supplier needs to be aware of what can sell in which retail outlets. The product offer can be excellent but if incompatible with the retailer's market position, may not sell, at least for some time, by when the retailer will have already decided to de-list.

The other shoppers in the store and the staff are a relatively obvious clue to the retailer's market position, but the interaction between staff and customers may be important, particularly in creating an image for service. Mazursky and Jacoby's (1986) work implies that shoppers will infer a high level of service if they see a large number of staff or service points. Bradley and Taylor (1992) posit a more fundamental relationship between company culture and market position in the case of the John Lewis Partnership and its subsidiary Waitrose. Employees in both are also partners in the business and their annual bonus, in the absence of a shareholder's dividend, forms a substantial proportion of salaries. Davies (1992) analysed the ratio of customers to staff while attempting to explain the reason for Marks & Spencer's having an image for service in three different retail sectors, food, menswear and ladieswear (Fig 4. 9). His conclusion was that there was no absolute relationship between sheer numbers of staff and a perception of service. Some other

Retailer	*No of Shoppers in 1987 (millions)*[1]	*No of Employees 1987/88*[2]	*Shoppers per Employee*
Marks & Spencer	29.2	61,094	478
BhS	20.1	18,132	1,109
Woolworths	25.7	32,363	794
Debenhams	8.3	11,950	695
House of Fraser	6.1	19,451	314
John Lewis	3.9	21,549	181
Lewis's	2.2	4,000	550
Owen Owen	1.7	2,493	682

Figure 4. 9 Customer:employee ratios in department and chain store retailing (*sources:* 1. Gordon Simmons Research Ltd, *Chain Store Index*, London; 2. Corporate Intelligence Group, Research Publications Ltd, London, *The Retail Rankings*, 1989 edition)

factor, probably company culture and the way staff were selected and treated, has an effect on the relationship between staff and customers. The personal service element in retailing is created at the point of contact between some of the lowest-paid members of the retailer's staff, the shop assistants, and the customers. In an era of self-service and therefore less personal contact, the opportunities for the relationship to develop are limited. How staff manage the critical incidents when contact is made are likely to be important, but one wonders just how much the reputation of the retailer for employing the best and the visual presentation of the staff can also affect the customer's perception of service and therefore their predisposition to the service experience.

Strategy and financial performance in retailing

Too little has been *proven* of links between a retailer's strategy and its financial performance. Davies and Brooks (1989) link successful positioning to a high rate of growth in food retailing, relative differentiation to relative profitability in menswear retailing, and the higher differentiation in British department store retailing compared to the same sector in Germany to higher profits in the British sector. Bradley and Taylor (1992) argue a link between culture and profitability in explaining some aspects of the performance of John Lewis and Waitrose. Other attempts tend to be even more anecdotal, and most focus on explaining why certain retailers have been successful in the past (O'Neill, 1991). The explanations of success vary from retailer to retailer and individual retailers, who are seen as star performers one year, all too often tend to tumble down the list of rankings in later years. That said the fundamental strategy of a distinctive image with the shopping public does appear to be central to retail success for those who cannot isolate themselves geographically or who cannot achieve the lowest cost position in their sector.

In business in general relative 'quality' is argued to be the fundamental driver for relative business success (Buzzell and Gale, 1987). But what does 'quality' mean in a retail context? It may be to position oneself closest to the average view of the ideal retailer as described earlier but only one retailer in each sector can achieve this position. Such logic would imply that only two retailers at most can be relatively profitable in any one retail sector, the one who is successful at cost leadership and the one positioned closest to the ideal. But this does not explain the profitability of Marks & Spencer in food

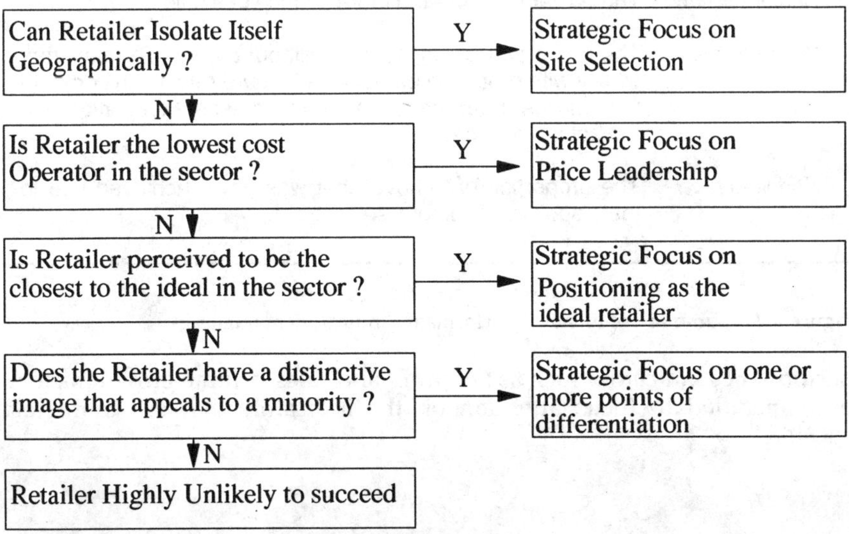

Figure 4. 10 The main strategic options in retailing

retailing, for just one example. Distinctiveness or differentiation will be all important for those retailers who cannot or choose not to be the ideal or cost leaders. In fact there can be as many successful retailers as there are dimensions along which a retailer can be distinctive. It follows that manufacturers need to identify which strategy dominates the retailer's philosophy and tailor their offer accordingly. How this might be achieved is debated in subsequent chapters. Fig 4. 10 attempts to summarise the strategic options any retailer might follow.

At the same time the supplier must be aware of the shorter term financial criteria used by the retailer to monitor its commercial performance. Those identified in this chapter are listed in Fig 4. 11. The more general business

GMROI	Gross margin as a ratio with the cost of stockholding. Potentially valuable in retailing high margin lines, but often misleading.
Profit or sales/sq ft	A useful measure of how well a retailer uses its main asset, space.
DPP	Direct product profitability, a better measure than sales or profit per square foot as more factors are considered. Difficult to calculate and not foolproof.
Profit or sales/employee	A useful measure of productivity in an area where cost saving on staff has been a goal of most retailers. Could be misleading to a retailer positioning on service.
Expenditure per customer visit	A useful measure of retail success. A high figure implies the product offer matches the customer's expectation and that the breadth and depth of product offer are right.
Customer flow	The busier the store the more chance of a sale.
Walkout rate	The proportion leaving a store without buying. This can vary widely with product type but a high figure relative to competition implies a gap between the customer's expectation and the actual retail offer.
Shrinkage	The proportion of turnover that was never achieved due to theft, spoilage or otherwise.

Figure 4. 11 Summary of financial performance indicators in retailing

performance indicators such as net profit and sales volume growth have not been included to focus attention on the indicators that are more retail specific.

Keypoint summary

1) Understanding a retailer's strategy may be difficult because a retailer may not have a long-term view of strategy itself.
2) Buyers assess product profitability but some measures, such as GMROI, are far from perfect, particularly for low margin products.
3) DPP is growing in significance as a method of stock selection but it is still more useful in outlets that sell prepackaged products from fixed shelving such as grocery and DIY. A manufacturer can benefit by providing planograms.
4) Shrinkage and staff costs are two of a number of areas of concern to retailers than can be addressed by their suppliers.
5) There has been a general trend to build larger shops and to increase the number of types of product on sale.
6) Understanding the financial measures used by retailers will be important in trade marketing.
7) Retail strategy can be dominated by market positioning or image. Suppliers could be well advised to tailor their offer to support a retailer's market position.
8) A supplier to a retailer whose position is the lowest cost retailer in its sector should consider matching the retailer's position by becoming the lowest cost supplier.

References

Andrew, A., Maier, J. (1989) The application of Direct Product Profitability in British Retailing, Proceedings of the 22nd. Annual Conference, Vol 1, M.E.G., July, p 136.

Boudet, A. (1991) PDP la mesure de l'efficacité, *LSA*, No 1241, 24 January, p 30.

Bradley, K., Taylor, S. (1992) *Business Performance in the Retail Sector*, Clarendon Press, Oxford.

Buzzell, R. D., Gale, B. T. (1987) *The PIMS Principles*, The Free Press, New York.

Corstjens, M., Doyle, P. (1981) A Model for Optimising Retail Space Allocations, *Management Science*, Vol 27, No 7, July, p 822.

Corstjens, M., Doyle, P. (1983) A Dynamic Model For Strategically Allocating Retail Space, *Journal of the Operational Research Society*, Vol 34, No 10, p 943.

D'Arcy, Masius, Benton, Bowles (1989), *Marketing*, Mercury Books, London, p 128.

Davidson, W. R., Sweeney, D. J., Stampfl, R. W. (1988) *Retailing Management* (6th Ed), Wiley, New York, p 375.

Davies, G. (1989) *What NEXT?*, Century, London, p 45.

Davies, G. J. (1989) Image and the Future for Grocery Retailing, *Grocery Business*, Institute of Grocery Distribution, January, Radlett, Herts.

Davies, G. (1991b) The Question of Expansion: A Case Study of the Independent Health-Food Retailer in Welford, R. (ed) *Small Business and Small Business Development: A Practical Approach*, Vol 1, European Research Press, Bradford.

Davies, G. J. (1991) *Advertising in Retailing*, Longman, Harlow.

Davies, G. J. (1991a) Retailer advertising strategies, *International Journal of Advertising*, Vol 10, p 189.

Davies, G. J. (1992) Positioning image and the marketing of multiple retailers, *International Review of Retail Distribution and Consumer Research*, Vol 2, No 1, p 13.

Davies, G. J., Brooks, J. M. (1989) *Positioning Strategy in Retailing*, Paul Chapman,

London, Ch 14.
Davies, R. L., Rogers, D. S. (1984) *Store Location and Store Assessment Research*, Wiley, Chichester.
Dyer, L. W. (1980) Instore Research at Publix, *Progressive Grocer*, Vol 59, p 98.
The Economist (1982) Spotting the Lemons, 27 June.
Elder, A. (1989) *Shrinkage in UK Multiple Retailing*, Institute of Retail Studies, University of Stirling.
Evans, E. (1989) Retail Buying, *Retail and Distribution Management*, Sept/Oct, p 17 (positions of Sears menswear outlets on price and age).
Feinberg, R. A., Koscica, D., Rocobs, S. J. (1983) Strategic Planning: What the top 100 Stores Say, *Retail Control*, 9 October, cited in Gilligan and Sutton, op. cit.
Gagnon, J. P., Osterhaus, J. T. (1985) Effectiveness of Floor Display on the Sale of Retail Products, *Journal of Retailing*, Vol 61, No. 1, Spring, p 104.
Gilligan, C., Sutton, C. (1987) Strategic Planning in Grocery and DIY Retailing, in Johnson, G. (ed) *Business Strategy and Retailing*, Wiley, Chichester, p 177.
Good, W. S. (1984) Productivity in the Retail Grocery Trade, *Journal of Retailing*, Vol 60, No 3, Fall, p 81.
The Grocer (1987) Merchandising fixtures by computer camera, 7 March, p 58.
Gronroos, C. (1980) Designing a Long Range Marketing Strategy for Services, *Long Range Planning*, Vol 13, April, p 36.
The Independent Grocer (1988), Feature, 1 July.
Johnson, M. (1989) The Application of Geodemographics to Retailing, *Journal of the Market Research Society*, Vol 31, No 1, p 7.
Kotler, P. (1991) *Marketing Management* (7th Ed), Prentice-Hall, Englewood Cliffs, NJ.
Lees, R., Worthington, S. (1989) Achieving Above Average Profitability in Retailing, *International Journal of Retailing*, Vol 24, No 2, p 17.
Levitt, T. (1980) Marketing Success Through Differentiation, *Harvard Business Review*, Vol 58, Jan/Feb, p 83.
Lewison, D. M., Delozier, N. W. (1986) *Retailing*, (2nd Ed), Charles Merrill, Columbus, Ohio, p 229.
Lusch, R. F., Moon, S. Y. (1984) An Exploratory Analysis of the Correlates of Labour Productivity in Retailing, *Journal of Retailing*, Vol 60, No 3, Fall, p 37.
Martineau, P. (1958) The Personality of the Retail Store, *Harvard Business Review*, Jan/Feb, p 50.
Mazursky, D., Jacoby, J. (1986) Exploring the Development of Store Images, *Journal of Retailing*, Vol 65, No 2, p 145.
Moore, L. (1988) Stated Preference Analysis and New Store Location, in Wrigley, N. (ed) Store Choice, *Store Location and Market Analysis*, Routledge, London, p 203.
Murphy, J. (1990) *Brand Strategy*, Director Books, Cambridge, p 65.
NEDO (1979) *A Structural Model of British Retail Trade*, HMSO, London.
NEDO (1988) *The Future of the High Street*, Distributive Trades, Economic Development Council, HMSO, London.
The Observer (1986) Corporate Advertisement for the Burton Group, 23 Nov, p 9 (age group segmentation).
Omura, G. S. (1982) Strategic Design of Store Interiors, *Academy of Marketing Science Monograph*, Vol 2, No 1.
O'Neill, R. E. (1991) Who's Who Among High Performance Retailers, *Monitor*, May, p 89.
Outlook (1988) *For the Way You Live (Marshall Fields Price Fashion Lifestyle Matrix)*, BAT Industries, Jan, No 8, p 16.
Parasuraman, A., Zeithaml, V. A., Berry, L. L. (1985) A Conceptual Model of Service Quality and its Implications, *Journal of Marketing*, Vol 49, p 41.
Porter, M. E. (1980) *Competitive Strategy*, Macmillan, New York.
Porter, M. E. (1985) *Competitive Advantage*, Macmillan, New York.
Retail (1989) No Fears at Sears (segmentation of British Shoe Corporation store posi-

tions), Vol 6, No 4, p 23.
Reynolds, J. (1989) *Retailing in the 90's:Threats to Profitability*, Longman, London, p 61.
Rinne, H., Geurts, M., Kelly, J. P. (1987) An Approach to Allocating Space to Departments In a Retail Store, *International Journal of Retailing*, Vol 2, No 2, p 27.
Ryan, C. (1989) Brand Building – The Retailer's Secret Weapon, in *Proceedings of 'Adding Value to Retail Offerings'*, ESOMAR, Edinburgh, Apr, p 149.
Scarborough, N. M., Zimmerer, T. W. (1984) *Effective Small Business Management*, Charles Merrill, Columbus, Ohio, p 339.
Shostak, G. L. (1977) Breaking Free from Product Marketing, *Journal of Marketing*, April, p 73.
Sparks, L. (1987) Employment in Retailing: Trends and Issues, in Johnson, E. (ed) *Business Strategy and Retailing*, Wiley, Chichester, p 243.
Sparks, L., Lord, J. D., Moran, W., Parker, A. J. (1988) Retailing on Three Continents: The Discount Food Store Operation of Albert Gubay, *International Journal of Retailing*, Vol 3, No 3, p 1.
Stanley, T. J., Sewall, M. A. (1976) Image Inputs to a Probabilistic Model: Predicting Retail Potential, *Journal of Marketing*, Vol 40, July, p 48.
Stanley, T. J., Sewall, M. A. (1978) Predicting Supermarket Trade: Implications for Marketing Management, *Journal of Retailing*, Vol 54, No 2, p 13.
Swindley, D. (1992) The Role of the Buyer in UK Multiple Retailing, *International Journal of Retail Distribution Management*, Vol 20, No 2, p 3.
Touche Ross (1989) *Retail Shrinkage: The Drain on Profits*, London.
Whyte, R. (1988) Direct Product Profitability, *Retail Technology*, September, p 59.

5

CONSUMER TRENDS

The purpose of this chapter is to identify many of the customer/consumer influences that have affected retailing and some of those that may do so in the future. The focus is not on short-term changes in social taste nor on the 'megatrend' analysis of the like of Toffler (1971), but on those social changes that are more likely to be drivers of retail change.

Social trend analysis, according to Codeluppi and Weber (1989), is concerned with identifying change that persists over time allowing predictions to be made about the future. Wack (1985) distinguished between two types of event that can be usefully identified, those that are 'predetermined' because they have occurred or almost certainly will do so, and those that are 'uncertainties', because they are reactions to events which can be based upon both fact and perception. Thus for example it is predetermined that the population of most western countries will age. What is uncertain is how retailers will react and how therefore manufacturers should shape their strategies. Given that retailers appear to exhibit a hesitancy towards strategic planning, predicting social change and leading a partnership with retailers to exploit any trend successfully would be one positive way forward for suppliers. That said, in the last few decades, retailers rather than manufacturers have tended to benefit from exploiting social change. Marks & Spencer pioneered cook-chill foods (EIU, 1989) with an own-brand offer. Next exploited the growing affluence of the working woman – not the makers of manufacturer branded clothes. Healthfood retailers and then the likes of Tesco left suppliers behind in developing healthy eating lines. Body Shop gave us caring cosmetics. Ratners mass marketed unbranded jewellery. MFI did more than most to promote the fitted kitchen. In electrical products, vehicles, many toys and a few other areas, manufacturers are more clearly in the van of technical innovation. When it comes to market innovation, British retailers appear to do more than hold their own.

Identifying social trends and predetermined events and uncertainties is far from easy. This chapter will inevitably be selective in its coverage, both because of space and an attempt to identify only those consumer trends that are likely, in the author's opinion, to shape the whole retail industry in the future. So apologies are offered for omitting any obvious trends that are important, particularly those that impact more upon individual retail sectors than upon retailing in general.

Society and the economy

At the time of writing, the world appeared to be teetering on the edge of a slump the length and depth of which had not been seen since the 1920s. Repossession of mortgaged property, business failures, unemployment and stagnation seemed to imply that the long-term growth in consumer expenditure would go into reverse. Yet short-term down-turns in the business cycle have disguised the long-term growth in virtually every developed economy since the industrial revolution. From 1900 to 1980 for example gross domestic product in Britain grew by a factor of four in real terms. Real compound growth of around 2% per annum has been achieved since the last war.

As personal disposable income grows, expenditure on the real necessities of life, food and basic shelter and clothing, falls as a proportion of total expenditure. The volume of food consumed remains approximately constant and the value of the food sector increases only slowly. The total value of product areas such as clothing and household goods tends to increase in line with the growth in disposable income, while expenditure on consumer durables, particularly electrical goods, tends to rise faster than the average rate of growth in expenditure.

However the proportion of consumer expenditure made in retail outlets has fallen even through retail sales have increased. People have tended to increase spending on services such as eating out and holidays and on their homes, in the last case largely it must be said because of house-price inflation rather than a genuine increase in value of purchase. It could be said that retailers of one sort or another have benefited from even these trends. Estate agents, travel agents, hotels and restaurants all regard themselves as 'retailers' and many traditional retail businesses have encompassed such services-retailing as their activities.

Forecasts of demand

Forecasts of consumer expenditure tend to assume that long-term economic growth is a fact of life and that the increased emphasis on purchasing services and durables will continue. Within these overall trends, forecasters try to spot combinations of social and economic trends that modify such a broader picture. For example Mintel (1991) were reported as being bullish about expenditure on children's products partly because of a growth in the number of adult relatives a child has in an era of high divorce rates.

So the apparent inevitability of real economic growth means future growth in the retail sector, particularly among those retailers selling consumer durables and even more so in the electrical sub-sector. Retailers who can offer services such as restaurants or travel agencies might also achieve above average growth. In the less buoyant sectors such as food, real growth can only be expected in novel areas or those where value is added to the basic food product such as in convenience meals. Suppliers to retailers of product areas exhibiting little growth in expenditure can expect greater price sensitivity if the retailer cannot diversify and seeks to reduce costs as the only means of improving profit. Where retailing capacity grows ahead of expenditure, price sensitivity can also be greater. Price insensitivity may well result if the product area is growing faster than the available retail selling space and retailers find it easier to meet their contribution targets because demand exceeds supply. One example in Britain during the 1980s would be greetings cards, where real sales increased but not as fast as value. In those retail sectors where overall growth is slow, individual retailers can still grow relatively quickly – if they have an innovative format or innovative product.

Perhaps the one consumer durable whose purchase has had the greatest impact on the retail sector in recent years is the motor car. By the end of the 1980s nearly 90% of Britain's population had the regular use of a car, an increase from below 40% at the end of the 1950s (CSO, 1991). The increase in car sales and associated purchases, significant as they have been, is nothing besides the mobility given to shoppers in its impact on retailing. Car mobility was a factor in the growth of larger stores at the expense of the local shop and home delivery services. A car means the ability to buy in bulk and the possession of other consumer durables, such as the fridge and freezer, means that shopping for routine food products can be done less frequently.

Social trends

Elsewhere in national statistics there has been evidence of a rise in single person households, accounting for 10% of the population by 1989 as young people leave home earlier and the elderly live on their own. Less stability in family life as the divorce rate increases has contributed to an increase in family units of a single parent and child, accounting for 14% of all families by the late 1980s. The proportion of women at work in Britain is one of the highest in the world and second only to that in Denmark in Europe. Many households now enjoy two or more substantial incomes, while in others a single parent works part time to supplement state benefit aid and/or maintenance.

These and other trends have led to a greater polarisation in the distribution of household incomes. In 1979 the bottom fifth of households had 10.1% of all income while the top fifth had 33.4%. By 1987 the relevant figures were 8.9% and 39.1%. Half the lowest quartile of households were headed by someone unemployed or by a pensioner. The proportion of wealth owned by the top 10% in society increased between 1976 and 1988, a reversal of the longer-term trend of greater equalisation of wealth between different levels in society.

Households seemed to be polarising when measured by their ability to spend, with an increasingly wealthy group at the top and an increasingly disadvantaged group at the bottom of society.

Fragmentation and homogenisation

Society, it is said, is becoming simultaneously more homogeneous and easier to subdivide into a much larger number of sub-groups than traditionally could be used to segment the consumer market. In addition to the economic trends identified above, a number of social factors have become more important. What appears to be happening is that people are feeling more independent and perhaps have acquired the confidence to take more of their own decisions rather than look to what are the norms of a large affinity or reference group. At the same time market research and computer analysis of research data have become more sophisticated, allowing businesses to be more analytical about their customer bases and more able to differentiate between what have become, in reality, smaller and less stable social groupings.

In practical terms, subdividing markets using variables such as social class, socioeconomic group (A,B,C_1,C_2,D,E), age and sex have become less useful in segmenting markets, because people appear to be less likely to have expenditure or behaviour patterns that are predictable from using such measures. Unfortunately the use of socioeconomic grouping in particular is both so easy to apply and so ingrained in business language that the application of many of the more complex measures of social groupings, that do appear to be more predictive, is far from widespread. But first, what is driving the apparent trend towards market fragmentation?

Codeluppi and Weber (1989) suggest ten factors that are summarised and retitled by the author in Fig. 5. 1. Doubtless this list is neither correct nor

Role exchange The increased willingness of individuals to exchange roles, e.g. women to become breadwinners, men to become shoppers.
Individualism The demand for products and services to be tailored to us as individuals, not mass marketed.
Convenience As time becomes a scarcer resource people are prepared to pay more for products that save time or time-saving services.
Need for identity Coupled with individualism, the need for products that allow individuals to express their identity.
Style symbolism Many products used to be purchased as symbols of status, now style is more important, but more difficult to express.
The need to belong A counteraction to individualism, the need to belong to a group but one which may be defined more by activities than ownership.
Health Particularly in an ageing population, concern for the effect on ones body of what is consumed and what activities one participates in.
Consumerism An awareness of legal rights that has become an ideology for what is right.
Context The recognition that the same person can act a different role depending upon the context and thus appear to be a different type of consumer.
Brand polygamy Loyalty to one brand being replaced by loyalty to a group of brands as individuals become more selective but still retain certain preferences.

Figure 5. 1 Ten drivers for social change (after Codeluppi and Weber, 1989)

complete but it does offer a useful framework to make some sense of the fragmentation effect. The notion of brand polygamy as a replacement for brand loyalty as a possible outcome of current social trends could be particularly useful. A picture emerges of a desire by individuals to express themselves and establish their individuality at least to themselves, but at the same time a need exists for help to create the look, the lifestyle that gives form to those desires.

As an example of the practical impact of market fragmentation, Zeithaml (1985) examined a number of demographic changes that have been affecting grocery retailing. By the 1980s it was being recognised that the 'typical' family – husband, wife and two children – no longer dominated society. In the case of food shopping some 30% of grocery shopping trips were conducted in the USA by males. A number of sub-groups could be identified such as the male grocery shoppers and working females. So while, traditionally, grocery retailers might be justified in assuming that their core market was the housewife shopping for her family, the needs of other significant segments now have to be considered. One issue that follows for the manufacturer supplying retailers is that the trends relevant to retailing and the segmentation methods they apply will not necessarily match the segmentation structures used by themselves. As retailers become better able to identify the segmentation variables that support their overall positioning strategy and the measures that allow them to describe those who value their distinctive attributes, then the pressure on manufacturers to use the same methods of segmentation will grow. If manufacturer and retailer are to join forces to develop a market, it seems counter-productive for them to be using different methods of segmentation. Later in this book the significance of local marketing, so-called geodemographics, used more and more by retailers, is considered. But first what are the other specific consumer trends particularly relevant to retail business?

An ageing population

Increased life expectancy and a reduced birth rate mean that the average age

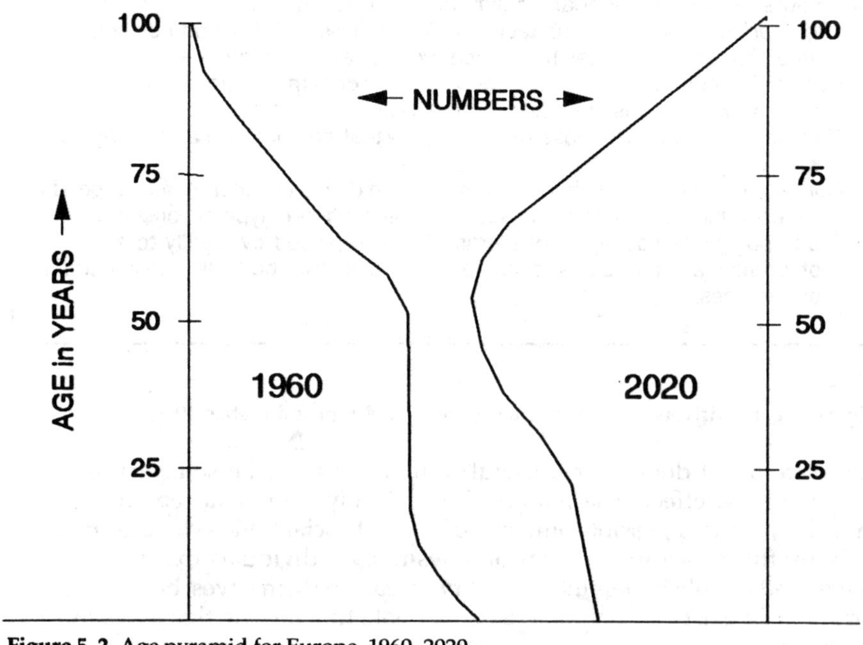

Figure 5. 2 Age pyramid for Europe, 1960–2020

of most western societies is growing. Fig 5. 2 expresses this trend using the change in the shape of the age pyramid for the European Community between 1960 and 2020. A number of effects might be noted. First there is the shifting population bulge; those born in the 1960s are moving up the age band. Thus the most populous group by the year 2020 will be in their 50s.

Put another way the 16 – 44-year-old group will see significant change in many countries, declining from 42.8% of the population in Britain to 36.4% by 2031, a decline of two million, of which one million will go by 2001 (URPI, 1990). At the same time the proportion of the population over retirement age will have grown. Allowing for a projected increase in the duration of full-time education in those at the bottom of the pyramid, the proportion in work in the economy will fall and this shrinking group will need to be economically productive enough to support the rest of us. At the same time there will be a relative decline in the number of young people entering the job market and an increase in their expectations from work given their higher levels of qualification. The numbers of the elderly who cannot cope totally or partially without help will increase, at the same time as the numbers of traditional carers, women, available for such work will decline.

At the moment the numbers in employment have grown, as more women have sought work for more of their lifespan, so there has been no shortage of labour. Indeed retailers have benefited from their desire for part-time hours. In the future retailers, as employers, may need to become more attractive to the younger age groups and will also need to increase their proportion of older staff. But the change in age profile of customers will be just as relevant. Between 1931 and 1981 the proportion of the population aged over 65 more than doubled in Britain. By 2025 the proportion over 65 will be five times that in 1901 (Diamond, 1989). The elderly tend to retire to certain parts of the country and increasingly to warmer counties. A population shift might even be expected towards the south of Europe for the retired. This is on top of other significant regional trends within countries, such as the process of suburbanisation and a movement away from centres of traditional heavy industry (URPI, 1990).

It is possible to see the rise in the number of older people in the population as a problem for society. It is also an opportunity and one that has not yet been addressed by retailers. Age is not necessarily a dominant variable in buyer behaviour but studies on the attitudes of older groups to shopping paint a picture of the older shopper emphasising service (Braus, 1990), perhaps because they recall an era of more personal service and less self-service in retailing. Other motivations include comfort, security, convenience, sociability and 'old fashioned' values (Schewe, 1990). But quite often the motivations of the elderly appear not to differ from those of lesser years and segments such as 'grandparents' have been difficult to target in practice (Schlosberg, 1990). Factors such as mobility do not appear to be as important in the patronage behaviour of the elderly as might be expected (Lumpkin and Hunt, 1989). Finally the elderly may not even represent a particularly coherent sector to target as, for example, sub-groups exist in attitudes to food shopping (Tantiwong and Wilton, 1985).

Retailers, such as Toys 'R' Us, Mothercare, Adams and Early Learning Centres, have been more successful at targeting the younger end of the market. Broader-based retailers such as Woolworths and Boots have children's sections or group products together that appeal to children or those buying for them. But examples of retailers targeting the other end of the age spectrum are far more difficult to recall. Some retailers have a customer profile that is older than the norm, such as some Coops, Littlewoods and Post Office Counters, but none of the large chains seem to focus on this group. The proportion of consumer expenditure accounted for by the over 60s is significant. In the past it seems to have been assumed that this group had limited resources, but this has changed as many more enjoy occupational pensions and draw lump sums upon retirement. Indeed for those years immediately after retirement, the potential level of disposable income and the predisposition to spend it must offer an opportunity. Both retailers and their suppliers seem all too focused on younger groups, who in turn are still weighed down with mortgages, the expense of children and, increasingly, alimony.

Lifestyle

WASP	White Anglo-Saxon Protestant
YUPPIE	Young, upwardly mobile professional
SWELLS	Single women earning lots and lots
OPALS	Older people with active lifestyles
DINKS	Dual income, no kids
NILKS	No income, loads of kids
SITCOM	Single income, two children, outrageous mortgage

Figure 5. 3 Examples of demographic acronyms (*sources:* Crispell, 1990, and others)

Who or what we are is one way of categorising people and segmenting markets. Numerous acronyms have filtered through into the popular press such as those in Fig 5. 3. Some are merely humorous but many represent a useful shorthand for a lifestyle, the most famous being the YUPPIE, a label that conjures up an image of a sharp suit holding a mobile phone in one hand and the wheel of a sleek imported car in another. Such stereotypes are transient and the markets they represent difficult to target. Recognising the potential value of describing people in terms of what they are rather than who they are, a number of attempts have been made to produce categorisation systems where occupation, age and sex are only part of a number of dimensions defining different lifestyle groupings. Individuals can be categorised into a number of groups by their responses to a battery of questions designed to assess their 'psychographic' profile or, more understandably, their activities, interests and opinions, as well as their demographics, such as age, occupation and stage in life cycle (Engel *et al.*, 1990). For example in the VALS system three broad groupings which subdivide into nine sub-groupings can be defined (Mitchell, 1983; Fig 5. 4). Each sub-group has its own buying patterns but for the purposes of this chapter the distinctions between the three main groups are adequate.

The spending of the Need Driven, sometimes called Sustenance Driven group, is dominated by need rather than preference and the group includes a

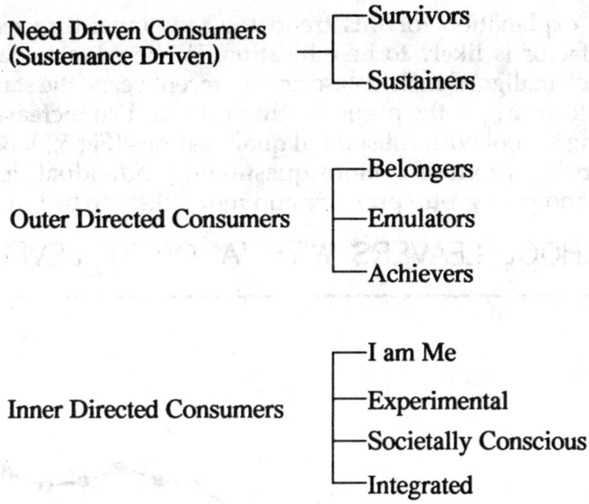

Figure 5. 4 VALS lifestyle groupings

high proportion of the economically disadvantaged. The Outer Directed group are those whose purchases are dominated by social influences. They are more brand conscious and brand loyal and tend to follow fashion trends. Inner Directeds buy more to please themselves, are less influenced by branding but are often trend setters themselves. Something that starts among Inner Directeds can diffuse out to society as a whole, particularly if the Outer Directeds perceive it as the 'right thing to do'. However a trend that originates among Outer Directeds will probably only last as long as it is fashionable (MacNulty, 1984; Powderly and MacNulty, 1990). The proportion of society who are Sustenance Driven in Britain has been falling while the Inner Directed group has been growing. The proportions in various countries vary, with higher levels of Outer Directeds in America and Japan, and higher levels of Inner Directeds in Britain and The Netherlands (Applied Futures, 1991). Inner Directeds in Britain tend to prefer specialist shops rather than the 'major shop in town' preferred by the Outer Directeds. The same potential trend setters became less well disposed towards teleshopping in the 1980s. Powderly and MacNulty (1990) suggest a revival of intown shops, especially local and speciality stores, because they are favoured by the Inner Directeds, a forecast that runs counter to research on out-of-town centres such as the north east's Metro Centre and Sheffield's Meadowhall (Howard, 1991). That said Americans seemed to be deserting their mall-dominated retail sector in the 1990s suggesting that there is indeed an element of fashion in patronising the mall.

The VALS approach and others that segment markets in terms of motivation as well as behaviour, are useful in that they provide not only a method of segmentation but also a means of studying market diffusion – that is how ideas move into the mainstream from being minority interests. The growth of the Inner Directed group is also interesting as it could imply less interest in heavily branded goods. Not that Inner Directeds do not buy brands, but if they do, they buy to satisfy their own internal needs not from a desire to be 'doing the right thing'. This topic is returned to later in Chapter 6.

Is there an explanation for this trend towards inner-directedness? One contributory factor is likely to be education. While educational standards have been much maligned in British society in recent years, the statistical evidence shows a lowering of the pupil/teacher ratio and an increase in the percentage leaving school with substantial qualifications (Fig 5.5). Better education will probably produce a more questioning individual, less likely to accept media and peer group pressure and more likely to be Inner Directed.

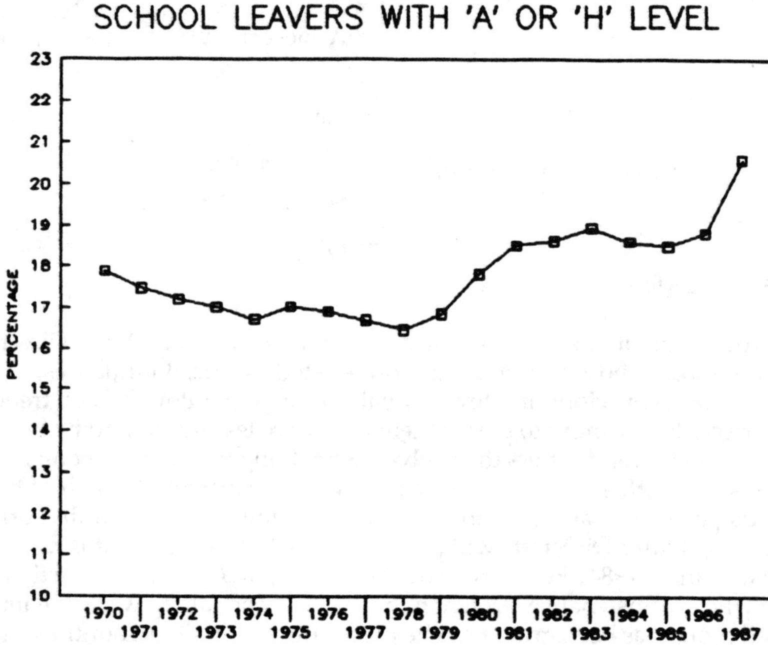

Figure 5. 5 Increase in attainment (*source:* DES, 1970–89)

A more concerned consumer?

The 1980s in Britain saw an unprecedented rise in consumer spending, much of it in retail outlets. Retailing was described as the 'Atrium over Thatcher's Britain' and shopping centres as 'temples of consumption' (Gardner and Sheppard, 1989). The 1990s were predicted to see a move away from materialism to 'mature realism' (McLoughlin, 1991). 'New' man would emerge to take his share of household duties in a society more dominated by female values.

One area of concern was certainly that of 'greenness' and associated with it, views on health, ethics and conservation. Some of the issues here can be regarded as minority ones, associated with fringe groups in society, but not all. Jowell *et al.* (1991) record a sustained rise from 78% in 1985 to 88% in 1989 in the numbers agreeing to the notion that 'industry should be prevented from causing damage to the countryside, even if this sometimes leads to higher prices'. The use of aerosols containing CFCs declined rapidly on fear of damage to the ozone layer. In 1990 64% of adults stopped using them (*Guardian*, 1990). Surveys by the Department of the Environment indicated

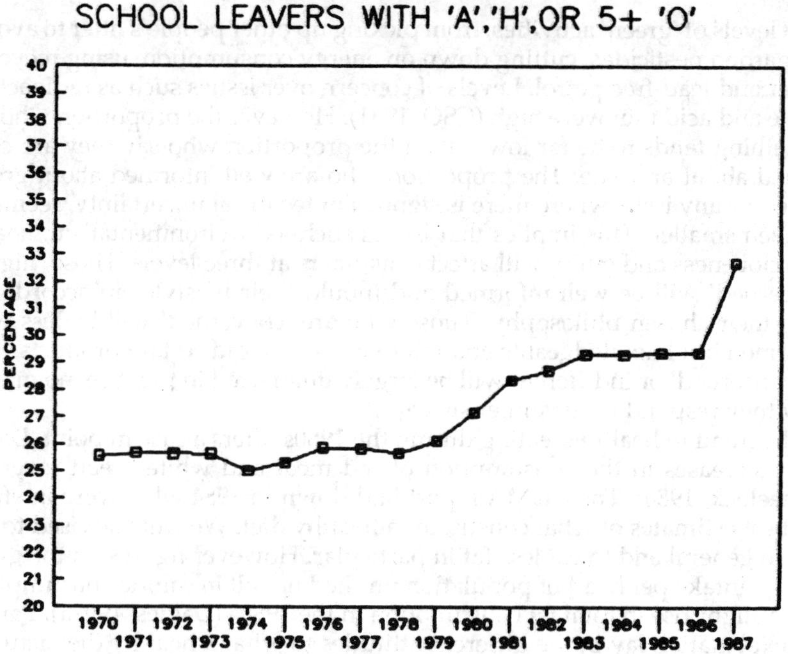

Figure 5. 5 Increase in attainment (*source:* DES, 1970–89)

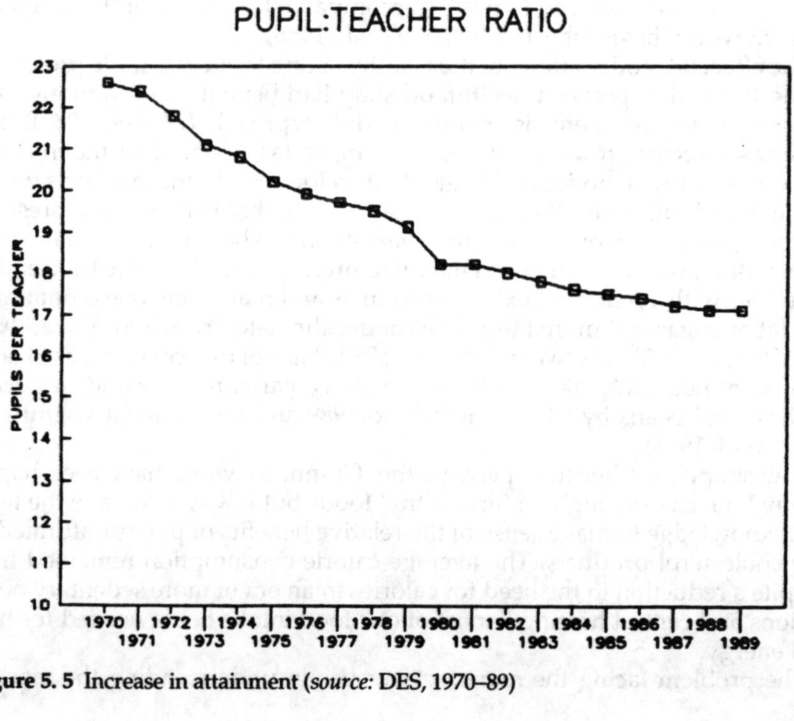

Figure 5. 5 Increase in attainment (*source:* DES, 1970–89)

high levels of 'green' activities, from picking up other people's litter to avoiding garden pesticides, cutting down on energy consumption, using recycled paper and lead-free petrol. Levels of concern over issues such as radioactive waste and acid rain were high (CSO, 1991). However the proportion who do something tends to be far lower than the proportion who say they are concerned about an issue. The proportion who are well informed about green issues, or any issue where there is significant technical uncertainty, seems to be even smaller. This implies that issues such as environmentalism, health consciousness and ethics will affect consumers at three levels. Those 'highly concerned' will be well informed and mould their lifestyles in accordance with their chosen philosophy. Those who are 'concerned' will be less well informed but knowledgeable enough to want to avoid certain products. The 'unconcerned' or indifferent will be largely unaffected in practice, no matter how they respond to consumer surveys.

The trend to healthier eating during the 1980s offers a case in point. Long-term increases in the consumption of red meat and white bread reversed (Wheelock, 1986). The COMA report laid down in 1984 what were in effect the best estimates of what constitutes a healthy diet. We were advised to eat less in general and to eat less fat in particular. However figures on the gross energy intake per head of population implied no fall in calorie consumption and a slight rise in total fat consumption in the 1980s (Davies, 1992a). Part of the explanation lay in the different attitudes to what a healthy diet actually is. One study identified six different attitude groups including one labelled the 'Superfits', who embraced not only the recommendations of various reports on healthy eating but also did so as part of a lifestyle that included aerobics. Another group were labelled the 'Grannies'. They regarded a healthy meal as 'meat and two veg', accompanied by many of the foods the Superfit would have abhorred (D'Arcy *et al.*, 1986).

The effect on food retailing of the healthy eating trend was quite profound. In the 1970s, the specialist healthfood shop had benefited, even though the majority regarded them as 'cranky and overpriced' (Mintel, 1987). The healthfood sector grew by 15% per annum, so fast in fact that the multiple grocery sector took notice and began to develop own-brand products with a strong health platform. Products such as muesli, that had been the preserve of the specialist, moved into the mainstream when Weetabix launched Alpen. But most branded goods manufacturers followed the market trends a little later with versions of existing products and many new ones containing less fat or sugar and more fibre. Sales of decaffeinated coffee rose steadily in the 1980s, some 28% between 1986 and 1989. Sales of diet cola increased 66%, semi-skimmed milk 200%. Sales of healthier variants increased: reduced-sugar baked beans by 64% from 1987 to 1989 and very low-fat yoghurt by 35% (AGB, 1991).

Few shoppers other than perhaps the 'Grannies' would have been happy to buy high calorie, high fat 'unhealthy' foods but few would have the technical knowledge to make sense of the relative benefits of polyunsaturated or low cholesterol products. The average calorie consumption remained high despite a reduction in the need for calories in an era of more sedentary occupations and central heating – most of our food intake being needed for heat and energy.

The problem facing the manufacturer lies in understanding the marketplace well enough to commit to the expense of establishing brand images that are appropriate to changes in consumer attitudes. The retailer, on the other hand, can experiment more in the knowledge that their risk is less should they guess wrong. The retailer also does not need to wait for the results of extensive research to begin experimenting. As one retail marketer once put it, 'The ring on our till is our main form of market research' (Ornstein, 1976).

Future trends

There are a number of current social trends that could have a major impact on retailing in the future. Two are discussed in some detail as illustrations of the need for suppliers to understand how such phenomena can affect their businesses because of an impact upon the retailer's business. The first is the male shopper, the second changing attitudes to shopping as an activity.

Men shopping

The housewife has been regarded as the stereotypical shopper with her husband in the role of influencer, together with their children. Not only is the four-person family no longer the most common social unit but also the roles of many males and females both in and out of the family have changed. Men in a heterosexual partnership have always been heavily involved in certain types of shopping (Putnam and Davidson, 1987), particularly consumer durables. Here they are expected to focus on technical and financial aspects while the female is supposed to be more concerned with design and with initiating the purchase. However by the late 1980s it was reported that 30% of British males claimed to be in charge of household shopping (Falconer, 1988), and 27% of males claimed to be 'competent' grocery shoppers (Mintel, 1988). Views differed as to whether men shopped differently from women when buying groceries. Davies and Bell (1991) tested a number of assertions on the relative speed of shopping of the sexes and found no significant differences when the task was the same but recommended targeting the male shopper by increasing his involvement particularly though greater emphasis on technology and on products with greater appeal to the male, such as alcohol. All retailers are likely to have to take the male shopper more seriously and to expect the female shopper to become more involved in technical aspects of products.

Shopping as an activity

All shopping can involve social activity, even if it is only talking to a check-out operator, but is shopping a true leisure activity? Much depends upon the meaning of the word leisure – is it freedom from necessary activity, in other words unnecessary activity? Hardly so, but most shopping purchases will be regarded as 'not unnecessary'. Some studies of leisure differentiate between essential shopping, mainly for food and other shopping that can be undertaken as discretionary activity, at least to some extent. Retailers and in particular shopping centres try hard to get us to see shopping as associated with leisure activity. Johnson (1990) differentiates between three 'models' of combinations of pure leisure and shopping:

Ambient leisure, where a shopping centre adds a number of services such as food courts, toilets, seating areas and some design features such as fountains and sculpture.

Magnet leisure, where some leisure experience such as a fairground, swimming pool or skating rink is added to a retail offer.

Heritage/destination leisure, where the heritage element, a castle or cathedral perhaps, acts as the magnet and retailers benefit from their proximity to the attraction.

Certainly shopping centres with a leisure element such as the Metro Centre in the north east of England are capable of attracting people from long distances, and over half will stay more than two hours if they make use of the leisure offer there (OXIRM, 1987). What is important in both cases is the ability of a retail centre to make people spend time both getting there and staying there. The issue becomes less one about shopping as a leisure activity and more about its being a time-consuming activity.

Many different perspectives on shopping as a time-consuming activity exist. Becker (1965) argued as an economist that time is allocated as a scarce resource. Sharp (1981, p 23) suggested that time is allocated between activities by individuals to obtain maximum utility. Jacoby *et al.* (1976) used the economist's perspective on time to suggest studying how people allocated their time using diaries as a useful approach for the marketer.

Some social scientists have claimed that the economist's view of time is valid only in an industrial society and suggest that time has fundamental social as well as economic associations. Sorokin and Merton (1937) for example as mentioned in Chapter 1 suggest that one of our major measures of time, a week, is not a quarter of a lunar month but the time between food markets. They illustrate their argument by referring to societies, including Roman, who had weeks that did not consist of 7 days.

Hassard (1990) quotes psychologist William James pointing out that time that is enjoyed passes more quickly than time that is bereft of interesting experience. However when one looks back, the period of enjoyment seems longer and of boredom, shorter. The most obvious concept of time is chronological. We measure time in minutes, hours, months and years, but this is again only one way of looking at time.

Time-buying shoppers

The number of weeks of annual holiday given to workers has increased (CSO, 1991), and the average number of hours worked in the week has decreased over the long term. However people appear to feel that there is less time to spare. They feel more rushed and this feeling is most noticeable among working women (Robinson, 1990). People now have more to do, more money with which to do it but the time available appears to have shrunk.

There appears to be a growing segment of consumers who can be labelled as 'time-sensitive shoppers' (Berry, 1982; Umesh *et al.*, 1989) or 'time-buying consumers' (Berry, 1979). Such shoppers tend to be employed full time and to be well educated. They also seem to spend more on each shopping trip. The time-insensitive shoppers tend to divide their purchases between stores more. Fram and Axelrod (1990) interpret the trend as working women regarding shopping as a 'stressful chore that interferes with leisure time'. Bradbury (1987) however differentiates between different types of shopping reporting that 80% of respondents to a survey cited shopping for groceries as an 'essential chore' while only about 30% labelled shopping for clothes and expensive household items in the same way.

Morello (1988) and Bergadaa (1990) cite Jung's work on psychological typology where individuals are said to be categorised by their involvement in the past, present or future. Bergadaa identified two groups, one orientated towards the future who sought to enrich themselves while keeping control over what they did (absolute determinism) while another group aimed to simplify their lives and tended to rely more on others (exogenous determinism). Davies (1992b) identified two similar groups in a larger survey, the characteristics of which are shown in Fig 5. 6.

The time concious majority (68% of adults)
Look to the future for success, but believe others will determine that future. Don't like to eat alone. See products such as washing machines as necessities. Fundamentally they believe that there isn't enough time in the day.

The inertia driven minority (22% of adults)
Prefer society the way it was because there was more excitement and romance. Don't like change and couldn't contemplate living anywhere else. Believe fate will decide what happens to them. Prefer not to do things in their leisure time, particularly reading informative books. Prefer package holidays to organising their own. Don't play sport or take exercise. Don't go to the dentists regularly. Are middle aged to elderly with children away from home. Don't invest for the future.

Figure 5. 6 Time perception groups

The smaller group corresponded roughly to Bergadaa's exogenous determinists but could be better labelled as 'inertia dominated'. The larger group, accounting for some two thirds of the adult population, have different attitudes towards activities and products. Above all they are time conscious, believing that there is not enough time in the day.

Over a decade earlier Bellenger and Korgaonkar (1980) were claiming that 69% of their survey could be classified as 'recreational' shoppers, who might be influenced by factors such as atmosphere and display. By the 1990s Davies (1992c) and Popcorn (1992) were recording what appeared to have become a general antipathy towards shopping with the latter predicting a substantial increase in direct delivery from manufacture to household over the years, bypassing the retailer. The significance of ideas such as these to manufacturer trade marketing strategy is considered later in this book. Suffice it to say that one way of countering retailer power is for suppliers to bypass them and to sell direct to 'shoppers', particularly those who hate the idea of spending time on shopping.

Keypoint summary

1) Over the longer term consumer expenditure has grown consistently but people are buying more experiences than products and some product sectors such as food are unlikely to show substantial growth.
2) Society is becoming more fragmented. Traditional measures of market structure are becoming less useful.
3) The segmentation methods relevant to retailing may differ from those used by manufacturers. Some commonality may be important if manufacturer and retailer are to cooperate.
4) An ageing population will mean fewer potential employees and a growing market opportunity, the 'greys'.
5) Lifestyle analysis suggest trends against the need to purchase brands because of a need to impress others and a preference for specialist shops.
6) An era of conspicuous consumption is giving way to a concern for the effect we are having on our environment, but people's actions do not always reflect with their opinions.
7) Manufacturers need to understand consumer trends thoroughly before committing themselves to capital investment. However retailers can react more quickly by trying out products on their shelves with minimal risk.
8) Two trends are identified as significant for the future: the increased involvement of men in shopping and whether people will want to spend as much time on shopping.

References

AGB (1991) *Healthy Eating*, AGB Market Information, London.

Applied Futures (1991) Private Communication, see also Mitchell, A. (1984) Nine American lifestyles, *The Futurist*, No 18, August, p 4.

Becker, G. S. (1965) A Theory of the Allocation of Time, *The Economic Journal*, pp 493–517.

Bellenger, D. N., Korgaonkar, P. K. (1980) Profiling the Recreational Shopper, *Journal of Retailing*, Vol 56, No 3, p 7.

Bergadaa, M. M. (1990) The Role of Time in the Action of the Consumer, *Journal of Consumer Research*, Vol 17, Dec, p 289.

Berry, L. L. (1979) The Time Buying Consumer, *Journal of Retailing*, Vol 55, No 4, Winter, p 58.

Berry, L. L. (1982) Retail Positioning Strategies for the 1980's, *Business Horizons*, Nov/Dec p 45.

Bradbury, D. (1987) Retailing and Leisure, Leisure Futures, Henley Centre for Forecasting, Summer.

Braus, P. (1990) What is Good Service?, *American Demographics*, July, p 36.

Codeluppi, V., Weber, D. (1989) The Ten C's: How to Use Socio-Trend Analysis in Marketing Strategy, *ESOMAR Proceedings*, Vienna, November, p 293.

Crispell, D. (1990) From WASPS to IMPS, *American Demographics*, June, p 51.

CSO (1991) *Social Trends*, HMSO, London.

D'Arcy, Masius, Benton, Bowles (1986) *Healthy Eating Study*, London.

Davies, G. (1992a) Healthier Eating and the Effects on Health Food Retailing, *British Food Journal*, Vol 94, No 4, p 30.
Davies, G. (1992b) Investigating the Time Orientation of Individuals and the Time Association of Products and Activities, Working Paper, Manchester Business School.
Davies, G. (1992c) 9 Reasons why Shopping has become Boring, *Aspect Retail Week*, Issue 7, Vol 5, p 2.
Davies, G., Bell, J. (1991) The Grocery Shopping: Is He Different?, *International Journal of Retail and Distribution Management*, Vol 19, No 1, p 25.
DES (1970–89) *Annual Abstract of Statistics*, HMSO, London.
Diamond, I. (1989) Ageing and Migration in Contemporary Britain, *Economic Review*, Jan. p 38.
EIU (1989) Chilled Foods *Retail Business*, No 382, December, London.
Engel, J. F., Blackwell, R. D., Miniard, P. W. (1990) Consumer Behavior (6th Ed), Dryden Press, Chicago, p 344.
Falconer, K. (1988) Gone Shopping, *Guardian*, Nov.
Fram, E. H., Axelrod, J. (1990) The Distressed Shopper, *American Demographics*, Oct, p 44.
Gardner, C., Sheppard, J. (1989) *Consuming Passion: The Rise of Retail Culture*, Unwin Hyman, London.
Guardian (1990) Environmental Survey Report, 14 September.
Hassard, J. (1990) *The Sociology of Time*, Macmillan, London, p 48.
Howard, E. (1991) Evaluating the Success of out of Town Regional Shopping Centres, OXIRM Working Paper No A23, Templeton College, Oxford.
Jacoby, J., Szybillo, G. J., Berning, C. K. (1976) Time and Consumer Behaviour: An Interdisciplinary Overview, *Journal of Consumer Research*, 2 March, p 320.
Johnson, S. (1990) The Leisure Market: Consumer Choice and Consumer Activity, in Howard, E. (ed) *Leisure and Retailing*, Longman, Harlow, pp 25–42.
Jowell, R., Witherspoon, S., Brook, L. (1991) *British Social Attitudes, 7th Report*, Gower, Aldershot.
Lumpkin, J. R., Hunt, J. B. (1989) Mobility as an Influence on Retail Patronage Behaviour of the Elderly: Testing Conventional Wisdom, *Journal of the Academy of Marketing Science*, Vol 17, No 1, p 1.
MacNulty, C. (1984) The Three Faces of the Consumer, *Large Mixed Retailing*, July, p 22.
McLoughlin, J. (1991) *The Demographic Revolution*, Faber & Faber, London, p 136.
Mintel (1987) *Health Food Shops*, London, January.
Mintel (1988) *Men 2000*, London.
Mintel (1991) British Lifestyles, as quoted in *The Financial Times* 31 January, p 14.
Mitchell, A. (1983) *Nine American Lifestyles*, Macmillan, New York.
Morello, G. (1988) Business Requirements and Future Expectations in Competitive Bank Services – The Issue of Time Perception, The Search for Financial Services, Seminar, ESOMAR, Milan.
Ornstein, E. J. (1976) The Retailers *Associated Business Programmes*, London.
OXIRM (1987) The New Regional Shopping Centre Phenomenon, Seminar Proceedings, Templeton College, Oxford.
Popcorn, F. (1992) quoted in *Retail Week*, 14 Feb, p 5.
Powderly, J., MacNulty, C. (1990) A Turbulent Time Ahead, *Marketing*, 11 Oct, p 33.
Putnam, M., Davidson, W. R. (1987) Family Purchasing Behaviour, *Management Horizons*, London.
Robinson, J. P. (1990) The Time Squeeze, *American Demographics*, Feb, p 30.
Schewe, C. D. (1990) Get in Position for the Older Market, *American Demographics*, June p 38.
Schlosberg, J. (1990) Stalking the Elusive Grandparent, *American Demographics*, July,

p 33.

Sharp, C. (1981) *Economics of Time*, Martin Robertson, Oxford.

Sorokin, P., Merton, R. (1937) Social Time: A Methodological and Functional Analysis, *American Journal of Sociology*, Vol 42, p 615.

Tantiwong, D., Wilton, P. C. (1985) Understanding Food Store Preferences Among the Elderly using Hybrid Conjoint Measurement Models, *Journal of Retailing*, Vol 61, No 4, p 35.

Toffler, A. (1971) *Future Shock*, Pan, London.

Umesh, V. N., Pettit, K. L., Bozman, C. S. (1989) Shopping Model of the Time Sensitive Shopper, *Decision Sciences*, Vol 20, No 4, p 715.

URPI (1990) Population Change: National, Regional and Sub-Regional, October No 90/4, Reading.

Wack, P. (1985) Scenarios: Unchartered Waters Ahead, *Harvard Business Review*, Sept/Oct, p 73.

Wheelock, J. V. (1986) Coping with Changes in the Food Business, *Food Marketing*, Vol 2, No 3, p 20.

Zeithaml, V. A. (1985) The New Demographics and Market Fragmentation, *Journal of Marketing*, Summer, p 64.

6

THE OWN-BRAND ISSUE

In Chapter 2 the rise of manufacturer power over the distribution chain in general, and over retailers in particular, was associated with the rise of the brand. At the same time the example of Boots the Chemist was used to make the point that many 'retailers' are capable of owning and developing branded products. But nowhere is there greater controversy in trade marketing than over the issue of brand manufacturers supplying retailers, who do not own or control their own factories, with own-brand products. The aims of this chapter include developing in greater depth an understanding of the significance of own-branding for the manufacturer. Just what are the strategic options the growth in own-brand represents? First, however, what are we talking about?

The terms own-brand, dealer own-brand, house brand, generic, own-label, sub-brand and many more litter the articles written on the subject. For the purpose of this chapter the following terms will be used to represent a number of different concepts:

- *Brand* A label that, when applied to a product or service, differentiates, signifies quality, has associated financial and psychic values and can command a premium over a commodity for the product.
- *Manufacturer's brand* A brand owned or controlled by a supplier to a retailer.
- *Own-brand* A brand owned or controlled by a retailer.
- *Own-label* A product whose name fails to achieve brand status but which carries a retailer's name or one associated with a retailer.
- *Generic product* A product which is unlabelled or where the labelling merely indicates the type of product (often referred to as yellow packs or economy lines or unbranded products).

In this chapter the term own-label will be used when it is unclear whether the retailer has developed a genuine brand.

Distinguishing between the four terms

One way to distinguish between the four terms is the relative price asked for each type of product. In grocery retailing the prices of generic products in one survey were between 25% and 45% below those for corresponding manufacturers' brands (*The Financial Times*, 1982). In this and another survey, the price advantage of own-label over manufacturers' brands ranged between 17% to 29% and from 9.6% to 20.9% respectively (*Marketing*, 1984). The issue of the relative price to the customer tended to dominate the debate over retailers' use of own-brand and own-label in the 1980s, but this diverted attention away from a whole raft of reasons about why retailers wanted to stock them. McGoldrick (1990), adapting earlier work by *Euromonitor*, suggests three categories of reason:

- Store image/customer loyalty.
- Competitive edge/extra turnover.
- Higher profit/better margins.

Summarising the potential benefits to the retailer, own-label or own-brand products can differentiate the retailer from its competition, give higher margins because the manufacturer's promotional cost is absent from the selling price, and offer a means of price promotion to build custom and loyalty. The issue is often seen as one where a manufacturer's brands compete with those of the retailer. This is certainly true in the grocery sector, but in other sectors own-branding dominates the retail offer – there is little or sometimes no competition within the store between manufacturer and retailer. The outlets of Marks & Spencer, Body Shop, MFI, the Gap, the Limited, Next, Tie Rack, Sock Shop, Thorntons, Benetton and many more are stocked almost exclusively by own-brand/own-label products. And what of the majority of car dealerships? The franchisee's name may be over the garage facia but the offer is dominated by the car maker's name, which is outside the retail outlet as well as inside the outlet. The issue of what *can* be called a manufacturer's brand and what is own-brand becomes more confused because of retailers such as Benetton and Body Shop. Is either business a retailer or even a manufacturer? Both have manufacturers and retail outlets associated with them but neither own the lot. What kind of business are they – and does it really matter to the customer? The issue should not then be seen in terms of retailer, manufacturer, designer, logistics company or whatever label you care to use, but who controls the supply chain. One way to control the supply chain is to control the brand. Indeed probably the only real asset companies such as Body Shop and Benetton possess is the brand their name represents, all else can be replicated by competition.

Retail brands

One problem many retailers have is whether some of the names they control can be considered to be brands. The business press see retailers as brands (*The Economist*, 1988; Jones, 1991), as do retailers themselves. Laura Ashley's chief executive referred to a 'portfolio of retail brands of which Laura Ashley will remain pre-eminent', (Bunce, 1989). W. H. Smith purchased the record retailer Our Price in 1986 and justified the premiums they paid because of the 'strength of the brand name', even though Our Price did not sell products under its own name, only suppliers' brands. As mentioned in Chapter 2, Tesco argue that 'the shop itself, its location, its atmosphere, the service it offers and the range of goods and prices can become the brand' (Murphy, 1990). Their Chairman, Ian MacLaurin, explained it slightly differently: 'To my mind the concept of 'the Tesco Brand' embraces everything that customers think of when they hear the name Tesco – our people, our products, our stores' (Tesco, 1991). Davies (1992) proposed that a retailer's product brand should be seen as distinct from a retailer's process brand, the branded *experience* (if it exists) that represents the shopping experience. The presence of true own-brands rather than own-labels will enhance that experience, and some aspects of the imagery will spill over from one to the other. Unless, however, the retailer-controlled products are genuinely seen as brands, then the risk to the retailer is that the store's image will decline by emphasising own-label over manufacturers' brands.

Sainsbury reduced its dependency on its own-brands in the late 1980s probably for this reason. In America Sears, J. C. Penney and K-Mart moved to increase their sales of manufacturers' brands for the same reason (*Stores*, 1988). Such concerns have led to the view that there is a limit to the market penetration of retailer-controlled products (Salmon and Omar, 1987). Figures of around 30% are sometimes quoted (Nielsen, 1988; Piper, 1988). Davies (1990) challenged this concept by proposing that all that was ultimately inhibiting own-label penetration was the concentration level in the retail sector and the power this represents. Fig 6. 1 correlates the penetration of own-label in different European countries with the retail concentration that existed in each country. Fig 6. 2 correlates the rise in own-label penetration in Britain with retail concentration in grocery.

The penetration of own-brand in Switzerland (Sz) was the highest in Europe at the time of the study. One retailer Migros holds a dominant market share. In the UK there are a number of grocery chains with over 5% of the market. The same is true in Germany (G) and The Netherlands (NL). In France (F) retail concentration is high but many chains are relatively decentralised, which may have inhibited own-brand growth. In Sweden (Sw), Norway (N), Austria (A) and Belgium (B) concentration levels and own-brand penetration are both low while Italy (I) has the highest proportion of

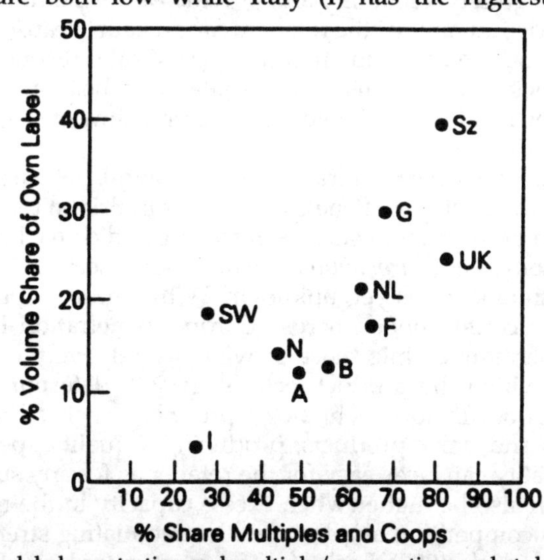

Figure 6. 1 Own-label penetration and multiple/cooperative market share in European grocery retailing (*source:* data from Nielsen, 1988)

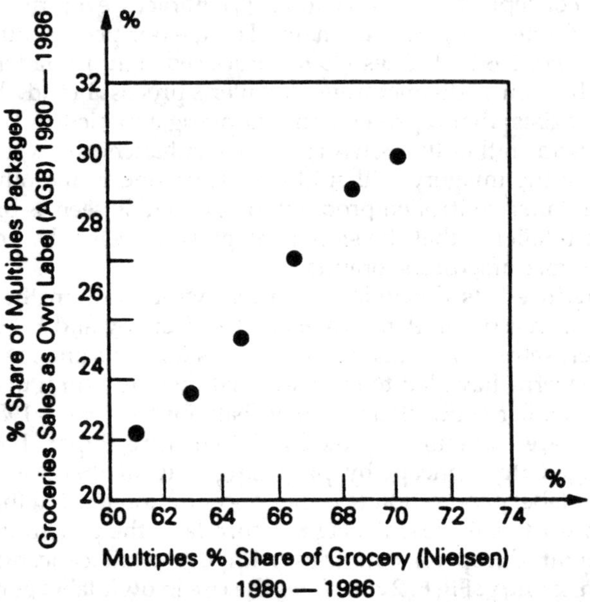

Figure 6. 2 Own-label penetration and the rise in multiple power in UK grocery retailing (*sources: Food Retailing*, 1987; Carter, 1989)

independent retailers in Europe of those countries analysed.

The correlations are both statistically significant and suggest there is no practical limit to own-brand/label penetration other than the respective abilities of retailers and their suppliers to create the stronger brand image. If retailers can get their customers to accept their own products as equivalent to or better than (in quality, reliability and psychic value) manufacturers' products, then any price advantage the retailers can sustain because of lower marketing costs can be used to erode manufacturers' sales. Economy of scale is one important factor in achieving this; a retailer must be large enough to purchase the volume needed to achieve a selling price low enough to undercut the manufacturer's brand.

As Fig 6. 1 illustrates, the penetration level of own-label varies by country. It also varies by product type. Penetration levels in Britain for example have been very low in product areas such as hardware and china, but very high in footwear and menswear (*Euromonitor*, 1986). In some sectors such as cars and newspapers own-label is, as yet, unknown. Within grocery penetration levels also vary. In confectionery, across Europe, penetration levels are low other than in Germany, while those in wine are relatively high (Frost and Sullivan, 1990). Often the product technology will determine the possible level of penetration. In low technology products, such as fresh produce, paper products and dairy products, producing a quality specification and maintaining quality can be as easy for the retailer as for any supplier. Penetration levels can also be higher when excess capacity in the manufacturing sector increases competition and reduces the negotiating strength of manufacturers (Davies *et al.*, 1985). Lack of differentiation or lack of branding can also make it easier for the shopper to believe that there is no real difference between similar products. Finally, where there is a gap in a market that is otherwise branded, a retailer will often fill it with its own product.

Generic products

Generic or unbranded products were a feature of grocery retailing in the 1970s. By the 1990s they had virtually disappeared in Britain but such products still maintained a significant presence elsewhere. French-based hypermarket retailer Carrefour are credited with launching *'produits libre'* in 1976. Such generic products have no visible branding, the name on the packaging describes the physical product and that is all. McEnally and Hawes (1984) described generics as a 'celebration of austerity', but the available research, including their own, suggested that generics were bought more extensively by the better-off than by the disadvantaged in society. Only one of the thirteen earlier studies reviewed by McEnally and Hawes reported a higher purchase rate among low income customers.

The demographic characteristics of the generic purchaser have been found to include a higher level of education, which might imply a greater willingness to assume the risk that might be inherent in a generic purchase. Some studies suggested low levels of brand loyalty among generic purchasers. Still more identified psychographic characteristics such as being more innovative and information seeking. Overall, generic buyers are price conscious. McEnally and Hawes' own research suggested significant behaviour differences between those who did and those who did not purchase generics. The generic buyer shops more frequently, has a higher product usage rate, is price conscious, store loyal and slightly less brand loyal. A picture emerges of a customer group who are 'involved' shoppers, price conscious and more reliant upon the retailer but people who do not buy generics because they are hard up.

Many explanations are possible about why the less well off are not buyers of generics. Perhaps they are more influenced by advertising or perhaps they cannot afford to risk a wasted purchase and seek instead the reassurance of manufacturers' brands. Whatever the reason, generics failed to attract the sustenance driven in society. Instead the better-off, but price conscious, traded down for a bargain. Instead of gaining custom the retailer lost margin from its own, loyaler customers. Small wonder that generics have declined in significance in many markets.

What has continued to grow have been the retailers' own-label and own-brand offers. So what do we know about the customer's views of these?

The customer's view

What matters often enough is the customer's perception of the product sector and the various offers within it. Where branding is weak or absent, as in fresh produce, probably in petrol and in all other 'commodity type' products, the retailer is in a fair position to benefit from an own-label, or generic, without having to create an own-brand. Where the psychic value to the shopper is high, as in cigarettes, fashion and cars for example, branding is likely to be crucial.

In one Gallup study for the Private Label Manufacturers' Association, in 1984, 63% of Americans 'mostly agreed' that stores offering a variety of what were referred to as 'store' brands usually offer them better value. Of these, 65% mostly agreed that store brands are made by the manufacturers of national brands, 50% mostly agreed that store brands perform or taste as well as national brands; 74% said that price was very important in buying store brands and 80% that quality was very important.

Interestingly 53% mostly agreed that stores that had a range of store brands 'cared more about their customers' (PLMA, 1984). This is the concept of the retailer acting as the shopper's buying agent yet again. Even allowing for some bias towards the sponsors of the research in the way questions were put, this survey supports the view that many shoppers have a positive view of retailer-controlled products.

Livesey and Lennon (1978) reported on earlier studies that suggested the penetration of own-label was higher in the higher socioeconomic groups. Their own work on who would accept own-label grocery products contained some apparently odd results. Own-label acceptance was higher in washing-up liquid and tinned peas than for the other products they tested, even though advertising and branding were very high in the former and low in the latter sectors. Uncles and Ellis (1989) found no difference in the purchasing patterns for own-labels/brands and manufacturers' brands. They concluded that own-label was bought just like any other 'brand' with a similar market share.

De Chernatony (1989) offered a different view and presented evidence that shoppers saw manufacturer's brands, own-label/brands and generics as a distinct hierarchy for five of the six product fields he tested. The previous work he quotes suggests a possible convergence of the three as quality specifications of brands declined, the price differential between own-label/brand declined and retailers moved to develop a personality for their own lines.

Another way of looking at own-label or own-brand products is that they represent minor brands in those markets where they exist. But if the 'market' is defined as the retail store, then many of these 'minor' brands become major brands. Whatever one's view, the manufacturer of brands must not assume that own-label or own-brand products are somehow inherently different in nature from brands. To the manufacturer and retailer they clearly are; to many customers they may not be. Successful and unsuccessful brands exists in all markets. An unsuccessful brand is one which has not established a consumer franchise above and beyond the product itself. The only difference is that the retailer can sustain an unsuccessful own-brand longer than the manufacturer because the retailer can delete it in favour of a competitor's line.

The management of own-brands by retailers

The case study following this chapter illustrates how one food retailer went about developing an own-label/brand range. Much of the procedure used will be familiar to readers working for branded-goods manufacturers, other than the speed of 'development' and the low level of real innovation.

The simple way for a retailer to establish an own-label is for the buyer to work with a manufacturer to establish the offer. The manufacturer retains the roles of product technologist and market researcher and shares the marketing role with the retail buyer. However many retailers now employ their own marketing and technical staff working alongside the buyer in a team that is much the same as a new product team in a manufacturer.

Senker (1987) examined the rise in the numbers of and the change in the role of the retailer's technical department. Many technologists employed by retailers are concerned with quality control but many work on product development. Fig 6. 3 takes some of Senker's data and presents it in a way that illustrates a link between the number of technical staff employed by the major grocery retailers and their dependence on own-brand, measured as a percentage of total turnover. The number of technologists has been adjusted by dividing Senker's count of technical staff by the retailers' market share, so as to compare like for like. Retailers such as Marks & Spencer appear to support their dependency on own-label/brand with a substantial technical effort. Retailers such as Kwik Save, who sell only manufacturers' brands, have little or no use for technologists.

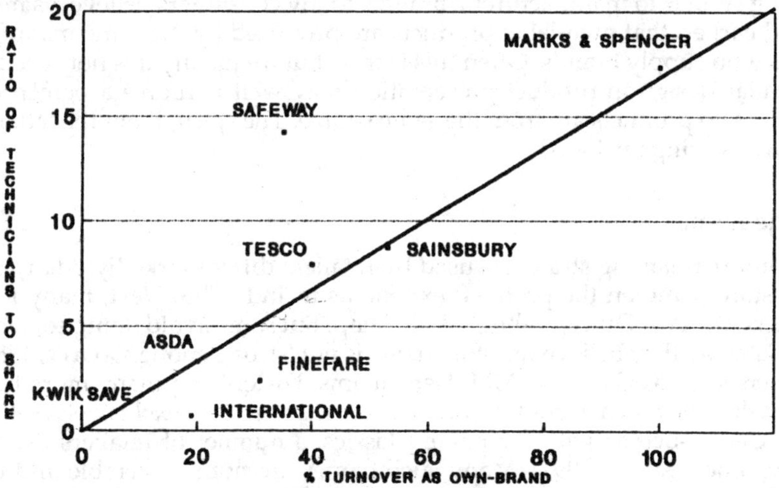

Figure 6. 3 Technician index and level of own-brand (*sources*: Senker, 1987; author's estimates)

FineFare and International Stores, now subsumed within Gateway, were both exponents at this time of generics. Their dependency on product technology as part of their overall strategy was, not surprisingly, lower than the correlation line suggests it should be. On the other hand Safeway, even before its acquisition by Argyll, was developing a strong own-label range which required a significantly higher technical effort.

Despite the increased involvement by retailers in product technology, own-label marketing strategy is often imitative rather than innovative. There are exceptions, such as Marks & Spencer with chilled food, Next with a particular fashion offer and the vertically integrated businesses of Boots, Jaeger and MFI. The norm in much grocery retailing is to imitate the brand leader and to follow rather than lead the market.

Passing off

Imitation might be the most sincere form of flattery if one accepts the old adage but it can be illegal. Passing off, as mentioned in an earlier chapter, is the wrong committed by someone who presents their goods as if they were those of another. The use of a brand name registered by another company or a breach of a patent on a product are extreme examples of illegal copying. Passing off is more concerned with assessing the 'get up' of a product, taken to be the packaging, its shape, colour and design. In one legal action, market research presented to illustrate the confusion that can occur when two products with *similar* but not identical 'get up' was dismissed as a critical point of evidence because, side by side, the products were clearly different (*Fleet Street Reports*, 1980). In this case two manufacturers were involved but the issue of imitation is even more general in own-labelling.

The main point of concern in the author's opinion is the use of similar packaging by retailers when presenting their products both in the use of shape and colour. It cannot be coincidence when own-label lines end up looking similar to manufacturers' brands. Many consumers believe, as mentioned earlier, that own-label products are produced by the same manufacturers who supply brands. Often this is true, but frequently it is not. The use of similar design in product presentation may well reinforce a perception that the two products are from the same source. The spirit, if not the letter of the law, is being infringed.

Range names

The product-naming strategies used by retailers differ markedly. Many use their store name on the product; exponents include BhS, Next, many food retailers, the Post Office, Habitat, Body Shop. But some avoid doing so, when like Gateway they believe the store name is not 'strong enough' (Urry, 1988). Retailers such as Gateway, MFI, Debenhams, Fosters and many more have names that they own or control for the products that they, exclusively, sell. In some cases, such as with the name Classics, a number of retailers use the same name (Davies, 1992). Many such names are not registerable and can best be regarded as range names or sub-brand names, useful more to the retailer than to the consumer. Such products are unlikely to be considered as brands. The names have no separate existence, no image of their own and no psychic value to the consumer.

Umbrella branding

When the retailer uses the same name on the product as on the store, the naming strategy could be regarded as 'umbrella branding': a number of different products carry the same name with perhaps a secondary name denoting the product type. The name appears again on carrier bags, staff uniforms and signage. But often the design work falls far short of the standards expected for manufacturers' brands. Lewis (1991) criticised FineFare's use of an 'inflexible design grid' which imposed the same look on soup as on tights. The problem here is one of a basic error in branding, the assumption that the brand's personality is suited to any kind of product.

The Cadbury name is a prominent example of successful umbrella branding. It is synonymous with quality in chocolate and can be used both on its own or as an indication that the product name it is used with carries the same attributes as all other such products. It is strong enough to be licensed to other manufacturers. But would even the name Cadbury add value to a soap powder or to a coffee table?

When the retailer gets it right, the store name can act as a successful umbrella brand name to a range of different but associated products. Next can be applied to clothing for both sexes, to furnishings and to furniture. St Michael still has relevance on both food and clothing even though the association between products is less obvious. The problem for many retailers is, however, that the name over the store would not be the one you would choose for a product brand name! Retailers may struggle to establish the brand imagery that is normally associated with successful manufacturers' brands because of a basic problem with brand names. Instead they tend to use price as a promotional tool coupled with heavy display, perhaps allocating up to three times the facings given to the leading manufacturer's brands (Bond, 1984).

That said there are signs that retailers are beginning to use elements of the marketing mix more usually associated with the manufacturer such as couponing and advertising to promote their own-label/brands (*Private Label International*, 1991a).

True brands

Real brands are few and far between. The acid test for a brand is the existence of added-value evoked by the name itself, independently of the product. The clearest demonstration of the power of branding comes from comparisons of products where consumers' preference shifts depending upon whether the identity of the product is known or not.

For example, in blind taste tests, conducted in the 1970s, where members of the public were unaware of which two colas they were tasting, Pepsi, on average, was preferred to Coke. When the tasters are told that one was Pepsi and the other was Coke, Coke was preferred to Pepsi (Sculley, 1988). Feldwick (1991) likens this phenomenon to the placebo effect that is found when a patient responds positively to a pill that contains nothing medicinal. It shouldn't exist but it does – the suggestion of benefit from the brand name is enough to convince the supposedly rational human being that it exists.

Product testing, rather than brand testing, is then only part of the answer to assessing a brand's acceptance. When products are tested on their own and compared to competitive lines, some remarkable preferences can be revealed. In one taste survey leading brands such Heinz beans, Walkers crisps, Tetley Tea and Flora margarine seemed to lose out to the own-label/brand products of retailers (Consumer Association, 1991). In the marketplace the preferences are reversed. However similar preferences for own-label over manufacturer's brands are becoming widely reported, reinforcing the view that manufacturers have paid too little attention to the relative quality of their products (*Woman*, 1992).

A genuine brand has the ability to change the customer's perception of reality. If it can do so as an umbrella name to another supposed brand, what chance has a retailer's own-label which carries with it the problem of being under the umbrella of the store name? The answer is as much chance as any other brand would have against a competitor that can offer the perceived benefit of extra value. Value in turn is the complex relationship that exists between quality and price. Quality in turn is the managed perception of benefit implied by all the customer is told about the product. Once the customer believes the retailer's own-label has the same quality as the manufacturer's brand, the latter will suffer because of the saving the customer makes by buying the own-label. If the retailer can establish its own-label as a brand, then all the manufacturer can do is segment the market, and treat the retailer's product as just another competitive brand. Easy enough to say but seen this way every retailer's own-label becomes a potential competitor.

Monitoring the market is not about seeing own-labels as a homogeneous collection of products. Each has its own position in the market, defined by the branding of the retailer owning it. Each retail chain within which the manufacturer competes against an own-label must be considered as a *separate* market.

Brand positioning

The implications of the last statement are profound for the marketer. It is bad enough having to analyse a national market, but to be told that a national market is too coarse a picture of reality might be difficult to accept. Is there much doubt, however, that the market represented by a Tesco store is different from that in a Kwik Save or a Sainsbury? Would the same product positioning strategy be as effective in a Wickes as in a B and Q? Fig 6. 4 represents a brand positioning model for the instant-coffee market constructed in the

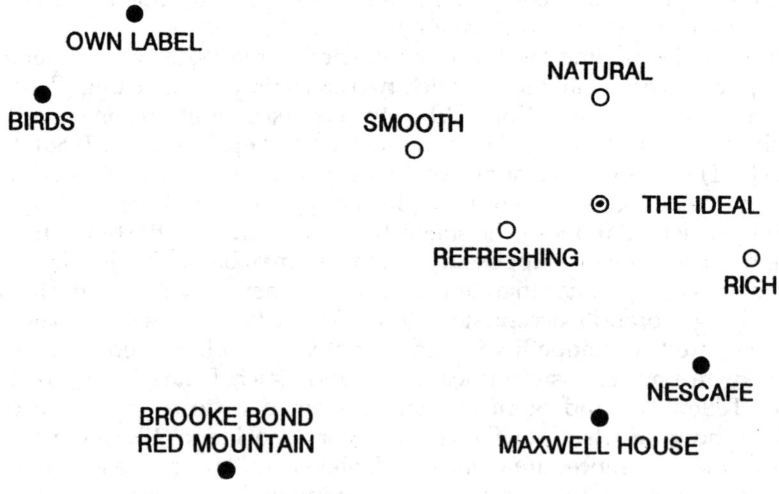

Figure 6. 4 The instant coffee market, 1982–83

early 1980s. Own-brand is shown as a single entity, which could be a dangerous assumption. The imagery surrounding Marks & Spencer's own-label coffee would be different from that with say the Coop name on it, even though the physical product may be the same. The model is constructed by asking consumers about what they see as similar and what as different. What is similar is then represented as close together, what is different as wide apart.

The brand managers of each of the manufacturers' brands on the market model would be able to identify a number of options to improve the positioning of their product. But those nearest to 'own-brand' need to know how close they are to *each* of the retailers' own-brands. If they were seen as similar in image to any one own-brand then they become immediate targets for delisting by the retailer concerned because they do little but duplicate the retailer's offer.

This can be a strategic dilemma for manufacturers, many of whom have developed secondary brands so as to protect their leading brands. Are they still able to supply retailers with a product whose positioning is based more on price than added value? Thus in electrical goods one manufacturer might market a similar product under a number of brand names but find itself competing with the retailer's own-brand directly in one or more of its own names.

In its interim report in the 1990, the electrical retailer Dixons appended a report by Consultancy Interbrand placing a valuation on its own-brand names. These were Matsui, used in hifi, radios, televisions, video recorders, microwaves, refrigerators and telephones, Miranda on cameras and binoculars and Saisho on a similar range to Matsui. Matsui and Saisho products were on sale in both Dixons and Currys, also owned by Dixons. In 1988/89 own-brand accounted for 26.7% of turnover. It follows that any secondary brand offered to Dixons would risk being seen by both retailer and customer as a substitute for Dixons' own-brand. Dixons could not afford to display products that competed directly with its own range.

The manufacturer's response

The danger for the manufacturer of leading brands is a gradual erosion of market share by retailers' own-brands. Own-label is less of a competitive threat unless the market sector becomes commodity-like and customers stop believing that any brand could hold any added-value over the basic product benefits. The competitive position against an own-brand is basically the same as against any brands with one essential difference, the retailer controls access to the customer and can give preferential treatment to its own lines.

Two long-term views are possible on the own-label/own-brand phenomenon. First that further erosion of the manufacturer's position is inevitable because of the advantages large retailers have in marketing and distributing products. This view is given further support by the possibility that customers will become less brand conscious over time. Even in Japan, said to be the most brand conscious market of all, own-label/brand penetration is substantial and growing (*Private Label International*, 1991b).

A second view is that strong brands will always prevail, particularly those that can retain and sustain the elementary appeal of the successful brand. It is irrelevant to the consumer who in the supply chain controls the brand and it is difficult to accept that there will cease to be a substantial segment of the market who rely upon the added-value of the brand. The same brands have often led individual markets for decades (*The Economist*, 1988), suggesting that leading brand names can be immune to attack from secondary brands and own-brands.

These two views are, frankly, irreconcilable and the long term outcome is likely to vary by product sector, distribution channel and country. The rest of this chapter is concerned with illustrating the different ways manufacturers and suppliers have chosen, strategically, to respond to own-brand/label.

Become solely own-label/brand suppliers

Bond (1984) reported the rapid change made by Whitworth who once held 75% of the dried-fruit market in Britain as brand leader. Within six years 70% of the market became own-label but Whitworth was still the dominant supplier. It switched strategies as the market changed.

Smith (1985) pressed Irish companies to use own-label/brand as a market entry strategy to develop a foothold in the British market. The same logic is being followed by many manufacturers, keen to take advantage of the reducing costs of cross border trading within the European Community.

Robert McBride, part of BP, are a major supplier of own-brand/label detergents. The cost advantages such companies have may prove significant. The branded detergent companies need to buy their raw materials from such as the oil companies. The suppliers of many raw materials see commercial advantage in forward integration (aluminium refiners into aluminium foil is another example) and selling directly to the retailer. On a much smaller scale farmers are working directly with retailers to supply speciality cheeses, particular types of bacon and much more.

Many companies are organising themselves as exclusively own-label suppliers. The problem inherent in own-label supply is having to rely upon the retailer. If the retailer fails to market the product, the supplier also loses out. If the retailer decides to switch supplier, the supplier may be bankrupted by the loss of business. Retailers such as Marks & Spencer insist on their own standards of quality control, hygiene and even staff welfare being adopted by their suppliers. They seem to prefer suppliers who do not serve other retailers. Supplying own-label can be profitable but the links to the retailer can become handcuffs albeit made of gold when things go well.

The threat to discontinue supply can be far more serious than if the supplier is selling to a number of retailers and if their brand name is strong enough to discourage shoppers from patronising a store that does not stock it. How to manage the relationship with the retailer is central to the success of being an own-label supplier, as will be discussed in later chapters.

Supply own-label and manufacturer brands

Supplying a retailer with a mixture of own-label and branded product appeared to be a logical solution in the early days of retailers' involvement in developing their own ranges. Retailers wanted low prices, far lower than they bought manufacturers' brands for, but manufacturers were often all too keen to obtain the extra volume so as to use their production capacities to the full. Own-label production was often marginally costed. Fig 6. 5 illustrates the financial logic of doing so.

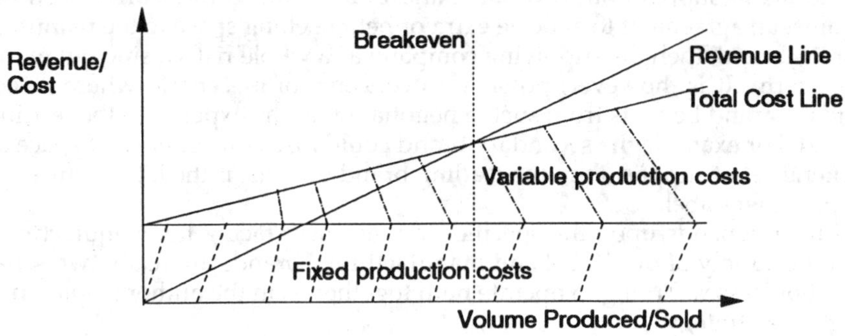

Figure 6. 5 Marginal costing of own-label production

Costs in manufacturing tend to fall into two broad types, fixed and variable. Those that are fixed do not vary much no matter how little or how much is produced. They include the cost of depreciating the plant, overheads such as rent and rates and any labour costs that have to be paid even if nothing is produced. Variable costs are only incurred once something is produced and they tend to rise in direct proportion to how much is produced. They include the cost of raw materials and much of the labour costs.

Once the breakeven point has been reached in Fig 6. 5, the manufacturer has covered all of its fixed costs. If it produces and sells a higher volume, it needs only to sell at a price to cover its variable costs before it makes some profit.

Fig 6. 5 is a simplification of reality. In the real world fixed costs do rise, in steps more often than not. Variable costs do not rise evenly in proportion to output and selling goods at a price that covers just the variable costs will often reduce demand for the full price product. But the principle of marginal pricing still holds. Above breakeven, a manufacturer can still make money by selling at below the breakeven price. This marginal costing approach has been used by many to justify making own-label at low prices for retailers. But if the retailer's own-label sells well, the manufacturer comes under pressure to produce more at the same price. If the manufacturer's brand begins to suffer and sales fall, the logic of producing a mix of two products selling at different prices falls apart.

Keen to protect the position of their own manufacturer's brand, companies often attempt to reduce the quality of their own-label products. In one instance a manufacturer decided not to spray coffee oil onto its own-label instant coffee. The consumer would not benefit from the coffee smell in the jar. Little or no difference would be noticed once the product was in the cup. Such subtle attempts to maintain a quality advantage may work, but for how long? The retailer's technologists and its own market research would pick up on any real difference. If the technical specification is rewritten so that the supplier has to provide a match for its brand, then the benefit will be short lived. Is it also really worth while changing a manufacturing process just to distinguish between the two products?

The problems of one company trying to manage two, near identical, products are just as acute on the sales and marketing side. The trade marketing manager dealing with the retail buyer will be under pressure to agree to better terms to supply both own-label and brand. Unless these are traded off against an agreement to allocate extra or better selling space to the manufacturer's brand, then the supplying company as a whole risks losing out in the long term. It is, however, possible to conceive of a scenario where a secondary brand benefits from such a negotiation at the expense of the leading brand. For example the secondary brand could insist on better shelf space or general retail support than the leading brand obtains, if the latter refuses to supply own-label.

Much depends upon the specific circumstances facing the manufacturer, but the supply of own-label and manufacturers' brands are really two separate businesses. Trying to operate both together is, in the author's opinion, a high risk strategy.

Supply manufacturer's brand only

A number of manufacturers have refused to contemplate own-label supply. Examples include Kelloggs' in cereals, Nestlé in coffee and Lever in detergents. Many have run advertisements pointing out that they do not supply own-label in an attempt to counter the view that the own-label products in their sectors are made by leading brand suppliers.

Such companies deny themselves access to the own-label sales of retailers and access in particular to the likes of Marks & Spencer who sell nothing but own-label/brand. As this sector of the market is growing and growing faster than the branded sector, such decisions cannot be made easily. Their plans for growth must be based elsewhere, either on replacing secondary brands or on benefiting from the expansion expected with a totally open European Market.

There are as yet few truly international consumer brands by comparison with the number of local or regional brands. In some cases manufacturers who have an international presence do not market the same product under the same name in all markets. Either the product or the name varies. Under EC law it is expected that it will be possible to sell whatever is legal in one country in another country within the Community, so the effect of local legislation will be minimised. Formulations, styling and sizing to suit local needs will continue but the development of truly pan-European brands is an important step in developing manufacturer's brand power. The threat to delist by a retailer is reduced if the manufacturer can switch supplies to another part of Europe. Retailers at present are national rather than international in their nature and would be unable to exert as much power as they do within a national market.

Manufacturers such as Unilever have introduced pan-European brands (in their case Timotei and Radion) but some names do not travel – the Danish chocolate brand Plopp, any product with the word 'mist' in it would have problems in Germany (because it means manure), the Spanish soft drink Revoltosa might struggle in Britain, as would Fairy Liquid in America (Hindle, 1990). The Mars group are one of many who have renamed individual brands, Marathon becoming Snickers, and Munchies moving to Brekkies for the sake of commonality and transferability. In the consumer-durable sector, the same cars, hifi, even furniture have been sold for some time throughout Europe under the same brand names, but a similar problem exists to some extent even here in commonality of product and the use of different brand names for the same product.

Pan-European or even international branding could be a short-lived advantage in the grocery sector. A number of pan-European retail alliances have been formed, the most active of which is the European Retail Alliance between Argyll (Safeway) in Britain, Ahold in The Netherlands and Casino in France. They were involved in a share swop and together form the heart of a wider association, Associated Marketing Services, involving other European retailers. The benefits expected from the alliance include sharing expertise but also the development of own-label.

Some of the implications of these options will be discussed in later chapters. The two inherent strategies, produce own-label and produce manufacturer brands, are totally different in terms of their implications for the manufacturer and all suppliers must be clear on which options they select and as to the consequences of their choice.

Keypoint summary

1) The market share of own-label/brand sales has been rising in most product sectors.
2) Views differ as to whether there is a natural limit to own-label/brand penetration.
3) Retailers can have problems establishing products sold under their own names as genuine brands.
4) Unbranded or generic products appear to have had their day but purchasers of these and own-label products do not tend to be the less well-off.
5) Customers often believe that own-label products are made by the manufacturers of national brands.
6) Manufacturers do not always enjoy the protection they should in law because of attempts to associate the physical look of retailers' products with their own-brands.
7) The management of own-label by retailers is becoming more sophisticated. It would be advisable to assume that a retailer's product is bought just like any minor brand. The relevant market to research becomes the retailer not the national market.
8) Manufacturers have two main options open to them: to supply or not to supply own-brand. Such options have their own separate implications and the two options may be mutually exclusive.

References

Bond, C. (1984) Own-labels vs the Brands, *Marketing*, 8 March, p 27.

Bunce, M. L. (1989) The International Approach of Laura Ashley: Adding Value to Retail Offerings, ESOMAR, Edinburgh, April.

Carter, D. (1989) Shifting Power Patterns in Groceries, *Retail Marketing and Manage-*

ment, Vol 14, No 8, (Nielsen *Grocery Trade Report* data).
Consumer Association (1991) Own-brand Foods, *Which?*, Nov, p 629.
Davies, G. (1990) Marketing to Retailers: A Battle for Distribution, *Long Range Planning*, Vol 23, No.6, p 101.
Davies, G. (1992) The Two Ways in Which Retailers can be Brands,. *International Journal of Retail and Distribution Management*, Vol 20, No 2, p 24.
Davies, K., Gilligan, C., Sutton, C. (1985) Structural Changes in Grocery Retailing: The implications for Competition, *International Journal of Physical Distribution and Materials Management*, Vol 15, No 2, p 3.
de Chernatony, L. (1989) The Impact of the Changed Balance of Power from Manufacturer to Retailer in the UK Packaged Groceries Market, in Pellegrini, L., Reddy, S. K. (eds) *Retail and Marketing Channels*, Routledge, London.
The Economist (1988) The Year of the Brand, 24 Dec, p 106.
Euromonitor (1986) The Own-brands Report, London.
Feldwick, P. (1991) Defining a Brand, in Cowley, D. (ed) *Understanding Brands*, Kogan Page, London.
The Financial Times (1982) 28 October, p 12.
Fleet Street Reports (1980) Tetrosyl Ltd vs Silver Paint and Lacquer Co, Court of Appeal, 15–11. 79, *Fleet Street Reports*, London, p 68.
Frost and Sullivan (1990) Report abstracted in *Private Label International*, Sept, p 24.
Hindle, T. (1990) No Holds Barred in Making a Name Stick, *Daily Telegraph*, 23 July, p 27.
IGD (1987) AGB data quoted in *Food Retailing*, Institute of Grocery Distribution, Radlett, Herts.
Jones, H. (1991) Tesco Shows its Shelf Interest, *Marketing Week*, 17 May, p 28.
Lewis, M. (1991) Brand Packaging, in Cowley, D. (ed) *Understanding Brands*, Kogan Page, London, p 143.
Livesey, F., Lennon, P. (1978) Factors Affecting Consumer's Choice between Manufacturers' Brands and Retailer Own-labels, *European Journal of Marketing*, Vol 12, No 3, p 158.
Marketing (1984) Own-brand vs the Brands, 8 March, p 24.
McEnally, M. R., Hawes, J. M. (1984) The Market for Generic Brand Grocery Products, *Journal of Marketing*, Vol 48, Winter, p 75.
McGoldrick, P. (1990) *Retail Marketing*, McGraw Hill, Maidenhead, p 246.
Murphy, J. M. (1990) *Brand Strategy*, Director Books, Cambridge, p 65.
Nielsen, A. C. (1988) Private Labels Strong but Stabilizing in Europe, *Private Label International*, June, p 8.
Piper, R. (1988) The Death of the Big Brand? *Admap*, December, p 24.
PLMA (1984) *Store Brands vs National Brands: The American Consumer Speaks Out*, Private Label Manufacturers Association, New York.
Private Label International (1991a) TESCO's Got (Almost) the Whole Product Mix in Its 'Hands', June, p 6.
Private Label International (1991b) Brand Conscious Market Bows to Private Label, September, p 11.
Salmon, W. J., Omar, K. A. (1987) Private Labels are back in Fashion, *Harvard Business Review*, May/June, p 99.
Sculley, J. (1988) *Odyssey*, Perennial Library, New York.
Senker, J. (1987) Technological Cooperation between Manufacturers and Retailers to meet Market Demand, *Food Marketing*, Vol 2, No 3, p 38.
Smith, J. (1985) Market Entry to the British Grocery Trade Through Private Label, *Journal of Irish Business and Administrative Research*, Vol 17, No 2, Winter, p 37.
Stores (1988) How big is the private label boom?, June, p 10.
Tesco (1991) *Annual Report and Accounts*, Chesham, Bucks.
Uncles, M. D., Ellis, K. (1989) The Buying of Own-labels, *European Journal of Marketing*, Vol 23, No 3, p 57.
Urry, M. (1988) Why Gateway Believes it is Leading a Retail Revolution, *The Financial Times*, 3 Nov.
Woman (1992) We Test the Best, 17 Feb, p 20, 24 Feb, p 18.

Case Study: ASDA BRAND

Asda Stores

Asda as an organisation can trace its antecedents to the sale of produce by the farming community of Yorkshire. But the most significant factor in the early days of their involvement in retailing was probably the purchase of two superstores in 1965 at Nottingham and Crossgates, opened somewhat earlier by an American company testing the potential for that style of food retailing in Britain. The two stores were enormous in their time and size of outlet became one of the significant differences in Asda's operation compared with its competition. Even by 1988 when the company could boast 126 stores and when most major multiples had moved into larger units, the typical Asda was nearly twice the size of the average supermarket.

Asda's product range was also large at over 30,000 line items, many of which were non-foods including clothing, small electrical goods, household and DIY products. Until the early 1980s Asda's own-label range had been very limited, accounting for some 6% of turnover compared to Sainsbury at over 60% and Tesco at over 20.

1985 saw a significant change in Asda's strategy. Stores were to be redesigned and two thousand own label lines were to be produced, providing up to 35% of sales (Stockdale, 1986). The target was an ambitious one and involved a number of major changes in organisation and in relationships with suppliers.

Changes in organisation

A number of key personnel were brought in from other companies to manage what was inevitably a considerable expansion of head-office staff. One of the new recruits, trading director Keith Clarke, summed up the organisational issue thus: 'Before, there had been perhaps four or five merchandising people, a very slim buying team and hardly any marketing people. The groceries and provisions portfolio, for instance, was in the hands of two people' (Clarke, 1985).

By the middle of 1985 a new organisation structure was in place based around the concept of what was termed the Trading Group. Each Trading Group was responsible for the coordination of a product area. Four functional areas were also defined. Their responsibilities were summarised as follows:

- *Marketing:* Defines, creates and communicates the proposition.
- *Buying:* Implements and maintains the proposition.

- *Merchandising:* Organises and presents the proposition.
- *Operations:* Is part of the proposition and delivers it.

Within each function there was a management hierarchy headed by a functional controller. The overall organisation structure represented a matrix. A team made up of specialists from each area would be responsible for a particular product or group of products. They would report progress to their respective Trading Group controller but, as individuals, they were responsible to their respective functional heads. The matrix approach was central to the development of Asda Brand merchandise. Keith Clarke explained in a conference speech: 'The secret here is *teamwork* and it's that growing sense of teamwork between different departments, between Asda House and our stores that is enabling us to get more and more out of all the hard work that everyone is putting in'. The development of Asda Brand also required a substantial increase in services to support the major departments. Thirty of Britain's leading design agencies were used in the preparation of labels and packaging (*Campaign*, 1987). The brief of the R & D department located in the company's dairy business was rewritten to allow it to expand to make 'a more forceful contribution'. From 1986 to 1988 the food technology and home economics group had expanded from 26 to over 100 people (*Retail*, 1988). A packaging department was created. A Trading Standards Manager was employed to ensure that all pack copy complied with legal regulations relating to product labelling.

Imitation or innovation?

A manufacturing company might evolve one successful new product every few years. Asda's ambitious programme required a new product launch every few minutes at one stage. A manufacturer could have examined twenty prototypes before selecting a new line and even then require considerable technical or marketing development to refine the product during a test market. The retailer, particularly one who was not manufacturing its own products, could short circuit the manufacturers' new product development programme in two ways: by imitating an existing line and by monitoring the initial sales of any new line and quickly withdrawing, or asking the manufacturer to modify any product not selling well.

Asda's policy on selecting lines for Asda Brand was to innovate where possible in both product and pack design. Examples cited by Asda of innovative lines included Low Salt Bacon, Corn Fed Chicken, Double Cream and Butter Ice Cream, and Pink Fabric Conditioner. An emphasis on quality led to design and product quality awards. Bleach bottles featured childproof caps and labels in the blind languages Braille and Moon. Inevitably however Asda had to depend upon the manufacturer to a great deal in terms of product formulation. In some instances companies were willing to offer products close to those they sold as their own national brands particularly where their brand was not a leading product. Few manufacturers were strong enough in terms of brand portfolios to ignore retailer requests for own-label lines; many welcomed the opportunity to concentrate on manufacturing rather than on marketing.

The development process

The Asda Brand *Launch Procedures* manual identified a number of phases in the process of evolving a new line. Phase I was concerned with identification. New opportunities were identified by a Trading Group. Buying established whether it was possible to source the product and Marketing estimated sales potential and profiled competition. Technical Services were called in to advise on an outline product specification and Merchandising were asked to identify any space considerations and other issues that would be raised instore by the new line. The Trading Group could now be asked to make a formal recommendation to the Divisional Director for a go/no-go decision.

Phase I included a full feasibility study by Marketing and Buying for a final decision by the Divisional Director. A favourable decision initiated Phase II, the detailed product development. Five processes were needed to be coordinated at this stage: design, technical, pack copy, buying and merchandising. Responsibility for this lay with a product manager in marketing, acting very much in the same way as a brand manager would in a manufacturing company.

The design of packaging was not delegated to the manufacturer selected to provide the product. Some manufacturers preferred to take responsibility for packaging arguing for example that they were better placed to specify the appropriate quality of materials. Asda on the other hand preferred to control packaging themselves not only for creative reasons but also for better control over costs. This approach in turn required the formation of a substantial packaging department responsible for all technical aspects of packaging, with the product manager overseeing design.

In some cases the pack designs were researched once the pack design had been selected. Final approval required the say so of a technologist and the Trading Standards Manager for Asda Brand. They were responsible for ensuring that the presentation of the pack met all formal legal requirements especially those of concern to Trading Standards such as statement of contents, illustration of contents and declared weight. Of particular concern was the potential for action by brand manufacturers for passing off. Brand manufacturers were highly sensitive to any own-label presentations that could confuse the consumer into believing that their brand had been repackaged for the retailer to sell at a lower price, particularly if the contents had not in fact been made by them.

The product manager had to ensure that packaging, legal, technical, design, merchandising and senior management were each aware of the Asda Brand proposed packaging design and had approved it. At this stage a high-quality mockup was produced for presentation to a weekly meeting chaired by a Trading Director who had the final responsibility for approval.

Once approved the pack design could be used to brief a packaging manufacturer, the company printing the packaging (and often another company making the print cylinder). A critical stage was the 'signing off' of artwork to be used to produce packaging. The same managers (technical, legal, etc.) who had appraised the original pack design were required to review their decision now that the final artwork had been produced. It was at this stage that the appropriate barcode was added to the pack design.

The Packaging Department took the responsibility for liaison with printers and supervising the production of the packaging itself. They also checked to ensure that the barcode could be read in practice by the electronic point of sale (EPOS) equipment used by Asda.

In parallel with the design work was the development of the product itself. In some circumstances a benchmark product was used to invite samples and costings from suppliers. An outline product specification was prepared by the Technical Department and the Buying Department contacted potential suppliers.

Samples of food products were tasted by a panel made up of a home economist, a technologist, a buyer and the product manager. Selected samples were submitted for any physical, chemical or microbiological tests by the technologist who had to form a view on the technical capability of the supplier and agree a technical specification. Of particular importance in assessing the supplier was their control over raw materials, process and hygiene.

Once a supplier had been selected by buying and received a positive vetting by the technologist, the supplier could begin manufacture but the first production run had to be attended by at least the technologist.

A third strand in the development process was that to provide pack copy. In some cases products were given names which might require registration. Registration involved the Legal Department searching the records of the Government Registrar of Companies to ensure no other company had rights to the chosen name. In most instances a generic name (tissues, fruit pastilles, baked beans, etc.) was used beside the Asda name and registration was not an issue.

The amount of information on most product packaging was considerable. Apart from the name, the product weight, ingredients, nutritional information, sell by date and storage, instruction on how to use or cook the product were also required. Recipe and cooking instructions were provided by a home economist to the product manager. The product manager might also choose to add copy emphasising particular product features and benefits such as 'high fibre' or 'made from the finest ingredients'. All pack copy had to be approved by the technologist and legal adviser and added to the design for the final artwork.

A fourth strand was mainly in the hands of the buyer. Once selected, the supplier received a letter of appointment including a specification of how many units were to be included in each outer pack. It was company policy that the minimum display space allocated to the product should carry the contents of one and a half outer packs. The display space in turn was calculated by the Merchandising Department using the sales projections of the product manager. The company tried to ensure that shelves or displays did not become empty of product by allocating more space to products that had higher rates of sale.

Another critical element in the letter of appointment to the supplier was a statement specifying Asda's maximum liability for stocks of packaging and product so that, if the product were to fail, Asda's financial exposure was clearly defined.

The technologist was also involved in this activity to specify recipes and processing methods. Samples of products supplied for approval and of production runs were kept to help monitor quality and assess shelf life.

Launch coordination and administration

The product manager's role included mapping out the various development strands using a critical-path analysis. The demands of the business meant that certain products could only be introduced at certain times of year. For example so many changes occurred normally around Christmas that the company tried to minimise the number of other changes introduced into stores at this time. In many instances new products had to be developed and launched against very tight deadlines.

Asda's stores were not all the same size. This and the fact that demand for certain products varied regionally meant that not all lines were carried in every store. The launch of an Asda Brand also often involved deleting an existing line. The responsibility for defining what products were carried where and for any deletions lay with Buying and Marketing, in conjunction with Merchandising whose role included designing the shelf display. To help Merchandising in this latter role, product samples were made available some months before launch for a display mockup in the company's model store situated in the head office building. The Trading Group needed to agree the proposed layout before any briefings could be prepared for stores and any special fixturing ordered.

Store management were informed by the Product Manager about the new line in *Asda Brand News*. The briefing included data on the market, the reason for launch, the sales projections and photographs of products. Any other administrative details were supplied by the buyer.

The product had been researched, designed, and specified packaging had been ordered, shelf space allocated, production had been sanctioned and finally the product had been delivered to the stores. The whole process might have taken only a few weeks or many months. Twelve weeks after launch the new line was reviewed against sales targets. The Technical Department were also monitoring product and packaging quality. Between 1985 and 1988 sales of Asda Brand rose from 6% to over 30% of Asda turnover. Some 2,500 lines had been launched, with more to come.

References

1 *Campaign* (1987) Anonymous article, 21 August.
2 Clarke, K. (1985) *Marketing*, 12 December.
3 *Retail* (1988) Anonymous article, Vol 6, Issue 1, Summer.
4 Stockdale, N. (1986) *Management Today*, April.
5 Street, G. (1986) *Admap*, December.

Note

The case study on Asda Brand shows clearly the level of control used by some retailers in the development of own-label. It is not just a matter of putting the retailer's name onto the packaging. That said the fundamental product innovation is still the responsibility of the supplier. Compare this with the example of M & S where even this role is subsumed by the retailer.

7

SUPPLY CHAIN MANAGEMENT

The purpose of this chapter is to use the perspective of supply chain management to appraise some options for manufacturers in their dealings with retailers.

Physical distribution management

The concept of supply chain management has evolved from two earlier ideas, physical distribution management (PDM) and logistics management. PDM evolved from the realisation that the physical movement of goods could be better coordinated by seeing stock management, warehousing, order processing and delivery as related rather than separate activities. The idea seems simple enough but the problems caused by lack of coordination can still be seen today. For example in Russia after the breakdown of communist rule, there was little in the way of formal systems to ensure that even the basics such as food could be moved from farm to processor to shop and thus to the customer. Even in Western economies large amounts of wealth are still tied up in stock. The money used to produce the stock is unavailable to the business owning the stock. If that money is borrowed money, it represents a direct financial burden on the firm. Whatever the source of funding, stock can represent 'dead' money, part of the apparent wealth of the business, but not necessarily wealth that is creating profit. Worse still, stock dilutes the asset value of the business making it more difficult to make a return on the capital employed to run it, probably the most important measure of a business.

Some stock is necessary in most businesses. Becoming out of stock is a major issue in retailing. A lost sale is bad enough; a lost customer because a competitor can manage its supply chain better is far worse. Suppliers who cannot guarantee availability risk prejudicing their relationships with retailers.

PDM is seen as a term used to 'describe integrated operations concerned with the movement and storage of finished products' (Bowersox *et al.*, 1981). Emphasis should be placed on the words 'integrated' and 'finished products'. In the context of this book PDM largely refers to the interface between manufacturer and retailer. Often this interface involves a separate transport company and sometimes a wholesaler. Where there is a wholesaler between manufacturer and retailer, there may be two entirely separate PDM systems.

Who, if anyone, is in control of the entire delivery system will determine the locus of control of the system. If no one is in control, then it is likely that there will be at least some inefficiencies within the system. Inefficiency in this instance means poor delivery and too high or too low a level of stock. Too high a level and money is wasted, goods may become stale, damaged or generally out of date. Too low a level and customer service to the retailer is put at risk, sales may be lost through an inability to meet particularly sudden increases in demand.

The main driving force behind PDM in the 1960s as a business concept was cost, or rather the cost of stock, with service a secondary issue. PDM was seen as a way of managing what had previously been seen as unrelated areas of business in a coordinated manner by making a series of trade-offs. If stock levels are reduced, then transportation has to become more reliable. Dramatic changes in stock management may affect both customer service and transportation needs, as in the following example.

Fig 7. 1 illustrates two different ways of managing a PDM system. Pattern A involves larger deliveries to the customer than Pattern B, but the strategy of using smaller delivery lots in Pattern B needs a more regular delivery cycle, adding to cost, but the stock level in the system is reduced. One cost can be traded off against the other. This example would be relevant to many

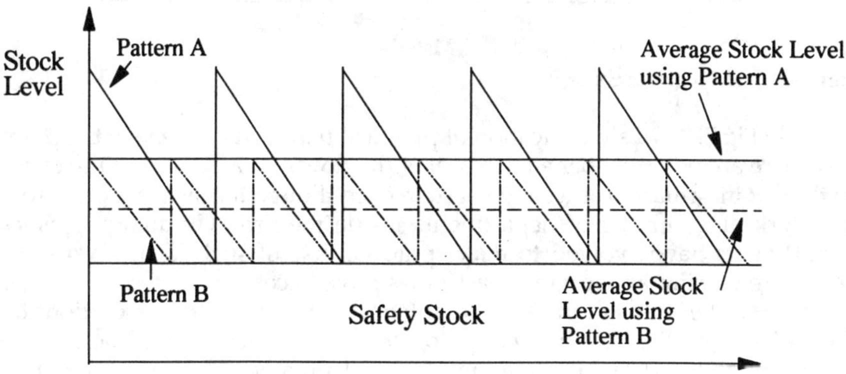

Figure 7. 1 Trade-offs in PDM

fast-moving consumer goods such as grocery and DIY products. But what of the safety stock in Fig 7. 1? Businesses hold safety stock because they need some stock to work with between deliveries but mainly because they find it difficult to forecast sales, and are worried about going out of stock at critical times. Many do not trust their suppliers to maintain the regular delivery pattern implied in Fig 7. 1.

What is needed to help manage the flow of goods is a counterflow of information to aid forecasting and planning. By the 1970s advances in information systems made it feasible for businesses to make reductions in safety stock. In the retail sector the process of concentration, meaning fewer, larger retailers in each sector, made it easier to think of a PDM as a number of goods flows supported by counterflows of data linking manufacturers and retailers together.

Logistics management

PDM is essentially about the management of finished goods. It assumes a guaranteed supply of such at the factory gate. It became clear that PDM on its own was not enough to ensure good supply management or to reduce stock to its bare minimum. What happens within a factory and to the raw materials before they reach the factory is relevant to whether finished goods appear on time at the factory gate.

Logistics is defined as: 'The process of strategically managing the movement and storage of materials, parts and finished inventory from suppliers, through the firm and on to customers' (Christopher, 1985). Logistics combines PDM with the allied concept of materials management, once the preserve of the manufacturer's purchasing department, into a single system. Fig 7. 2 presents a picture of how this looks as an overall concept (Davies, 1984).

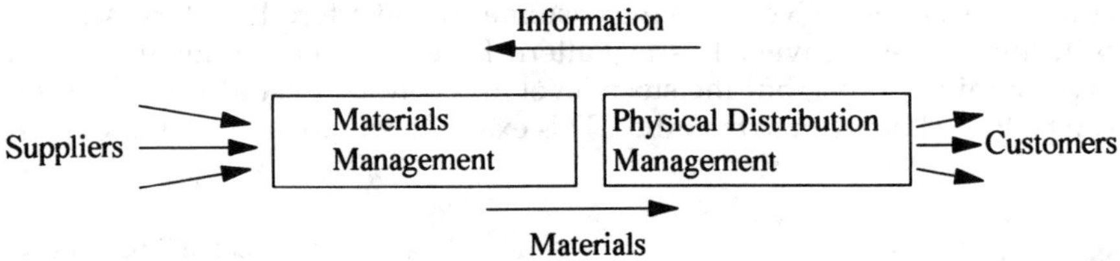

Figure 7. 2 The logistics concept

While Fig 7. 2 is a simplification of practical reality, it does make the point that there are potential benefits in seeing the flow of materials and the counterflow of information as a single system even though the system cuts across the work of a number of departments inside the firm. Gradually logistics departments have evolved to make practical use of such ideas. Transport and warehousing as individual activities have become elevated from their Cinderella-like status in the 1950s to integral parts of logistics operations by the 1980s. So-called 'leading edge' logistics departments could be seen to contribute to the strategic planning of their companies (Bowersox, 1988), as the need to coordinate what had always been significant parts of the business became apparent. With this came a change in focus for logistics management, away from cost saving, although this is still important, and towards a focus on better service, reduced order cycle times and greater responsiveness to the customer's needs.

Just in time

The ultimate in logistics management is when only the right amount of materials or finished goods reaches the appropriate point at the last possible moment. This concept, just in time, (JIT), is said to have originated in Japan but its impact is worldwide (Delbridge and Oliver, 1991). JIT represents the practical limit in terms of material supply and customer service. To achieve it requires both excellent coordination and information. JIT also presupposes that errors have been virtually eliminated particularly in product quality.

The idea of controlling quality by inspection (quality control) is replaced by ensuring that the production process does not produce faulty products in the first place (quality management).

In some sectors of industry, JIT has meant building component plants next door to the customer's assembly lines. Such an idea is impractical in most if not all retail situations, but the idea of JIT is important in distributing short-shelf-life products such as dairy produce, records or chilled meals or time-sensitive products such as spare parts. Over or under delivery of any of these wastes money.

Time to market

One of the advantages of operating a JIT philosophy in a business is that the time taken for a minor change to a product to be implemented can be minimal. There is no stock in the system. A change in the colour of a car, the covering of a sofa or the flavour of a boiled sweet can be made and taken into the market in no time at all.

The reduced time taken to make a more significant change such as a new product introduction is another, related benefit. Japanese car companies have made substantial reductions in the time it takes to develop and launch a new model. A significant time advantage in managing innovation is being viewed as a source of competitive advantage (Stalk, 1988). The innovation cycle consists of a number of phases within the manufacturer and outside. Market research with consumers and convincing the retailer to stock the product are two of these. Cutting down on the innovation cycle will depend upon an ability to influence the distribution chain. The car manufacturer can rely upon its tied dealerships, but can every manufacturer claim a similar relationship with its retailers? That said retailers generally welcome genuine innovation. It brings people into their stores and creates interest in the market generally, but more of this in a later chapter. The picture that emerges from this chapter thus far is of a growing realisation of the benefits from ever wider coordination first across a company and then linking that coordination through to suppliers and retailers.

Supply chain management

To achieve JIT requires a wider span of control than that inferred by either PDM or logistics management. Coordination is now required right back to the raw material supplier at one end and forward to the ultimate consumer at the other, in other words across the whole supply chain. The 'supply chain' is the shorthand for the connected series of activities that deal with planning, coordinating and controlling material, parts and finished goods from suppliers to customers (Stevens, 1989) and payment and information as reverse flows. Effective management of the supply chain is seen as a way of competing for retailer patronage (Tyndall, 1988). Managing it, however, requires coordination of both the material flow and information flow (Scott and Westbrook, 1991), particularly in a situation such as a more integrated Common Market when the physical scope of supply chains is likely to increase (Underwood, 1989).

The term supply chain management (SCM) implies a need for one party within a supply chain to take control. Within the academic literature the supply chain is a similar concept to that of the marketing channel, which has been defined as: 'The external contactual organization which management operates to achieve its distribution objectives' (Rosenbloom, 1991). In making this definition Rosenbloom limits the scope of control or influence by the channel manager to the product itself. Channel management appears to focus therefore on managing the relationships from manufacturer to consumer. Most manufacturers also manage the relationship with their suppliers. What is important is to see such upstream relationships as part of the single system that ends with the customer. The distribution channel is but one element of the supply chain.

When Marks & Spencer develop a new line they involve themselves not only in the factors that effect the buying and distribution of the product but in the minutiae of how the product is made and the source and nature of the raw materials used to make it. The company established its own textile laboratory in 1935 and about this time began an association with the chemical and fibres giant, ICI (Sieff, 1970). M & S did not sell ICI's products directly but an understanding of dyestuffs and man-made fibre technology enabled the retailer to gain competitive advantage by influencing manufacturers to use such materials in making products for them.

A direct involvement in other aspects of the supply chain was recorded by Briggs (1984) in bringing the Iceberg lettuce to M & S's shelves year-round. M & S technologists visited the United States to study the product's technology. British farmers were involved to grow the product, but to ensure year round supply the company established sources in Spain and Israel. Airfreight was necessary to ensure the product arrived in a suitable state. Such behaviour cannot adequately be described as channel management. It subsumes PDM and JIT and time-to-market as concepts. M & S do not own any component in the supply chain other than their stores, but they do own the customer franchise to be able to make it work. They control the supply chain without owning it.

Supply chain management can therefore be described as: 'Organising the provision of goods to the consumer by controlling the relevant activities of all those involved in the supply or manufacture of those goods, their sub components and raw materials'. The keywords are 'organising' and 'controlling'. SCM is not necessarily about ownership although there is nothing in the definition that precludes it, but effective management of the supply chain cannot be guaranteed without control. In the case of M & S, their ability to control is based upon a technical ability in understanding the problems to be overcome *and* its presence in the marketplace. These provide it with both legitimate and referent bases for the power it needs to achieve control. Their suppliers' expectation of profit is also important!

There is nothing in the definition that excludes a manufacturer from being a supply chain manager. Indeed how to obtain or retain such power is the focus of this book. As discussed in earlier chapters, a source of manufacturer power can lie in the brand and in the franchise this achieves. But as retailer concentration has increased and the relative value to the customer of many manufacturers' brands has decreased, then this source of control has been fading. To redress matters, manufacturers need not only to re-establish their brand franchises but also to develop other ways of at least sharing in the control over the supply chain. At the same time trade marketing needs to become more concerned with the entire supply chain, from raw material through to what happens to packaging and to the product itself upon disposal. Supply chain or logistics management also presents an ideal opportunity for a more holistic, and greener, view on business (Sussams, 1991).

Information as a source of power and control

To quote yet another adage, 'information is power'. Fig 7. 3 illustrates a typical supply chain and the points therein that can and have been used to obtain information to control it. A manufacturer might undertake research to

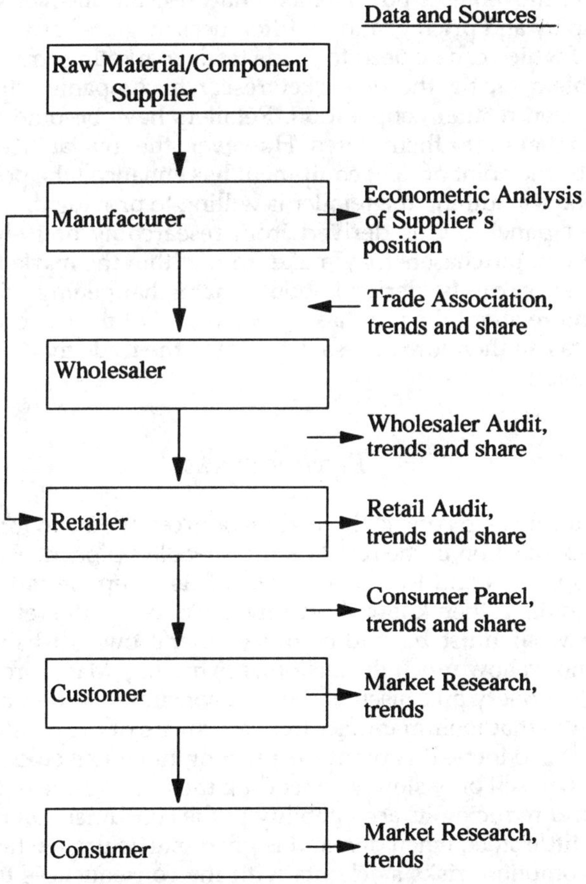

Figure 7. 3 Data sources in the supply chain

identify what is happening or might happen to its source of raw materials or components. For example most confectionary companies try to predict the cocoa harvest to help them take a view on forward buying. Car companies try to analyse the cost structures of their suppliers to take a view on the prices they should be paying for components. Car companies and confectionary companies belong to trade associations who collect market data from members that can be used to assess general trends and in particular market share.

In some countries or sectors where the wholesaler is dominant, market research into wholesaler despatches (a wholesaler audit) can be useful. This is a key source of data in pharmaceutical marketing in Britain and has been a major source of general marketing data in the USA for many products.

In Britain the two main sources of marketing data on distribution channels have been the retail audit and the consumer panel (Crimp, 1985). In the first, a panel of shops, chosen to be a representative sample of all retailers in the sector, is monitored as to their purchases or deliveries, their stock and sales. Top-line data on market trends and market share can be used to follow the main market movements but detailed analyses can uncover weaknesses in relative display and pricing, and in differences in share between market segments, all of which can be used to guide trade marketing strategy.

The problem facing those market research companies operating retail audits has been retailer cooperation. Retailers have become less willing to allow researchers into their stores. However, the availability of data from EPOS (electronic point of sale) equipment has enhanced the potential quality of data, always assuming the retailer is willing to provide it.

Consumer panel data is derived from researching households who are asked to record purchasers they make from within the market under study. Less information can be derived about what is happening within the retail sector but more about the purchasing behaviour of the customer. The value of panel data can therefore be less valuable to the trade marketer than to the brand manager.

Pipeline stocks

A manufacturer can reconcile the various sources of data to form a picture of its own stock position in the retail sector, so-called pipeline stocks. It knows its own despatches and to a point those of its competitors from any trade association data. It then knows how much is entering the retail channel and can derive what must be within the retailer's own distribution system. Finally it knows how much the customer is buying. Many products, such as crisps, confectionery and biscuits are best consumed within a limited time-span. It is vital that their manufacturers are aware of the pipeline stock position for their products. It is pointless pushing too much stock into the retail system if it will sell only slowly, extending the average age of the product in the shops and reducing its acceptability to the consumer. On the other hand having too little stock when demand is good, particularly when the product is under promotion, risks stockouts with the consequences that have been mentioned earlier in this book.

The whiplash effect

Products such as consumer durables are less likely to be monitored using an audit but the equivalent data would include an analysis of ownership and purchase trends. The 'whiplash' effect in consumer-durable markets can produce excessive and damaging stock movements that can be avoided through an understanding of such data. Retailers tend to hold stock in proportion to sales, so if sales suddenly rise they will reorder not only to replenish stock levels depleted by the sales increase but also to build stock levels to a higher level to support what appears to be a higher level of consumer demand. Fig 7. 4 illustrates this effect. It assumes that what the retailers order in one

	Index of Consumer Demand	Index of Retailers' Stocks	Index of Retailers' Orders from Suppliers
Period 1	100	100	100
Period 2	100	100	100
Period 3	100	100	100
Period 4	120	80	120
Period 5	120	80	140
Period 6	140	80	160
Period 7	160	60	260
Period 8	100	220	0
Period 9	80	140	0
Period 10	80	60	100

Figure 7. 4 The whiplash effect

period is delivered for sale during the next period. In Period 4, following three periods of even supply, demand increases. The retailers do not overreact but do order more. Demand remains high in Period 5 and retail stock levels now start to look too low. The retailers might be concerned about losing sales by being out of stock and place an order large enough to replenish the stock and increase the stock level. Orders placed on the supplier now run ahead of actual consumer demand. In Period 6 consumer demand increases yet again, and even though deliveries have been high they only match sales, leaving stock low. Orders are increased yet again. In Period 7 sales are still increasing and stock levels fall. To meet demand the retailers increase orders and add on more to build stock, to an index of 160. However in Period 8 sales fall back and retailers have a very high stock level. Reorder levels are cut to zero. In the next period sales decline yet again and yet again the retailer places no orders. In Period 10 stock is back into balance and orders suddenly pick up again.

Fig 7.4 illustrates the need for close coordination between members of a supply chain. In this example no one really is in control of what is happening. The system is being driven by retailer ordering levels not by actual consumer demand. The manufacturer is left with the problem of absorbing quite violent changes in demand, due to the whiplash effect.

This in turn is passed on to any component suppliers where the demand pattern is magnified yet again. What is needed is the gathering and sharing of consumer data. Any delay in the data moving back down the supply chain is likely to cause stock hoarding to compensate for any unexpected change in demand. As supply chains extend, for example across Europe over the coming years, such effects might become more prevalent (Willmott, 1989).

Electronic information

The greatest change in information management in the supply of consumer goods is happening now. Article numbering (AN), the system of allocating a unique code to every stock item in the world, is revolutionising the quantity and quality of information that can be used to manage the supply chain. AN provides a 'common business language' (Osborne, 1991) that can be used to support electronic data interchange (EDI). At the heart of the AN system is the barcode concept where each product line item has a unique number but to be of value the idea requires a high level of participation by manufacturers and retailers and a method of exchanging information. Osborne charted the progress made towards this goal by 1991:

1976 UK Article Numbering Association Constituted.
1979 First UK store introduces scanning.
1981 European Article Numbering Association changes name to 'International' after Australia and Japan join.
1982 Tradacoms EDI standards published.
1984 80% of grocery products using the system.
1987 A five-year timetable set to achieve 99% source marking.
1991 More than 6,000 UK stores using scanning. More than 2,500 companies using Tradacoms for EDI. Over 170,000 stores using EAN scanning or its American equivalent, UPC, worldwide.

Problems still exist in the system, for example the incidence of misreading on scanners is still too high, and scanner data is normally only analysed each night rather than in real time by retailers, but the rapid progress made to date is truly remarkable. Trading along many supply chains is already paperless and the benefit of better information is being used to improve their efficiency. Even the smallest of companies, a Welsh goat farmer supplying cheese to Tesco for example, and linked to them by his own PC, are benefiting (Ody and Newman, 1991). So by the 1990s the use of barcoding was widespread. Almost every stock item could be identified by a unique code. EPOS systems were widely used so that the sale of any barcoded item could be recorded. Standards had been agreed (Tradacoms) to facilitate the exchange of such data between often incompatible computer systems. A full review of EDI, Tradacoms and associated systems is available in Macpherson (1987).

Thus far retailers have tended to use EPOS information to aid the process of centralisation of control. Given the quality of the data that EPOS produces it is surprising that more use is not made of it to support decision-making at head office as envisaged by Beaumont (1988). Lockett and Holland (1991) formed the view that IT (Information Technology) in retailing is 'not really leading edge' and that the full value of information is still to be realised. Retailers are working on systems which will coordinate their entire trading and distribution activities. For example, a real-time system in a grocery store could analyse the customer's shopping basket and print out an appropriate discount voucher for the next visit, promoting the sale of an own-label product ahead of a manufacturer's brand. How such systems interface with their suppliers will be central to trade marketing. As the case study at the end of this chapter reveals, the introduction of EDI does not necessarily benefit all members of a supply chain. But first how do retailers manage the physical flow of goods from the manufacturer into their stores?

Retailer logistics

The structural changes in retailing have had a profound effect on the physical movement of merchandise. Individual companies have become larger and have centralised their buying. Individual stores have become larger and there are fewer stores in total. Wholesalers have all but disappeared from the main retail sectors in Britain such as grocery and larger retailers are dealing directly with suppliers.

Years ago, in Britain, most deliveries were being made by manufacturers or wholesalers directly to retailers' premises. Today the norm is for delivery to be made to a retailer's own or controlled central warehouse. So instead of a wholesaler delivering an assortment of merchandise to the retailer, the retailer has replaced this role with its own warehousing and transportation. McKinnon (1986) believes that it is unlikely that the multiples could have secured their market share growth without the economic and operational benefits of centralised distribution. However the advantages to the retailer do not stem from replacing the manufacturer's delivery system as much as from reducing stock levels, reducing the need for delivery procedures at store level, and freeing up storage space in retail outlets that can be converted to selling space. Other benefits stemming from better control may including fewer stockouts and lower shrinkage.

Retailers do not always adopt the same strategies for centralising distribution even within the same retail sector, but some generalisations can be made. Davidson *et al.* (1988) differentiate between predistribution and post-distribution philosophies. With a predistribution system merchandise is sent directly to the store against a plan sent to the supplier when the merchandise is ordered, thus circumventing the multiple retailer's centralised system.

Such an approach may be logical for both perishable items and slower-moving lines. For the majority of products in a country such as Britain where distances between major population centres are small, postdistribution is the norm – that is delivery to the retailer's warehouse where mixed deliveries are made up for each store. The postdistribution route reduces store deliveries from 60 a day on average in grocery retailing to 12 or less (Moore, 1991). Own-label and imported products also tend to move via the retailer's system (McKinnon, 1986).

How retailers organise and manage their own distribution systems varies. Some retailers insist on organising the collection of stock from their suppliers (McKinnon, 1986). Some own their transport and warehousing systems but many 'contract' out to third parties. Such contracts vary in their scope but can be very comprehensive, to include custom-built premises, incorporation of the retailer's order processing, vehicles painted in the retailer's corporate colours, specialist racking and much more (Burns, 1988). Contracting out releases a retailer's capital and allows it to focus on its core business of retailing (Sussams, 1989). The third-party operator can often achieve economies such as backloading for other companies or combine entire operations to make best use of its transport (Whitley and Cox, 1989). A third-party operation does, however, introduce another company and another organisation into the supply chain. Having absorbed the wholesaler's role many retailers are now recreating it in their third party relationships to some extent.

Quick-response systems

The benefits of EDI and coordinated physical distribution are gradually being realised in reducing inventory and in improving customer service at the same time. Coles Myer represents 20% of the Australian retail market. Its department store group, Grace Bros., operates a central distribution system and saw the value of cooperating with its suppliers of 'big ticket' items such as electrical appliances and furniture, to reduce stockholding, and improve service to customers (Campbell, 1988). Grace Bros. provides its suppliers with a 12-month sales forecast updated every month. Suppliers commit to a two-day lead time for all products and have to hold the appropriate levels of stock in their system. Merchandise is called off from any sales made each day for delivery into Grace Bros. warehouse during the second day following. Grace Bros. deliver to the customer the next day. 'Cooperation and trust' are cited as critical elements in making the system work.

Similar projects have been reported in other retail sectors, where sales and stockturn have been improved markedly, leading to higher margins and greater return on assets (Kurt Salmon, undated). Most North American retailers appear to be adopting quick response (Larson and Sijbrands, 1991). Coordination is required throughout the supply chain. Forecasting by retailers and manufacturers needs to be as precise as possible. Flexibility is needed at all stages in manufacture but, above all, the supply chain needs to work as one system.

Sharing information

A problem for all parties is how open they should be with each other over their internal information. A retailer would like to be sure that its supplier is holding adequate stock, but the supplier is also serving other retailers who might need the same stock. The supplier would like to know its level of sale in the retailer's outlets to make its own judgements on replenishment. The potential is there for a retailer to have access to the stock position of a number of alternative suppliers and to use information on excessively high stocks, for example, to renegotiate prices. How 'transparent' the members of a supply chain make their internal information systems to each other is an issue considered by Holland and Lockett (1991). They suggest five generic models of association between trading partners. In two models neither partner gains access to the other's information system. Trading is still 'adversarial'. In one model the customer has access to the supplier's data on stock, allowing it to make informed purchase decisions. The supplier remains 'blind' until it receives an order. In a fourth model the supplier has access to its distributor's data and retains responsibility for supply. The last model, of merged information systems, remained a hypothetical one at the time of their work as no example had been identified to illustrate it.

Which model is adopted within any one supply chain will depend upon the competitive posture of that supply chain to others. If the chain is supplying to and buying from only other members of the same chain, total integration of data systems would appear logical and low risk. As to the others, the case study that follows this chapter will illustrate one of the potential dangers for the supplier in an open relationship. Further, some products may eventually be traded on totally electronic trading systems, much as equities are on many stock exchanges today (Shulman, 1988). Totally different styles of trading relationships will exist, and the level of transparency between suppliers and retailers systems will be a key issue.

Keypoint summary

1) The concept of a quasi-unitary organisation between manufacturer and retailer when both participate in a number of similar relationships, as in grocery manufacture and retail, is perhaps more idealistic than realistic. But talk of a seamless pipeline is now with us (Rouland, 1991).
2) There is potential to optimise the efficiency of a supply chain in any circumstances.

3) There appear to be a number of principles that can be used to guide such a relationship even when both parties are also seeking to negotiate a position of commercial advantage that favours one rather at the expense of the other, principles that are valid inside of what might be described as an 'uneasy alliance'.

   The two main principles are these:

   - The reduction of total supply-chain cost.
   - Maximising the opportunity for customer purchase.

4) These in turn can be broken down into a hierarchy of goals.

   - Reduce supply chain stock to what is needed to supply forecast demand and eliminate out of stock.
   - Produce an agreed forecast of demand and agree to share the consequences of inaccuracy.
   - Make data and physical distribution systems compatible.
   - Identify surplus stock and work jointly on ways to eliminate it.
   - Identify costs that can be reduced by joint action and avoid trying to reduce one's own costs by imposing them on the other.
   - Work together to understand what the end customer wants in terms of service and on how to deliver these expectations.
   - Stock reduction and increased service is possible only when supply chain members cooperate, and is likely to depend upon one member accepting responsibility for structuring the chain and leading it.

References

Beaumont, J. R. (1988) An Overview of Decision Support Systems for Retail Management, *Journal of Retailing*, Vol 64, No 4, p 361.

Bowersox, D. J. (1988) Strategic Logistics, *Focus on Physical Distribution and Logistics Management*, Vol 7, No 9, p 4.

Bowersox, D. J., Calabro, P.J., Wagenheim, G.D. (1981) *Introduction to Transportation*, Macmillan, New York, p 312.

Briggs, A. (1984) *Marks and Spencer 1884–1984*, Octopus Books, London, p 68.

Burns, R. (1988) Retailing and Distribution Trends, in West, A. (ed) *Handbook of Retailing*, Gower, Aldershot, p 215.

Campbell, K. C. (1988) Department Store 'Quickship' Eliminates Inventory – Improves Customer Service, *Asia Pacific International Journal of Business Logistics* Vol 1, No 2, p 12.

Christopher, M. (1985) *The Strategy of Distribution Management*, Gower, Aldershot, p 1.

Crimp, M. (1985) *The Marketing Research Process* (2nd Ed), Prentice-Hall, London, Chapter 10.

Davidson, W. R., Sweeney, D. J., Stampfl, R. W. (1988) *Retailing Management* (6th Ed), Wiley, New York, p 542.

Davies, G. (1984) *Managing Export Distribution*, Heinemann, London, p 20.

Delbridge, R., Oliver, N. (1991) Just In Time or Just The Same, *International Journal of Retail and Distribution Management*, Vol 19, No 2, p 20.

Holland, C., Lockett, G. (1991) Forms of Association in Business Markets: The Impact of Inter-organisational Information Systems, 7th IMP Conference, Uppsala, Sweden, September.

Kurt Salmon (undated) *Quick Response Implementation*, Kurt Salmon Associates, New York, (promotional material).

Larson, P. D., Sijbrands, M. J. C. (1991) Quick Response Retailing in Canada and The Netherlands, *International Journal of Retail and Distribution Management*, Vol 19, No 7, p 10.

Lockett, A. G., Holland, C. P. (1991) Competitive Advantage using Information Technology in Retailing: Myth or Reality?, *International Review of Retail, Distribution and Consumer Research*, Vol 1, No 3, April, p 261.

Macpherson, S. (1987) *Data Communication for Retailers*, NCC, Manchester.

McKinnon, A. C. (1986) The Physical Distribution Strategies of Multiple Retailers, *International Journal of Retailing*, Vol 1, No 2, p 49.

Moore, E. J. (1991) Grocery Distribution in the UK, *International Journal of Retail and Distribution Management*, Vol 19, No 7, p 18.

Ody, P., Newman, S. (1991) Speeding up the Supply Chain, *International Journal of Retail and Distribution Management*, Vol 19, No 5, p 4.

Osborne, A. (1991) Article Numbering: The Language for Business, *International Journal of Retail and Distribution Management*, Vol 19, No 1, p 13.

Rosenbloom, B. (1991) *Marketing Channels* (4th Ed), Dryden Press, Orlando, Fla.

Rouland, R. C. (1991) Distribution Technology, The Seamless Pipeline Dream, *Discount Merchandiser*, Vol 31, No 4, April, p 48.

Scott, C., Westbrook, R. (1991) New Strategic Tools for Supply Chain Management, *International Journal of Physical Distribution and Logistics Management*, Vol 21, No 1, p 23.

Shulman, R. E. (1988) Now is the Time for a New Manufacturer/Retailer Relationship, *Supermarket Business*, Vol 43, No 12, p 13.

Sieff, I. (1970) *Memoirs*, Weidenfeld and Nicolson, London, p 156–7.

Stalk, G. (1988) Time the Next Source of Competitive Advantage, *Harvard Business Review*, July/August, p 41.

Stevens, G. C. (1989) Integrating the Supply Chain, *International Journal of Physical Distribution and Materials Management*, Vol 19, No 8, p 3.

Sussams, J. (1989) Logistics in the Distributive Industry, *Management Services*, May, p 6.

Sussams, J. E. (1991) The Impact of Logistics on Retailing and Physical Distribution, *International Journal of Retail and Distribution Management*, Vol 19, No 7, p 4.

Tyndall, G. R. (1988) Supply Chain Management: Innovations Spur Long Term Strategic Retail Alliances, *Marketing News*, Vol 22, No 26, 19 Dec, p 10.

Underwood, L. (1989) Strengthening the Supply Chain, *The Director*, Vol 43, No 1, August, p 71.

Whitley, R., Cox, B. (1989) Logistics in Retailing, *Management Services*, April, p 6.

Willmott, A. (1989) Extending the Supply Chain Into Europe, *Focus on Physical Distribution and Logistics Management*, Vol 8, No 2, p 30.

Case Study: THE APPLICATION OF EDI TO THE TRADING OF PERISHABLE FOODS

In the early 1980s a large food retailer was reconsidering the methods it used in reordering perishable merchandise. For one category of such products it had four major suppliers, three of whom acted as intermediaries for smaller companies supplying similar goods to the retail chain.

The ordering system in use at the time is shown schematically in Exhibit 1. Each store in the retail chain would be contacted by a supplier's telesales service. The orders received would be entered into the following day's production and despatch programme. Despatches were made from regional depots by each supplier directly to stores.

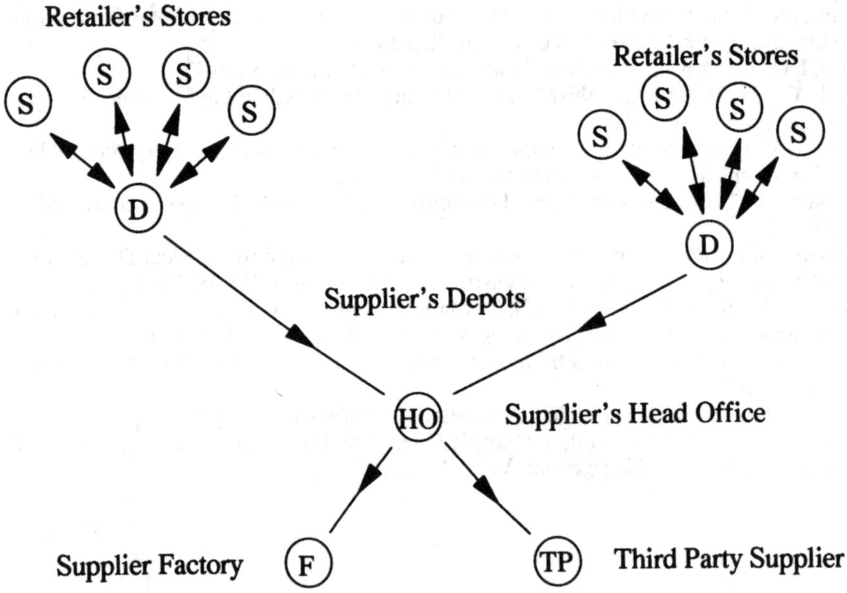

Exhibit 1 The original order system

As with most food multiples in Britain by this time, store managers had little discretion on what products were stocked and displayed. However they retained considerable discretion over stock and order levels for a wide range of perishable products.

In a review of order processing, the company's Computer Division identified a number of advantages for retaining the different and less centralised system for perishable products. The telephone calls from suppliers acted as a reminder to the store; the suppliers could advise stores directly on availability; the direct contact had other advantages from the exchange of information. However a number of disadvantages were also identified. Because stores did not take the initiative in placing orders, there was a possibility of inappropriate ordering; placing orders took up a great deal of time; errors were possible; there was no head-office control nor information; the whole process was labour intensive, particularly for suppliers who needed to maintain large numbers of telesales staff.

The Computer Division examined the potential for a commercial software package written to be compatible with the Article Numbering Association standards for electronic data interchange. The package was designed to present and accept data to the Tradacoms network format. It translated the data from one company's computer system into the ANA/Tradacoms format and reconfigured the data to be compatible with the system within another company. Thus any two organisations could communicate, even though their internal computer systems might be incompatible, using the proprietary software.

The new system

The retailer saw the potential from establishing computerised data interchange allied to a change in the way orders were configured. Exhibit 2 shows

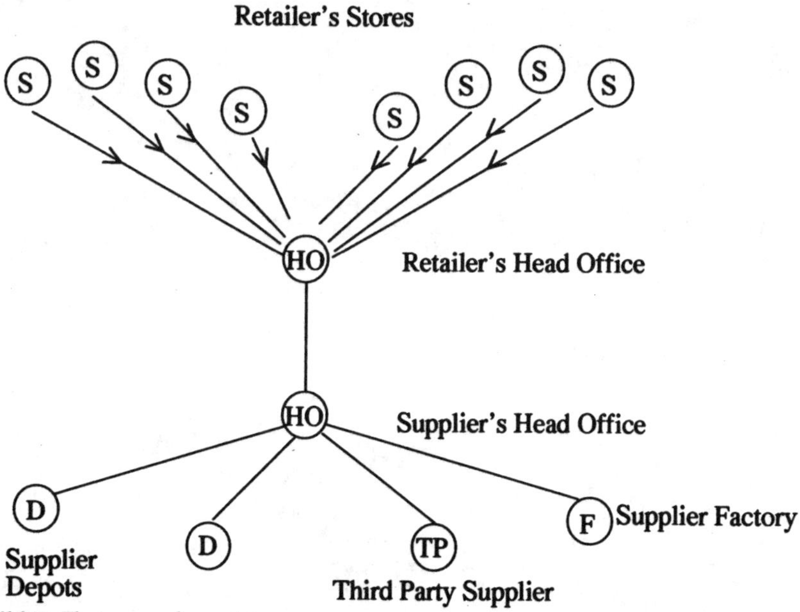

Exhibit 2 The new order system

the new system schematically. Orders for the range of perishable goods were sent by each retail outlet using portable data capture units and modems down standard telephone lines to the retailer's head-office computer. The data were encoded using the software package and transmitted to suppliers. At each supplier the data was decoded via the same package to be used within their own systems.

Soon after installation, the retailer added some refinements to allow a summary order to be sent quickly to each supplier, who could initiate their production scheduling. The details of the order followed identifying which product lines and what quantities were required by individual stores.

The advantages to the retailer included better control and management information. The suppliers had faster, more appropriate information. However the major benefit appeared to accrue to the retailer who calculated the savings suppliers could make because of the elimination of their telesales operations and negotiated substantial discounts from its suppliers.

Note

This case study was summarised from an original which formed part of a series of studies sponsored by SITPRO, the Simplification for International Trade Proceedures Board. The lessons to be learnt from the case study are that better links between retailer and manufacturer can save money but that the cost savings may be absorbed by reduced selling prices.

8

CHANNEL POLICY

In this chapter a broad range of strategic options in selecting and managing a distribution channel for a manufacturer are considered. The term 'channel' is used because the word evokes a picture of a river or a canal along which a product flows from source to user. A channel has clear edges or boundaries. A number can exist of varying length and width from which the navigator or trade marketer can choose. The broader the channel the greater its capacity and the larger the number of users. The danger of the analogy is that 'channel' suggests a passive system where a manufacturer might expect the wholesaler and retailer to serve as its selling agent. That said, how can a channel be seen as Hardy and Magrath (1988) suggest it might be seen, as a 'strategic asset'?

Channels and sub-channels

As mentioned in Chapter 4 a company should analyse its industry along four dimensions, one being the various channels open to the distribution of the products it and its competitors make. Fig 8. 1 lists many of the channels and

Wholesale – Cash and Carry – Buying Club
Franchise – Concession – Own Outlets
Direct Sale – Direct Response – Commission Agents
Retail (by type) – Independent – Multiple – Department Store
Retail (by price and service) – Discounter – High Service – Exclusive
Retail (by range) – Specialist – Category Killer – Multi-Product Store

Duty Free Shops, Hypermarkets, Market Stalls, Catering, Hotels, Leisure Centres, Railway Stations, Vending Machines, Car Boot Sales, Mail Order, Teleshopping, Hire Shops

Figure 8. 1 The diversity of retail distribution channels

sub-channels that might be considered by a manufacturer. The point is that the selection of a channel can be a source of competitive advantage on its own, if the manufacturer can specialise in or dominate that channel. Channel specialism can to an extent isolate a supplier from competition, even though similar products are being sold via other channels, because the manufacturer decides to focus on the needs of the channel and its customers. So Avon became a leading cosmetics company by not competing along the main distribution channels for cosmetics, but by dominating a channel virtually of its own creation, selling direct to customers' homes via commission agents. Body Shop has also become a leading cosmetics company by franchising its cosmetic products and retail format and dominating a channel of its own creation. Skil Handtools can choose a similar strategy, not by creating its own channel but by specialising in those serving the professional user of electric hand tools. Its competitor Black & Decker selected a different strategy, selling through a large number of channels. Once the channel strategy has been selected, the manufacturer needs to drive down its costs within each channel so as to out-perform those competing within the same channel and to promote greater patronage of the channel it alone seeks to dominate.

Cost reductions can be obtained in a number of ways, by reducing the manufacturing cost of the product, by achieving volume sales and an economy-of-scale effect, for example. Alternatively the channel costs can be reduced by working closely with any third parties to reduce the transaction costs in the supply chain, as illustrated in the case study preceding this chapter. Buzzell and Gale (1987) point to evidence from the PIMS database that market share is correlated with profitability, suggesting that, if a single channel can be considered to be a market, then maximising sales and share within each channel the manufacturer enters should be an objective. However Buzzell and Gale argue that increased sales are not driven directly by any price advantage, as might be implied from Porter's (1980) paradigm of business strategy, but by obtaining a quality advantage. This in turn can be used to obtain either increased sales (and therefore lower costs) or, alternatively, higher prices. Both increase the gross margin potential and therefore the opportunity to achieve higher net margins if costs can be controlled. The two perspectives are similar in some ways but not in others.

What can also be important is the negotiating position of the manufacturer when considering a choice of channel. There is evidence from PIMS that companies tend to be more profitable when they have few suppliers, perhaps because it is easier to form relationships and drive down transaction costs to mutual advantage. However profits can also be higher for suppliers where the product is unimportant to the buyer, although whether this can even be the case in any reseller market is unclear. Porter (1979) points to the key issue of the relative concentration levels in the supplier and buyer parts of the industry. Power tends to be held on the side where concentration levels are lower. Thus, as Segal-Horn and McGee (1989) point out, in the British confectionary market there are a limited number of large suppliers and a large number of small specialist retailers. In this channel the manufacturers, with their heavy branding, are in a stronger position than, say, in furniture, where supplier concentration is, or has been, far lower than retailer concentration and manufacturer branding has often been minimal (*Verdict*, 1986). In the case study on W. H. Smith News that follows this chapter, the wholesaler can be seen to hold power over both the fragmented magazine publishers supplying it and the largely independent retail sector it supplies to.

Fig 8. 2 summarises the points made in this section and some from earlier chapters by identifying channels which are likely to be more attractive to a manufacturer from general business theory.

- Concentration levels are higher on the supply side, lower on retail side.
- The channel offers a unique route to the customer.
- The manufacturer has or can achieve a quality or price advantage over any competition within the channel.
- The channel is more dependent on the manufacturer than the manufacturer is on the channel for financial success.

Figure 8. 2 Channel attractiveness, from a strategic perspective

The channel design process

With these general rules in mind, a number of writers advise much the same on the design of a company's distribution channel system. The starting point is an understanding of the entire market, the existing channels, the different customer and product segments that each represents. The key is the customer, although the stage in the lifecycle of the product can also influence decision-making. Lynn (1991) suggests that innovative products generally require high support channels. As the market matures, users may be prepared to forgo customer service for a cheaper price if they feel more confident about purchasing. An innovative electronic product might be better marketed via specialist stores in its introductory phase and move to a mass-marketing channel as the product diffuses into a wider customer base and that same customer base becomes more familiar with the product. It is important to quantify the market requirements for the product if it is new to the market, and segment the customer base, if possible in terms of the available channels (Novich, 1991). An understanding of how customers select and use different channels or types of retailer within a channel will be necessary (Magrath and Hardy, 1991). Finally the cost effectiveness of each channel needs to be known, including some idea of whether it is possible to enter certain channels. Timex, the watch manufacturer, for example, found it too costly to enter existing distribution channels and had to develop their own (Porter, 1979). Bacardi reportedly enlisted the help of Coca Cola in the distribution of its tropical fruit mixers in high-volume channels because Bacardi felt it did not have the specific expertise to develop mass-market distribution (McQuilkin, 1988). Certain channels may be deemed to be inappropriate for the product – the example of Levi Jeans in Sears in the USA was mentioned in an earlier chapter. But there can be certain synergies in distribution which can be ignored because at first sight they appear inappropriate. Brantley (1989) notes how American banks opened small branches in supermarkets alongside the automatic teller machines seen inside or outside many such stores around the world. Distributing financial services in a supermarket appears to have been a success.

What matters is what the customer wants and the manufacturer, via its brand, aims to offer. The desire for, and the ability to offer, exclusivity

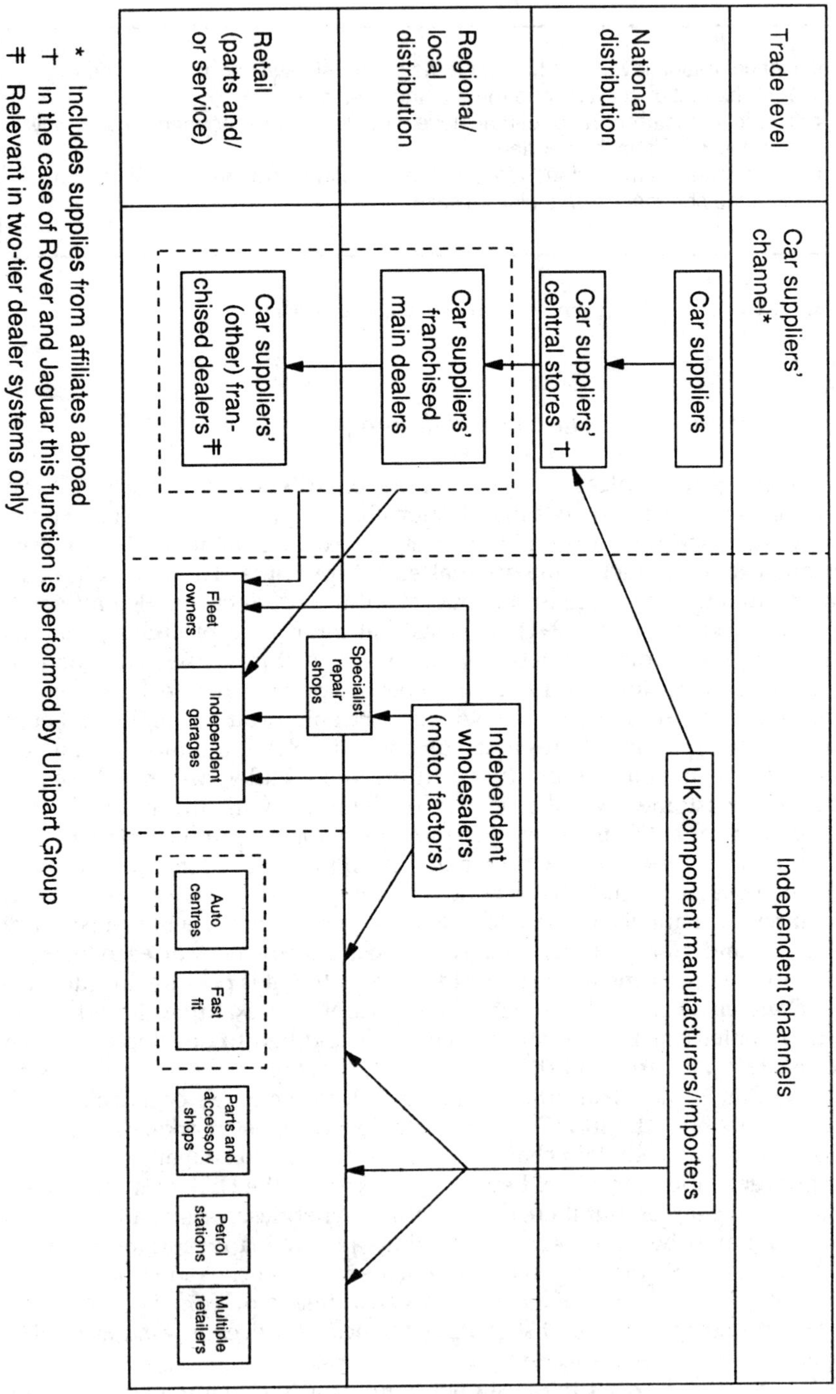

Figure 8. 3 Replacement car parts main distribution channels (source: MMC, 1992)

suggests a limited number of channels with a high level of service. Retailers would be selected for their own image with the customer and their ability to offer similarly positioned products. If the customer wants assortment, the manufacturer may be unable to insist on exclusivity. If exclusivity *can* be offered the retailer may demand the sole franchise to the product in a particular area. The customer may want convenience and to be able to compare. Mass distribution, of the product to retailers selling similar products, may be necessary. The various channels in the supply of car spares are shown in Fig 8. 3 as an example.

Wholesalers

Wholesalers provide an economic function in markets where the level of concentration among both manufacturers and retailers is low and the customer desires assortment. Rosenbloom (1989) argues that they also exist because of their abilities in marketing. He sees them as providing a number of functions for the manufacturer: market coverage, selling, stockholding, order processing, market research and customer support. For the retailer they provide availability, assortment, the breaking of bulk supplies into smaller units, credit, service and advice. His survey suggested a wider marketing role in the future for the wholesaler in America, a prediction reflected in an Arthur Anderson survey reported by Michman (1990) who explain the trend by the lower selling costs of the wholesaler.

The wholesaler is still important in American distribution, but less so than in Japan where there are proportionally many more wholesalers in a multi-layered structure of national, regional and local wholesalers. The system is complex, archaic and best described as part of an internal political economy where tradition is still important (Goldman, 1991). The system is changing but even large retail chains are supplied via wholesalers who act more as agents of the manufacturer than in other markets. This structure has been blamed for the problems businesses have in accessing the Japanese market, although actual discrimination in the retailing of foreign products, once they are in the distribution system, appears to be absent (Borin et al, 1991).

While wholesaler power varies by country, it also varies by product type. Even in Britain where the importance of wholesalers is lower than in most other countries, they still play a dominant role in the distribution of some products. By 1989 Britain still had over 108,000 thousand wholesale businesses, including commission agents, scrap dealers and builders merchants who may not be generally thought of as such (SDA26, 1989). One strong sector is fresh produce, where over 2,000 wholesalers account for about 60% of sales of fruit, vegetables and flowers (ICC, 1990a). Many have large import businesses as can be guessed from two of the leading company names, Geest and Fyffes. While the independent greengrocer and fruiterer have been losing out to the supermarkets, sales of flowers are still dominated by the independent florist.

There are a similar number of electrical wholesalers (ICC, 1990b) but they provide a good example of how misleading raw statistics can be in that their major role is not to sell to retailers as much as to electrical contractors. Indeed they could be regarded as commercial retailers. One leading business,

Newey and Eyre, owned by BTR plc even offer an own-label/brand, Newlec.

Some wholesalers provide a necessary processing role, such as the abattoirs operated by most meat wholesalers. In Britain 150,000 farms rear beef, 89,000 sheep and 21,000 pigs. There are significant imports of lamb that need distribution to 15,000 retail butchers who, although losing share to the supermarkets, still held over 40% market share in 1988 (ICC, 1990c). Meat accounts for around 20% of food expenditure, so the meat wholesaler's role is a significant one in the food channel.

Importing is an important function of British clothing wholesalers, who prospered in the 1980s by bringing in products from emerging manufacturing centres in developing countries. Manufacturing groups such as William Baird and Tootal own wholesalers, Caskitt plc own retailer outlets (ICC, 1989).

Equally complex is the grocery wholesale sector. Traditional wholesalers have lost market share to cash-and-carry businesses but still hold a third of the market. The sector is concentrated with ten operators accounting for 98% of turnover (ICC, 1990d). Cash-and-carry turnover is mainly in food but such companies have expanded into non-grocery items (KeyNote, 1991d). Symbol groups such as NISA/Today, Spar, Londis, Mace and VG could also be categorised as grocery wholesalers. Collectively they provide own-brand/label in grocery, hosiery, tobacco, confectionery and alcohol. The wholesalers are looking to support the narrower product range of the convenience store outlet, but many customers of the grocery wholesale/cash-and-carry are businesses such as hotels, restaurants, pubs, clubs, cafeterias and off-licences. The sector is strong and growing, but not from sales to traditional grocery retailers.

To add to the complexity of most wholesale sectors, many wholesalers deal with each other. Many import and export. Some have manufacturing businesses, some retail businesses. Understanding the markets they serve and value is important (Magrath, 1990), as they can provide access to significant numbers of end customers; sometimes ones that you would not expect.

Vertical integration

Given the problems of selling via intermediaries it is surprising that more manufacturers have not considered selling directly to the end customer or organising their own retailing. If the customer insists on assortment, variety, selection or comparison at the point of sale then selling what might be a limited product offer directly to the consumer may not be feasible, but many manufacturers do operate channels that are exclusive to them.

Historically vertical integration in the distribution chain does not appear to be an attractive business proposition particularly where such a move involves capital investment, although very high levels of integration can be more profitable than an intermediate level (Buzzell and Gale, 1987). Many breweries have profited by owning pubs, and more traditional retailers such as MFI sell mainly what they themselves manufacture. Such examples of complete vertical integration are rare and many such conglomerates have chosen to divest their manufacturing; examples include Burton in clothing and Greenalls in brewing. Shoe retailers C. J. Clarke have divided their retailing and manufacturing into separate profit centres, allowing the retail arm to source outside of the group.

Factory shops

There are examples of manufacturers opening or operating their own shops, the most significant examples being the manufacturers' malls opening in America where companies take limited space in malls designated solely for similar types of operation. Black (1990) suggests that apparel makers had seen such outlets as a way to sell off seconds, overruns and last season's lines but now view them as potentially significant channels for their mainstream merchandise. One company avoided the obvious problem of conflict with regular retail outlets by locating its own stores in tourist destination areas. In Britain factory or mill shops proliferate and many appear to combine retailing with some aspect of leisure as can be seen in guides to such outlets (Cutress and Stricker, 1991).

A recent trend is for leading brand name manufacturers of clothing to open their own shops in the high street, such as Levis, In-wear, Matinque, Naf Naf, Coppernob, Speedway, Piretta, Itom, Armani, Avitex. The reasons given are the downturn in the independent sector in Britain and the ready availability of retail sites (Lynn, 1992), but there are positive benefits to complement these rather defensive explanations, such as the complete control of sales and profit by selling direct to the end customer and learning about retailing as an activity.

A number of manufacturer/retailers exist in the apparel market in Europe (Barnes, 1992). Jacques Vert, for example, a women's wear manufacturer, entered retailing in 1983 and by 1992 had a small chain of outlets and its own wholesaling division. German-based Escada has become one of the largest manufacturer/retailers in Europe. By 1991 it had 470 retail outlets worldwide either wholly owned, shared ownership or concessions. At the same time as some vertically integrated businesses were expanding both manufacturing and retailing activities, others such as Laura Ashley were divesting of one or the other. It is impossible to say therefore whether there is an overall trend towards manufacturers opening their own outlets, as a response to greater retailer power or otherwise, as the involvement of one type of business in the other type of activity has been a feature of the marketplace for many years.

Concessions

A concession implies that a host retailer lets space to another business, possibly another retailer or a wholesaler, but often a manufacturer. The hirer can sell its own goods under its own name. By 1987 Mintel estimated that there were over 28,000 concession units in the UK operated by 301 different companies. From the retailer's point of view concessions can be a mixed blessing as it may lose control and coherence over its own image while at the same time adding to the diversity of its offer to the shopper. The opportunity for the manufacturer includes a relatively low cost of entry into retailing. Not all manufacturers will be able to be credible as concessionaires and the concept of a concession appears to be accepted in only a limited number of larger stores, but the concession offers an option for vertical integration that could be extended to many if not most retail sectors as the average size of retail stores increases. Smaller store operators such as Kwik Save also place significant emphasis on concessions.

Franchising

Franchising implies an agreement with a third party for the rights to sell a product or conduct an entire business in a prescribed manner. Hoffman and Preble (1991) suggest that franchising offers a low-risk option in achieving rapid growth. Because a franchise normally involves a legal agreement between the franchisee and franchisor, the franchisor can retain a reasonable degree of control. Because the franchisee bears most of the cost of establishing the retail outlet, and even pays the franchisor for the privilege, the costs of developing a retail chain can be relatively low. The motivation level of the franchised manager may well be higher than that of the employee.

Hoffman and Preble suggest three bases for a franchise: product, business or business conversion. And here lies the problem for the would-be franchisor. Few product-based franchises are large enough to justify an entire retail business and few manufacturers have the expertise to develop a full retail business franchise, such as a Benetton, Body Shop or McDonald's. The origins of many business-format franchises seem to lie less with manufacturers than with businesses who were, or still are, themselves intermediaries in the supply chain. Nevertheless franchising is predicted to continue its rapid growth in America and retail franchises to account for half of retail sales there. In Europe franchising offers a similar potential for many manufacturers seeking to move rapidly out of a domestic market but who want to retain or regain control over their marketing channel. Extensive retail franchises exist in Britain in car distribution, tenanted public houses and petrol stations (Stern and Stanworth, 1988), where the emphasis is as much on the product as on the business format.

There are drawbacks to operating franchises. Holland and Barrett and Sock Shop both withdrew from franchising because of inadequate control. When franchise agreements assign territories or fix prices, exemption needs to be sought from the relevant European Competition Laws (Sanghavi, 1990). Specific factors in the franchise agreement appear to be important in ensuring coordination. For example a royalty payments system can ensure that the franchisor has the necessary incentive to promote sales, while monitoring systems are important to ensure franchisees act in the best interests of the channel (Lal, 1990). Financial dependence can also influence whether franchisees meet the performance goals set by the franchisors (Lewis and Lambert, 1991). The franchise route can be attractive but the manufacturer who would be a franchisor needs to develop and test any business format with care.

Direct marketing/home shopping

One way of avoiding any issues with intermediaries be they owned or controlled is by selling direct to the end user in their homes. Two terms are used to describe this activity: direct marketing and home shopping. The first encompasses a range of activities that might not be directly concerned with selling goods or services and it includes sales to businesses. The second describes the activity at issue from the customer's perspective. May and Greyser (1989) talk of 'bringing the store to the home' as one perspective on home shopping and use the idea to assess to what extent many direct selling activities can be truly equated to home shopping. In many forms of home shopping there is no equivalent of the seeing/feeling of the merchandise that might be important in selection. Nevertheless they and others see a continued growth in home shopping, estimated to account already for as much as 27% of all American retail sales in all its forms (Conhaim, 1988).

Keynote (1990) points out that 'direct marketing' is difficult to define but suggest a number of activities that it encompasses including: direct mail, mail order, direct response, direct selling and telemarketing.

Direct mail

Early pioneers of direct mail included the Reader's Digest with their direct book business, but the largest British users are now mail order companies. Direct mail includes free sheet newspapers, leaflets and coupons. Over 2,000 million items a year are sent, two thirds to domestic premises. Of such mail, 53% is from an earlier contact and nearly 10% as a response to a request by the customer (Keynote, 1991a).

Mail order

The mail order industry in Britain has been highly concentrated in the hands of five large companies, GUS, Littlewoods, Freemans, Grattan and Empire. Traditionally mail order involved an agent who sold on commission. The motives for purchase included the easy credit on offer and mail order consequently appealed very much to the poorer in society. Mail order accounts for some 3% of retail sales in Britain although in a BMRB survey in 1991, 43% of the population claimed to have made a mail order purchase that year. Only 18% of respondents were 'agents' underlining the decline in agency and the rise in self-selection. An NOP survey identified clothing as the most frequently purchased item from a mail order catalogue (Keynote, 1991b). Many retailers and charities now run their own catalogues. Newspapers and magazines run small catalogues blurring the line between mail order and direct response. Companies such as credit card operators Barclaycard are using their list of clients by distributing catalogues of gifts. The 'club' format is widely used in the sale of books and CDs, a special offer advertised in the press attracts 'members' who agree to purchase a number of items from a catalogue sent to them in exchange for the benefits from the special offer.

In America mail order has a large market share. Its origins and in part its function as a service to rural settlements are one explanation its size. However, there are certain price advantages because not all mail order is subjected to sales tax, roughly the equivalent of VAT in Europe: as much as half according to one study (Mittelstaedt and Stassen, 1991). America is also a less compact market than Europe. Significant numbers of people live substantial distances from city centres making mail order inherently more attractive. It is unlikely therefore that mail order will grow to the same level in Europe as in America, but that said, the introduction of the *Next Directory*, a more upmarket catalogue, could be claimed as evidence of ways of expanding the sector.

Direct response

In many ways direct response marketing is similar to mail order – a single item can be displayed in a magazine or in a mailshot. Quite often the initial reply is part of building up a mailing list of individuals more likely to respond to such promotion. The initial advertisement loses money and its value is more for the mailing list it produces. As a means of direct access to customers, direct response is a means to an end more often than an end in itself. Financial services marketers have had some success using direct response to sell insurance, probably because of the repeat business stemming from the initial contact.

Direct selling

The success of Avon has already been mentioned, but many products are sold door to door, from encyclopedias to vacuum cleaners. Some companies such as Kleeneeze combine a limited catalogue with door to door selling. Other forms including party plan, one exponent being Tupperware, where the salesperson sells to an invited group in someone's house. The householder organises the group and receives some financial reward. Some financial services are sold door to door, the leading UK example being the 'man from the Pru'. Home improvement products such as double glazing and conservatories are marketed at least in part by direct methods.

Many products are delivered to and often sold at the customer's door such as milk, newspapers, coal, manure, ice cream and, in many rural areas, a full range of merchandise. How the selling is done varies, the latest example of a direct system being 'multi-level marketing' where individuals recruit others and receive commission on what their family tree of recruits sells as well as on their own sales. Combinations of direct methods are commonplace, the telesales person makes the initial contact, or perhaps a sales/prospector or the advertisement in the local paper prompts a call from the professional salesperson.

Telemarketing

Telemarketing or teleshopping, shopping at home in response to information from one's television set, is still in its infancy. Two broad types can be distinguished, those which are interactive and those which are not, although the latter can be enhanced by special electronics. Promotional television programmes can invite their audiences to call freephone numbers to place orders. The audience have limited control over what they see and any response is outside of the one-way communication system. Interactive, two-way systems, such as Prestel, include a keyboard search and can be used to transmit as well as to receive. Cable television systems are inherently capable of two-way interaction. But the simplest response method is still the telephone, supported by a catalogue and list; the home shopper phones or mails the 'retailer' who subsequently delivers the merchandise to the home or a local collection point.

Davies and Reynolds (1989) reviewed a number of experiments on home shopping using various communication systems. The failure of one initiative in America, Viewtron, was explained by a number of reasons, including the cost of subscription, too low a base of regular users, and the news-orientated nature of a system promoted by a newspaper group. Another, Grocery Express, had problems with the cost of computer equipment, inefficient manual picking and low customer loyalty. One success, Comp-U-Card, benefits because of both the wide range of consumer durables it sells (but doesn't stock) and from the company's ability to use more than one means of communication with the customer. Manufacturers and retailers can use their Comp-U-Mail System.

In Britain the forecasts for Prestel have failed to be realised. Cost of equipment is an issue. In France Minitel has achieved higher levels of penetration due to a decision to subsidise equipment costs. W. H. Smith's experiment with a television cable subsidiary found problems with the level of communication possible with the current generation of equipment. Club 403, another trial which attempted to combine teleshopping with other services, experienced problems with a complex charging system and customer enthusiasm. The food operation, Telecard Supershop, failed to meet its target of 1.4% penetration one year after its launch in central and west London. Davies and Reynolds query whether the costs exceeded the benefits the system could provide.

France's Minitel system remains the one outstanding national project with a high level of penetration. Even so teleshopping accounts for only 6% of services and even these include many minority or specialist services. Only 3% of users access the service daily. Serious users tend to be 25–35-year-old business people or skilled manual workers.

Despite numerous predictions that teleshopping represents the dawn of a new age in retailing, the only services to have shown substantial growth are the cable television shows where products are sold to viewers who then order by phone. Interactive systems appear to have failed thus far for the following reasons:

- The cost of equipment.
- The cost of service.
- The lack of a substantial customer base.

There is as yet no perceived value in interactive home shopping. However, both Davies and Reynolds (1989) and May and Greyser (1989) see the time-sensitive shopper and the 'grey' market as segments that could be attracted to teleshopping. As these two groups form the vast majority of society, perhaps teleshopping is still an idea waiting for its time.

In the author's opinion the potential for home shopping depends as much on the product as on the shopper. For high margin and highish price-point lines such as clothing the cost of picking, packing and delivering the merchandise is both low and absorbable into the gross margin. For food, the picking cost and delivery cost are both high as a percentage of selling price and gross margin. Unless the shopper is willing to pay for one or both, the idea cannot succeed. At present only the very well-off seem willing to justify the extra expense. The retailer can only absorb the two costs if the order size is high. Interestingly one grocery home-shopping service that claims viability has an average delivery order size of $1000 (Fensholt, 1988).

In theory teleshopping offers the manufacturer direct access to the shopper. There will be scale economies and one centralised order and despatch system would not be costly to create. Manufacturers of high margin products where the unit price is fairly high could well benefit *once* the marketplace accepts the value of teleshopping. There has been little published motivation research to explain why electronic shopping is or isn't fundamentally attractive to consumers. Brown *et al.* (1992) suggest that the perceived risk is too high – interestingly a perception that is increased the higher the social group. Generally the social risk (doing the wrong thing) and the financial risk are perceived to be lower when shopping in traditional retail outlets.

Vending machines

One final area that is worth considering for some products where technological advances could affect the significance of the channel is that of the vending machine. Britain and the rest of Europe are far behind America and Japan in the use of vending, but there are still some 637,000 machines in Britain alone (Keynote, 1991c). The channel is dominated by a few, large players such as GKN, TM and Sketchley and the products sold tend to be drinks, cigarettes, confectionery and other food, although tickets, books and condoms are also vended. The cigarette market alone via vending machines was worth £500 million in 1990. Could the future for fast food lie at least partially in the vending machine? Possibly, but the few companies controlling vending are in effect specialist retailers. To avoid the same issues as with all other retailers, manufacturers would need to develop their own 'chains' of vending machines.

Vertical integration in perspective

The cost of entry into direct retailing and the need to offer the customer a broad selection means that most manufacturers should be wary of adopting a strategy of selling directly to the end customer. The options of concessions, direct response or franchise appear to be more attractive. All involve manufacturers in learning new skills and moving away from their main area of expertise let alone the risk of upsetting existing channel members. Making better use of existing channels and moving out of traditional channels, if they become too competitive, are easier areas to address before considering such options.

The multi-channel option

There is evidence that selling via more than one channel, even when those channels overlap in their coverage of the end user, increases sales (Porter, 1976; Kestnbaum, 1984; Moriarty and Moran, 1990). The problem with a multi-channel strategy is that it risks conflict between the different channels. In their distribution of personal computers, American manufacturers use four different channels (Jenkins, 1988): local retail stores, who offer discounts, information and support; value-added resellers, who offer greater support but higher prices; mail order, which offers low price, speed but no aftersales service; and direct sales, normally volume sales to corporate customers. Segmentation is possible even within such channels as La Plante (1991) notes with the emergence of computer superstores. Such discounters had not managed to secure IBM or Compaq franchises at the time of writing, possibly because of the dangers of inter-channel conflict over relative selling prices.

If selling prices are to be allowed to vary by channel then the manufacturer has to ensure that there is a rationale for such differences. In the case of computers, the differences in service and volume could be used to justify different selling prices to customers and possibly different margins for resellers. Where the legislation permits, as in Britain, and volume discounts are possible, the effect can be to make the smaller resellers less viable if relative selling price is important in the market. Some variation in product type is one method of solving the potential conflict between the large volume retailer and the independent. For example different brand names have been used for nearly identical products, one sold via discounters, the other through higher price/service retailers. Levi Jeans used its Britannia brand to supply mass merchants, leaving its main brand name for distribution via more upmarket channels. This contrasted with Lee Jeans who tried to counter falling sales by selling to discounters, alienating the higher-margin department stores and losing prestige among customers (Morgenson, 1989). Another device is to produce a 'stencil product', a model number with some possibly cosmetic changes in design, that can be sold by a limited number of retailers. Sometimes manufacturers will supply a model still under their own brand name to a retailer where the model is unique to that retailer. The differences will again be likely to be largely cosmetic.

For grocery products one option is to provide different product sizes to different channels. Thus a 'catering pack' will be offered to wholesalers selling to hotels, restaurants and those retailers selling to consumers who like to buy in bulk. Problems can arise with selling multipacks, the multiple packaging of the standard unit, of say confectionery, direct to a superstore or a hypermarket, if the standard unit is also sold via wholesalers to the independent sector. In one instance known to the author independents were able to buy a leading confectionary brand cheaper per standard unit by buying multipacks from a local hypermarket than they could by buying boxes of standard units from their wholesaler. The manufacturer had got its price points too far out of line to avoid inter-channel conflict.

Frequently it is desirable to produce significantly different versions of the same product, or rather the brand, for different channels. For example Coca Cola is available in cans, small glass bottles, large plastic bottles and as bulk concentrate to be used in soda fountains. The concentrate could be found in pubs and cafeterias. The large plastic bottles could be found in supermarkets and off-licences. The small glass bottles could be found in pubs as mixers. The cans could be sold via vending machines, outlets such as confectionary shops or multipacked in supermarkets. The amount of Coca Cola one would get for a given amount of money as a customer might vary but few customers would object. Different retailers might also decide to stock more than one product form. One supermarket might decide not to sell multipacks of cans but sell them singly. The Coca Cola example illustrates how it is possible to tailor the product offer to a number of channels without affecting the brand or causing inter-channel conflict.

One problem with maintaining a number of marketing channels is that of 'leakage' between them. This can take two forms: either leakage between established channels that have different price structures, or leakage into channels that are not intended to carry the product. Parallel importing is a prominent example of both issues, where products are imported from a market where they are on sale at much lower prices because of market conditions in that market or where the manufacturer is trying to expand its sales by price promotion. Sometimes even changes in exchange rates are large enough to make it more profitable for a wholesaler for example to buy from another wholesaler abroad rather than from the manufacturer. One option is to cease supplying any intermediaries who participate in such actions (Weigand, 1991). But even within one geographical market any multi-tiered distribution system seems prone to what is also, confusingly, called 'grey' market practices (Lowe and McCrohan, 1989). The uncontrolled channelling of product increases price competition, reduces the incentive for some intermediaries to handle the product and erodes loyalty within the channel as a whole.

At the time of writing the issues of channel choice and grey market practices had attracted publicity in the distribution of premium fragrances, such as those marketed by Chanel and Christian Dior. The main distribution channel for such products was the department store where saleswomen, employed by the cosmetic house, sold directly to the public. The costs of this operation represented about a quarter of the selling price of the product.

Product was also available at a discount of some 20% in duty-free shops. A number of discount retailers began to obtain product from wholesalers abroad. Their retail prices tended to be about the same as in duty-free shops (*Which*, 1992). They demanded direct supply from the cosmetic houses who refused, claiming that their products' image would suffer if sold in less opulent surroundings.

Another way of looking at the problem was to consider the relative costs of what had become competing distribution channels. The high cost of personal selling in a concession within a department store was absent in the discount store. Whether the cosmetic houses could legally deny supplies to discounters was an issue. Their options included convincing the Office of Fair Trading that it was appropriate to restrict supply to upmarket retailers; to convert their direct selling operations to franchises to obtain exemption from free trading legislation; or to offer the discounters a different product offer that would not conflict with that channelled through department stores.

Customer and product profitability

The fact that a business makes a profit at the end of the year can disguise the reality that much of that profit comes from a limited number of its products and customers. Many products in any manufacturer's portfolio lose money or fail to make any substantial contribution to profits. With some products this is perfectly acceptable; they are new and will make a profit in the future; they are important to complete a range of otherwise profitable lines and the retailer will not stock an incomplete range. The case for other products is less easy to argue one way or another, because of the lack of reliable data. Such lines *seem* to be only marginally profitable but their deletion may reduce overall profitability. Individually they are less than successful but no one knows how unsuccessful. The problem for the business is often that its management *cannot* be sure about the actual contribution made by any one product. How do you allocate 'overheads' for example? What proportion of main board costs should be allocated to one product rather than another? Can the costs of any products made on the same production line be fairly allocated? Is it even worth spending the amounts needed in accountants' time finding out? The same issues facing the retailer trying to calculate a figure for a product's DPP are faced by the manufacturer. Ultimately both make certain assumptions, and trade off precision against practicality or expediency to come to their best estimates of product profitability.

The same issues are again relevant when considering the profitability to the manufacturer of supplying any one retailer, so-called customer profitability analysis. In theory any manufacturer can obtain data on both the profit it makes from each product and the profit it makes from each

		Products							
		1	2	3	4	5	6	7	8
	A								
	B								
	C								
Customers	D								
	E								
	F								
	G								
	H								

Figure 8. 4 Customer and product profitability matrix

customer. Fig 8. 4 represents such an ideal.In Fig 8. 4 the manufacturer has 8 product lines and 8 customers. Costs and revenues can be allocated to each and the matrix can be used to identify where the manufacturer makes its money. It would appear that few manufacturers have such data available to them.

Issues in customer profitability

Few manufacturers make frequent or detailed estimates of the differences in their costs of supplying different customers (MMC, 1981). The complexity of such calculation is the reason most often given for failing to do so. Quite often a manufacturer does not gather cost data in a form that can be used to analyse to which customers certain costs should be allocated. Instead major costs such as sales, stock, and distribution are treated as single costs. Costs are perhaps allocated by product line but not by customer account. The objective of a customer profitability analysis is therefore to assign the revenues, expenses, assets and liabilities of an organisation 'to the customers who cause them' (Howell and Soucy, 1990). In Howell and Soucy's experience many companies believe that their highest volume customers are their most profitable, when it is often the next level down where the company makes its money. They recommend the kind of analytical framework shown in Fig. 8. 5 as a starting point in analysing a company's customer portfolio.

% of Manufacturer's Sales / Net Margin	HIGH	MEDIUM	LOW
HIGH	Profitable Retailers	Likely Key Retailers	
MEDIUM			
LOW			Unprofitable Retailers

Figure 8. 5 Customer portfolio framework (after Howell and Soucy, 1990)

The principle is to identify those retailers in the bottom right-hand corner and move them towards the top left or, failing that, to delete them or seek to serve them in a different way. To make such decisions information is needed about the costs associated with each box in Fig 8. 5. For companies supporting more than one distribution channel, it may be preferable to use the same approach to analyse first the profitability of each channel. Once an overall picture has been obtained it can be decided whether more detailed analysis, at the level of individual customers, is worth while. If so, the business needs to assess the most cost effective way of allocating its main cost areas. For example, it may be impractical to impose a system of allocating telesales time to each customer based on the actual time involved, because of the cost of recording and analysing what telesales people do. But a useful surrogate for telesales activities could well be the number of calls made or received to and from each retailer. This data can be used to make a fair allocation of telesales costs.

For a manufacturer serving a concentrated retail sector, where relatively few, powerful retailers account for most of turnover, then the level of analysis can often become the individual retailer. Indeed, it is essential that a manufacturer has a clear understanding of its customer profitability in such circumstances and what costs 'drive' the profitability of each account. For example one food manufacturer found that it made more money supplying own-label products to two of its main retail customers than by supplying its brands to two others. The problem was that the advertising support for the branded products was not being recovered from the retailers selling the brands. Another manufacturer found that it made little net profit by supplying own-label products to one retailer despite what appeared to be attractive gross margins. The demands the retailer made on its R & D staff and the subsequent costs of modifying the manufacturing process made the products relatively unprofitable.

In both instances the manufacturer was able to identify the main 'cost drivers', those costs that vary so much between retailers and that they cause differences in profit. What was needed in both instances was either a reduction in the key costs, advertising in one case, R & D in another, or an increase in selling prices to the retailer. Knowing its cost structure in detail is not only important when identifying such issues but it is also vital when trying to negotiate a price rise with the retailer.

Problems in implementation

Anandarajan and Christopher (1987) claim that most accounting systems are geared to appraising the costs and expenditures of individual departments or functions, as an integral part of the budgeting process used to control the business. Furthermore they perceive a gulf between marketing and accounting personnel that militates against evolving accounting systems that reflect the marketplace the company serves. They cite examples of companies with clearly defined market segments but no way of assessing the relative profitability of serving each segment. They recommend a number of steps towards introducing customer profitability analysis. The following list is adapted from their original one, and it provides a useful summary to the second half of this chapter:

- Define the customer groups and segments served.
- Identify the main differences in the service needs of each group/segment.
- Identify the factors that produce variations in the costs of serving each group/segment.
- Identify the resources used to support each group/segment.
- Identify how the company responds to the different needs.
- Restructure the system of cost coding to facilitate the allocation of costs to customers.

In reality most businesses still do little more than identify the gross margin applicable to each distribution channel or individual customer (Bellis-Jones, 1989). Unless the true costs of serving each account are known, salespeople will continue to chase business without knowing whether it is profitable or not (Helfrich, 1991). Without the necessary data trade marketing as a concept is impractical.

In conclusion

The range of options open to manufacturers in designing their marketing channels is immense. As a supplier comes under pressure from one channel it can consider other options. Much will depend upon the volumes the supplier needs to sell, the product type, the realities of the market and the end customer's predisposition to where he or she is willing to buy. The objective of this chapter was to identify a broad range of strategic options for the manufacturer once it has developed and produced a product and decided on its branding strategy. There are a plethora of options for most products, limited only by the willingness of the manufacturer to think outside of any mind set that might constrain its thinking, a mind set constructed perhaps on what has been the norm, rather than what it might be. The objectives of any manufacturer in experimenting with 'retailing' or serving the customer directly can be many and varied. But consider why two manufacturers have opened 'shops', the household textile manufacturer, Dorma, in Wilmslow, and Rover Cars in Reading. Is the motive to support existing retailers or perhaps to learn about retailing or consumer wants and needs? In the latter case a customer cannot buy a Rover car in the outlet, all he or she can do is watch videos, seek advice and read but it raises the question of whether any car manufacturer *needs* a traditional garage to sell cars. Why not have a car on the drive the following day for a test drive having seen an advertisement or visited such a relatively low cost demonstration unit?

Keypoint summary

1) Marketing channels should be seen as strategic assets and as sources of competitive advantage.
2) Attractive channels are those that the manufacturer can exert power within.
3) What the end customer expects or desires in choice and range can constrain the options available.
4) Vertical integration, without the ownership involving capital investment, can be a profitable option.
5) Selling direct to the end customer is already an option which could become more attractive for some products if teleshopping develops.
6) Selling via more than one channel can make sense, although certain problems are inherent in multi-channel distribution.
7) Once channels have been designed, the true profitability of both individual products and channels must be assessed, particularly the costs of serving any one channel or any one large retail customer.

References

Anandarajan, A., Christopher, M. (1987) A Mission Approach to Customer Profitability Analysis, *International Journal of Physical Distribution and Materials Management*, Vol 17, No 7, p 55.

Barnes, P. (1992) Clothing Manufacturer–Retailers in Europe, *EIU Textile Outlook International*, March, p 107.

Bellis-Jones, R. (1989) Customer Profitability Analysis, *Management Accounting*, Vol 67, No 2, p 26.

Black, S. S. (1990) Factory Outlets Gaining Speed, *Bobbin*, Vol 31, May, p 70.

Borin, N., Van Vranken, C., Farris, P. W. (1991) A Pilot Test of Discrimination in the Japanese Distribution System, *Journal of Retailing*, Vol 67, No 1, p 93.

Brantley, R. L. (1989) Banking Products Appear to Sell Well in Grocery Stores, *Savings Institutions*, Vol 110, No 6, p 85.

Brown, J. J., Gray, J. I., Korgaonkar, P. K. (1992) The Effects of Social Class and Perceived Risk on Consumer Preferences for Electronic Shopping, *International Journal of Management*, Vol 9, No 1, p 97.

Buzzell, R. D., Gale, B. T. (1987) *The PIMS Principles*, Macmillan, New York, Chapter 7.

Conhaim, W. W. (1988) Electronic Shopping Services Augment Information Marketplace, *Information Today*, Vol 15, No 10, p 29.

Cutress, G., Stricker, R. (1991) *The Factory Shop Guide, NW England*, Cutress and Stricker, London.

Davies, R. L., Reynolds, J. (1989) *The Development of Teleshopping and Teleservices*, Longman, Harlow.

Fensholt, C. (1988) Grocery Shopping by Home Computer, *Supermarket Business*, Vol 43, No 5, p 39.

Goldman, A. (1991) Japan's Distribution System, *Journal of Retailing*, Vol 67, No 2, p 154.

Hardy, K. G., Magrath, A. J. (1988) Planning for better Channel Management, *Long Range Planning*, Vol 21, No 6, p 30.

Helfrich, R. W. (1991) Service, is it Worth the Effort?, *Sales and Marketing Management*, Vol 143, No 15, Dec., p 46.

Hoffman, R. C., Preble, J. F. (1991) Franchising: Selecting a Strategy for Rapid Growth, *Long Range Planning*, Vol 24, No 4, p 74.

Howell, R. A., Soucy, S. R. (1990) Customer Profitability, *Management Accounting*, October, p 43.

ICC (1989) *Clothing Wholesalers* (4th Ed), ICC Business Ratios, Hampton, Middx.

ICC (1990a) *Fruit, Flower & Vegetable Merchants* (5th Ed), ICC Business Ratios, Hampton, Middx.

ICC (1990b) *Electrical Wholesalers* (17th Ed), ICC Business Ratios, Hampton, Middx.

ICC (1990c) *Meat Wholesalers* (16th Ed), ICC Business Ratios, Hampton, Middx.

ICC (1990d) *Grocery Wholesalers* (14th Ed), ICC Business Ratios, Hampton, Middx.

Jenkins, A. L. (1988) PC Purchasing, *Computerworld*, Vol 22, No 19, p 18.

Kestnbaum, R. D. (1984) Retailing vs Direct Marketing Competitors or Confederates, *International Trends in Retailing*, Vol 1, No 2, p 25.

KeyNote (1990) *Direct Marketing* (4th Ed), KeyNote Publications, Hampton, Middx.

KeyNote (1991a) *Direct Marketing* (5th Ed), KeyNote Publications, Hampton, Middx.

KeyNote (1991b) *Mail Order* (3rd Ed), KeyNote Publications, Hampton, Middx.

KeyNote (1991c) *Vending Machines* (6th Ed), KeyNote Publications, Hampton, Middx.

KeyNote (1991d) *Cash and Carry Outlets* (9th Ed), KeyNote Publications, Hampton, Middx.

Lal, R. (1990) Improving Channel Coordination through Franchising, *Marketing Science*, Vol 9, No 4, p 299.

La Plante, A. (1991) Superstores: Appeal of In-stock Bargains, *Computerworld*, Vol 25,

No 48, p 113.
Lewis, M. C., Lambert, D. M. (1991) A Model of Channel Member Performance, dependence and satisfaction, *Journal of Retailing*, Vol 67, No 2, p 205.
Lowe, L. S., McCrohan, K. F. (1989) Minimize the Impact of the Grey Market, *Journal of Business Strategy*, Vol 10, No 6, p 47.
Lynn, F. (1991) Good Channel Marketing Means Getting Back to Basic Concepts, *Marketing News*, Vol 25, No 11, 27 May, p 25.
Lynn, S. (1992) The Branded Threat, *Retail Week*, 28 Feb, p 6.
Magrath, A. J. (1990) The Hidden Clout of Marketing Middleman, *Journal of Business Strategy*, Vol 11, No 2, p 38.
Magrath, A. J., Hardy, K.G., (1991) Six Steps to Distribution Network Design, *Business Horizons*, Vol 34, No 1, p 48.
May, E. G., Greyser, S. A. (1989) From-home Shopping: Where is it Leading?, in Pellegrini, L. and Reddy, S. K., (eds) *Retail and Marketing Channels*, Routledge, New York, p 216.
McQuilkin, C. (1988) Coke, Barcardi use Segmentation to Develop a Tasteful New Product, *Bank Marketing*, Vol 20, No 7, p 112.
Michman, R. D. (1990) Managing Structural Change in Marketing Channels, *Journal of Consumer Marketing*, Vol 7, No 4, p 33.
Mintel (1987) Retail Concessions, *Retail Intelligence*, Vol 5, p 4.1.
Mittelstaedt, R. A., Stassen, R. E. (1991) The Macromarketing Effects of the Taxation of Interitate Mail-order Sales, *Journal of Macromarketing*, Vol 11, No 1, p 46.
MMC (1981) *Monopolies and Mergers Commission, Discounts to Retailers*, HC 311, HMSO, London.
MMC (1992) *Motor Car Parts*, HMSO, London.
Morgenson, G. (1989) Sacrificial Brand, *Forbes*, Vol 143, No 3, p 41.
Moriarty, R. T., Moran, U. (1990) Managing Hybrid Marketing Systems, *Harvard Business Review*, Vol 68, No 6, Nov/Dec, p 146.
Novich, N. S. (1991) Getting the Most from Distribution, *National Productivity Review*, Vol 10, No 2, p 215.
Porter, M. (1976) *To Multi-Channel Interbrand Choice Strategy and Bilateral Market Power*, Harvard University Press, Cambridge, Mass.
Porter, M. (1979) How Competitive Forces Shape Strategy, *Harvard Business Review*, March/April.
Porter, M. (1980) *Competitive Strategy*, Macmillan, New York.
Rosenbloom, B. (1989) The Wholesaler's role in performing marketing functions, in Pellegrini, L. and Reddy, S. K. (eds) *Retail and Marketing Channels*, Routledge, New York, p 117.
Sanghavi, N. (1990) *Retail Franchising in the 1990's*, Longman, Harlow.
SDA26 (1989) *Business Monitor, Wholesaling*, Business Statistics Office, Newport, Gwent.
Segal-Horn, S., McGee, J. (1989) Strategies to cope with retailer buying power, in Pellegrini, L. and Reddy, S. K. (eds) *Retail and Marketing Channels*, Routledge, London, p 24.
Stern, P., Stanworth, J. (1988) The Development of Franchising in Britain, *National Westminster Bank Quarterly Review*, May, p 38.
Verdict (1986) Verdict on Furniture and Carpet Retailers, May, London.
Weigand, R. E. (1991) Parallel Import Channels – Options for Preserving Territorial Integrity, *Columbia Journal of World Business*, Vol 26, No 1, p 53.
Which (1992) Save £££ on Perfume, Consumers Association, December, p 3.

Case Study: W. H. SMITH NEWS

Newspapers

Britain is unusual in the high number of its national papers and the high, 60%, readership of newspapers generally among the population. The national press is relatively concentrated with four groups accounting for over 85% of all sales. Exhibit 1 presents the major groups in rank order of sales. In addition to the nationals there is a strong regional press. Thomson Regional Newspapers are the market leader with over 11 million copies per week of paid for and free papers (KeyNote, 1991a).

Owner	*Titles*
News International	*The Times, The Sunday Times, Sun, News of the World, Today*
Mirror Group Newspapers	*Daily Mirror, Sunday Mirror, People*
United Newspapers	*Daily Express, Sunday Express, Star*
Daily Mail and General Trust	*Daily Mail, Mail on Sunday*
Telegraph Newspapers	*The Daily Telegraph, The Sunday Telegraph*
Newspaper Publishing	*Independent, Independent on Sunday*
Lonrho	*The Observer*
Guardian and Manchester Evening News	*Guardian*
The Pearson Group	*The Financial Times*

Exhibit 1 Ownership of major national newspapers in rank order of sales (source: KeyNote, 1991a)

The nationals are highly competitive, particularly within the three major subsectors: the mass market dailies such as the *Sun* and *Mirror*, the mid market dailies such as the *Mail*, *Express* and *Today* and the quality dailies including *The Times*, *The Telegraph*, *Guardian* and *Independent*. The market for Sunday papers is, if possible, even more competitive as readers tend to be less loyal.

One of the most influential events in recent newspaper history was the launch of the *Today* daily by Eddie Shah in 1986. Although the venture was less than totally successful in itself, Shah's policies of combating restrictive practices and introducing new technology revolutionised the industry. All the major groups were forced to respond and costs were cut across the sector by between 33% and 60% (Jordans, 1990).

Total sales of newspapers have declined slowly over the years although the leading dailies have increased sales slightly overall. The one substantial area of growth in the 1980s was that of free papers, which eroded the sales of regional and local papers substantially. Two thirds of all newspaper revenues come from advertising. Newspapers are themselves major advertisers, the top ten nationals accounting for 72% of sector advertising expenditure in 1991 (KeyNote, 1991a), although overall volumes were cut as profits tightened in the late 1980s.

Consumer magazines

There are some 2,000 consumer magazines in circulation in Britain but 350 account for 95% of all sales. The number of titles has grown rapidly and at the same time the target readership of many has become more narrowly focused. In addition there are some 4,500 business titles such as *Progressive Greetings, Airtrade, The Grocer*. Consumer magazines are bought mainly by women and many are targeted at them. That said the largest circulations in 1990 were achieved by *Radio Times* and *TV Times*, each selling over 2.5 million copies a week. Women's weeklies form the largest single sector overall with a combined circulation of about 4 million. Some magazines such as *Woman* and *Woman's Own* have been selling well for many years, while many new names have been launched such as *Prima, Take a Break, Best, Bella, Marie Claire, Riva* and *Working Woman*. Many of the new arrivals have since departed (BZW, 1991). Exhibit 2 lists the names of leading magazines and their publishers.

Owner	*Titles include*
Reed International plc/IPC Magazines	*Ideal Home, TV Times, Country Life, Amateur Gardening*
DC Thomson & Co Ltd	*The People's Friend, My Weekly, Jackie*
EMAP plc	*Motor Cycle News, Smash Hits*
Argus Press	*Photography, Which Video?, Aero Modeller*
Haymarket Publishing Ltd	*What Car?, Autocar and Motor, Practical Caravan*
Condé Nast	*Vogue, Tatler, House & Garden*
BBC	*Radio Times*

Exhibit 2 Leading magazine publishing groups and their titles

Advertising revenue is not as important to a magazine as to a newspaper but about half of all revenue achieved by magazines still comes from that source. A number of publishers produce titles in all major sectors, national and local papers, consumer and business magazines, but in general the magazine market is separate from the daily and Sunday press as a sector and is far more fragmented.

Market segmentation

Readership of both magazines and newspapers varies significantly with demography and lifestyle. Socioeconomic group differentiates *The Telegraph* from the *Mirror* reader, age the buyer of *Smash Hits* from the *Oldie*, sex between the reader of *Woman* and *Men Only*, geographic area the buyer of the *Cheshire Life* and the *Western Mail*, and special interest the reader of *Angling Times* and *New Library World*. People who live in the same area tend to share many of the same demographic and lifestyle characteristics – consequently some papers and magazines sell better in one area than in another. What one newsagent can stock and sell will differ from another in both quantity and breadth.

Distribution

The distribution of magazines, daily national newspapers and Sunday national newspapers is dominated by two wholesale companies, W. H. Smith and John Menzies. Wholesalers distribute to an estimated 70,000 retail outlets of which 47,000 are CTNs (Confectionery, Tobacconist and Newsagents) (KeyNote, 1991b).

W. H. Smith News, a subsidiary of W. H. Smith Group plc, is the leading news and magazine wholesaler in the UK with 60 wholesale depots (known as houses) serving 24,000 retail outlets including 250 of its own retail shops. The company first began to distribute newspapers in 1792. Over the years it saw the total number of wholesalers grow to reach some 800, and by the late 1980s distribution had become a maze of longstanding relationships between publishers, wholesalers and retailers. Stimulated by the changes wrought by Eddie Shah and his *Today* newspaper operation, publishers began to re-examine many of these traditional relationships. Led by News International, publishers served notice on their wholesalers and put out to tender their distribution of newspapers and magazines for individual parts of the country.

News International launched its own operation to distribute its own titles such as the *Sun*, *The Times*, *Today*, *News of the World* and *The Sunday Times*. W. H. Smith saw its market share all but halve, finding itself competing with all and sundry (including milkmen) who had bid successfully for a local franchise.

Gradually smaller operations closed or were absorbed by the major wholesalers. The number of wholesalers declined from 2,000 to 200 over three years. News International withdrew from a market that was now radically altered. A major difference was the change in relationship between the various members of the supply chain. In the words of one W. H. Smith News executive,

> In the past the retailer was our customer, he had the choice of a number of wholesalers in his area. Now that wholesaler has a local franchise from a publisher, he has to come to us for the titles we are franchised to carry. Our customer is now the publisher.

W. H. Smith News

W. H. Smith News operate very differently from ten years ago. Organisationally they have divided their business into two: newspapers and magazines. Each newspaper allows the wholesaler a certain percentage of 'returns' or 'unsolds', papers that it will give credit for if they are unsold, ranging from 5% to 20%. The skill of the newspaper salesmanager is then to allocate newspapers to retailers such that sales are maximised and returns minimised. In making the allocation, the sales manager is aided by a computer model that predicts the sales of the leading 12 dailies from the recent sales history of each paper. The final prediction takes account of factors such as weather, holidays and the known promotional activity by individual papers. A newspaper itself might decide to increase its print run at the last moment if it believes it has a 'scoop': an exclusive story that will encourage casual readers to buy or to switch their allegiance. The retailer can vary what it receives, for example if a number of regular customers have cancelled orders during a holiday, but most rely heavily upon the forecasts made by the wholesaler, in the knowledge that they can return any unsold copies. The retailer completes a returns note and the publisher accepts the wholesaler's calculation of what has actually been sold.

The control exercised by the wholesaler is even greater with magazines. Here the salesmanager acts as a buyer as well as a seller by selecting the, minority of, consumer magazines that the wholesaler carries, some 50 to 60 titles from the 2,000 available. Another decision-support computer system can be used to assess which outlets should carry a new magazine or one under promotion and in what quantity. It does this by matching the magazine to others with a similar readership profile. The newsagent is advised on any changes made in the number or scope of the magazines it will receive. Again the retailer can modify the despatch by phoning the 'house'. The retailer could, if it wishes, do its own calculation on the number of magazines it should receive but agreeing to receive what W. H. Smith News calculate it should removes a great deal of work and attracts extended credit. The magazine publisher will estimate the returns level it will accept and most decide on levels far higher than that for newspapers, hoping to attract new custom and build sales by having their publication on display. If a particular publisher is under-represented in total within certain categories of newsagent then yet another computer program can be used to spread their titles over a wider number of outlets. The different programs and data bases can be used together to help decide what actions to take in various circumstances and which programs, Newscope, Magspread or Box Level Analysis (BLA) to use, as illustrated in the decision chart shown in Exhibit 3. The term 'Box' is trade jargon for a retailer.

Relationships in the supply chain

W. H. Smith News employ a team of merchandisers whose role it is to support any magazine promotion by influencing displays in retail outlets. Advice on shop development and store design is available as is a training and induction service.

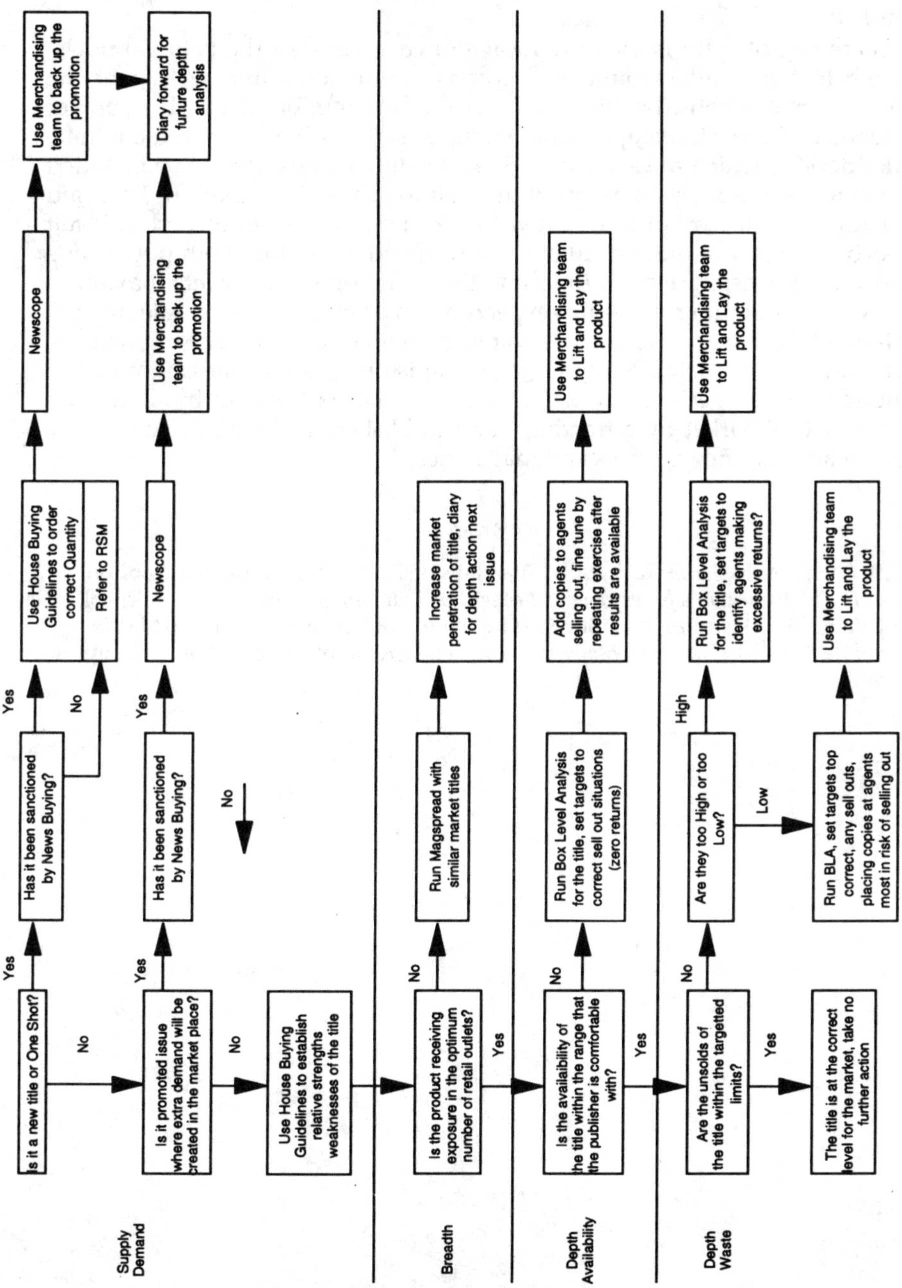

Exhibit 3 Decision system for magazines

The wholesaler decides whether to supply any would-be newsagent. If the catchment area is adequate supply would be given on a trial basis but supplies would be denied to any new outlet if it was felt that this would merely dilute the existing level of sales.

As the wholesaler is the only local source of most of the national newspapers that any outlet would need to carry to be credible as a newsagent, the wholesaler has considerable power in the distribution chain. This power extends to the relationship with the magazine publisher because the wholesaler decides which titles to carry. Some leading names have to be included but many minor magazines find it difficult to achieve distribution. That said a leading publisher could threaten to take its franchise elsewhere if it felt poorly served. The main conflict to be resolved is meeting both publisher's and retailer's aspirations at the same time. The publisher wants maximum sales and minimum returns but expects all its products to be on sale in what is limited shelf space. The retailer wants to retain its own franchise and see its total number of customers grow to maximise its own business, not just in publications. In between is the wholesaler who will benefit by increasing share of the market by attracting more publishers and by developing the total market for newspapers and magazines.

References

BZW (1991) *Media Sector Review 1991*, Barclays de Zoete Wedd Research, London.
Jordans (1990) *Britain's Newspaper and Magazine Industry*, Jordan and Sons, Bristol.
KeyNote (1991a) *Newspapers* (10th end) KeyNote Publications, Hampton, Middx.
KeyNote (1991b) *Consumer Magazines* (6th end) KeyNote Publications, Hampton, Middx.

9

THE TRADE MARKETING MIX

Borden (1965) used an earlier idea of the business executive being a 'mixer of ingredients' to discuss the differences in the marketing of different companies. He noted that companies allocated very different levels of expenditure to the same marketing activities. He suggested a list of 12 ingredients that companies seemed to balance in what he called the 'marketing mix'. This concept has been one of the most durable of ideas in marketing, reduced as it has since been to 4Ps and 2Ss: product, place, price, promotion, sales and service. In consumer marketing the mix is normally taken to refer to elements as they affect the end customer or the consumer. The purpose of this chapter is to identify the dimensions of the trade marketer's mix, where the focus is the retailer as 'customer'. Most of the discussion assumes the supplier is marketing branded goods.

The decision to see the retailer as customer rather than a distribution channel represents a significant change in orientation for the manufacturer. Phrases such as 'managing distribution channels' presuppose that the manufacturer holds a position of power and can use this to impose itself as the channel leader. Words such as 'intermediary' to describe the modern retailer are more than inaccurate, they imply a paradigm of marketing where the retailer will accept any and all products that the manufacturer determines will flow through the channel. This represents reality in fewer and fewer product markets each year. Retailers have always had some choice in the products they retailed, now they have more and the power to use that choice to better effect. Their motivations may be less fickle and more logical than those of the consumer, but the retailer needs marketing to as much as the consumer. So how should this be done?

Promotion: consumer advertising or price promotion?

In the marketing of fast moving consumer goods and particularly so with grocery products, the issue of where the marketing budget should be allocated has been much debated. Traditionally advertising was directed at the consumer to create market demand. The existence of this demand was enough to encourage the retailer to stock the products. During the 1990s the proportion of manufacturers' marketing budgets given to consumer advertising fell as expenditure was redirected towards consumer and trade promotions. Johnson (1988) was one of many to report on studies by Donnelley

Marketing of this shift in spending pattern in America. Of the estimated $100 billion spent by American companies on promotions in 1987, two thirds were on financial incentives to the wholesale and retail trades to stock and promote products. Buzzell *et al.* (1990) reported two other Donnelley statistics. In 1978 advertising accounted for 42% of all promotional spending and consumer and trade promotion, 58%. By 1988 the proportion allocated to advertising had slipped to 31%. They also quoted a Proctor and Gamble estimate that 25% of salesperson and 30% of brand management time is spent in designing, implementing and overseeing promotions.

In Britain the growth in the use of coupons designed to offer the consumer a financial incentive to repurchase or purchase has been remarkable. By 1990 over 5 billion coupons were being distributed annually, although only some 376,000 were redeemed (NCH, 1990). In America manufacturers were offering 20 times the number of promotions to retailers that the latter would accept (Curhan and Kopp, 1987). From the author's own experience consumer promotions can be an attractive alternative to advertising in stimulating sales, but was the explosion in consumer promotions based on price through special offers or coupons in the 1980s really sensible?

Trade promotions are intended to encourage the retailer to promote the product to the end customer. It is often hoped that any discounts offered by the manufacturer will be passed on in lower prices by the retailer by way of special offers, even to the point where the retailer is willing to cut its own margins and add to the price cut given to the shopper. Unfortunately retailers are as likely instead to buy a product under price promotion to stock up and sell at the normal price once the manufacturer's price promotion has ended (Buzzell *et al.*, 1990).

Many such price incentives to the retailer are used to increase the retailer's margins, at the expense of the manufacturer. This should really come as no surprise given the way the retail buyer is appraised (see Chapter 3), mainly on the gross margin achieved. Any possibility of enhancing the gross margin by absorbing a manufacturer's price promotion is going to be attractive. In America price discrimination is contrary to the Robinson Patman Act, so discounting to a larger retailer because it is large is, in theory, not possible. But elsewhere retailers are able to put pressure on suppliers for discounts and refunds for a wide range of support.

'Push' marketing, targeting expenditure on discounts of one sort or another to retailers, rather than 'pull' marketing, targeting the consumer, has become the norm in many product sectors (Johnson, 1988; Walters, 1989). Often the supplier needs to offer a discount merely to acquire shelf space, so-called slotting allowances. In France hypermarkets have even come to regard themselves as renters of shelf space. More recently there has been a move to reduce what are seen as increasingly sterile trade promotion techniques (Dagnoli and Freeman, 1988; Hume, 1988; Baum, 1990; Anon, 1991a).

Trade promotions, Curhan and Kopp (1987) assert, have been shown to be effective in changing sales volumes but research implies that they 'do not alter the brand's long-run sales trend'. The implication is that trade promotions merely move the volume around during the trading year, causing both manufacturing and distribution problems and to little lasting effect. If the discount is reflected in reduced retail selling prices, continual price promotion to the consumer is held to be deleterious to the brand franchise. Liesse and Dagnoli (1991) see the switch from advertising to price promotion to the consumer as eroding the position of brands in the consumer's mind, claiming that customers are already more loyal to the store than to the brand. So even if manufacturers succeed in shifting their promotional monies away from purely trade incentives and more towards the consumer, the chances are that the long-term risk remains of a reduction in brand franchise unless the brand itself is sustained (Scott, 1988).

The traditional way of building a brand image is through advertising. The problem with advocating advertising as an answer to the disadvantages of price promotion is that it is difficult to prove that advertising has any effect on sales whereas price reductions often have a more visible and immediate impact.

The role of consumer advertising

Joyce (1967) proposed a model as to how advertising works and how advertising and purchase by the consumer might be linked that has not been improved upon significantly in 25 years. The model proposed two such links: a direct effect where advertising through its suggestive powers prompts a purchase directly; and an indirect effect where advertising's role is to change attitude. The change in attitude arouses interest in the brand which eventually leads to purchase. An attitude change can be measured but it is difficult for any manufacturer to disentangle the effect of any attitude change from other market variables. The link between advertising, measured as expenditure, and sales is a difficult one to prove. Indeed there is a view that advertising is not a dynamic force capable of engineering change in the marketplace, but instead a weak force that is used by manufacturers more to defend a position, established presumably by other means, than to develop a brand's sales (Jones, 1990). Other writers are clear in their views that the effect of advertising can be proven and measured by separating its effects particularly from other means of promotion (Hollis, 1990; Holstius, 1990). Some argue a more straightforward relationship between share of voice (the share of all advertising volume in the sector) and market share implying a clear link between the two (Schroer, 1990). Some practitioners argue that the only direct link between advertising and revenue is that consumer advertising costs a great deal! Investment in advertising is a matter of faith, a belief that such investment is mandatory in building a successful brand over the longer term (Haselhurst, 1988). Much may depend upon the quality rather than the quantity of advertising. Successfully identifying what levers need to be pulled in a particular situation and with a particular product may be more important than obtaining a high budget (Vaughn, 1979). In practice, companies all too often set a budget for advertising as a percentage of sales (Hooley and Lynch, 1985) rather than to achieve a particular goal linked to building the brand, which *must* be the main long term role of consumer advertising.

What is needed is a more analytical approach to advertising, offering greater proof of effect to support its use, better ways to pre-test advertising and a better understanding of how advertising can be made effective. Some such insights have been forthcoming from an IRI study (Lodish and

Lubetkin, 1992; Sylvester, 1992). Pointers from the research on TV advertising include the following:

- There is no direct relationship between expenditure level and sales.
- Heavy expenditure in peak viewing time is preferable.
- There is synergy between advertising and consumer promotion, but not with trade promotion.
- Copy testing does not appear to be reliable in improving advertising effectiveness.
- 'Burst' (concentrated expenditure) is better than 'drip' (even expenditure over a longer time period).
- Advertising does have a long term effect on sales.

Advertising and consumer promotion

Identifying the effectiveness of advertising is then difficult but it becomes more complex when advertising is used in combination with other attempts to influence the consumer, particularly price promotions. Abraham and Lodish (1990) assert that companies often spend too much on both and fail to measure the combined effects involved because they do not use a single source of market research data. But perhaps the basic issue is a lack of an accepted model to define the roles of promotion and advertising in consumer marketing. Moran (1982) proposed a 'ratchet effect' to represent how the two tools should be used in combination. Price promotion exploits any upside demand elasticity, the increase in customers or purchases due to a price reduction. Advertising then reduces the downside elasticity once the price promotion ends, making it less likely that the new customers are lost after the price advantage is withdrawn. Thus using promotion followed by advertising raises the sales of repeat purchase products in a series of stages.

The same effect is unlikely to be observable in marketing consumer durables, where the sequencing of promotion and advertising is probably better reversed in timing. Advertising may be used to develop interest, possibly for the generic area as much as for the brand being advertised. A special offer on price could then ensure the customer buys the right brand.

Advertising and the retailer

Evidence of a substantial advertising campaign to consumers will encourage a retailer to stock and feature a product. Advertising to retail buyers via the trade press is also important, despite the centralisation of retail buying (Cobb, 1988). In one survey 90% of suppliers rated the trade press highly for promoting products to retailers. In Britain one trade magazine, *The Grocer*, has a paid circulation of 54,000, emphasising the wide coverage of such media.

Cooperative advertising, where the retailer and manufacturer collaborate over the advertisement, is commonplace, an activity representing over £50 million of expenditure a year in Britain (Mintel, 1988). What proportion the manufacturer pays for varies, but McGoldrick (1990) quotes one American study implying that in 98.7% of instances the proportion was 50% or above. The philosophical issue with cooperative advertising is whether the simultaneous promotion of both retailer and product is in either's interest. The retailer *may* benefit from its association with the product and vice versa, but what of the other products the retailer wishes to sell or the other retailers the supplier needs to influence?

The role of the salesforce

The change in the role of the salesforce because of the increased centralisation and concentration of retailers has been noted earlier. In the 1950s according to Grant (1988), the salesperson had considerable influence inside a retailer's store. This influence remains in many sectors and particularly with the larger independent but the salesperson's role in dealing with the modern multiple is very different. Many do not allow salespeople into stores at all. Salesforces have declined in size: by an estimated one third in grocery between 1977 and 1987 alone. But the number of national account managers has increased as has the number of merchandisers, whose role is to ensure a product is well presented in store. According to Grant the typical salesforce in Britain selling to the grocery sector used to consist of a small central team and a large field team. The field force is still substantial but has reduced in line with the decline in outlet numbers. The central team has grown to reflect the importance of the manufacturer's key accounts.

The role of the trade marketer

The trade marketing manager is not a totally new role: most salesforces have always had to recognise the significance of key accounts. What is new is its importance and professionalism. Trade marketers are now business managers, not just salespeople, advisers or planners, but people with an indepth knowledge of their customer. They have the financial and marketing data to support an objective of maximising the volume of their company's product lines by understanding the market position of the retailer. How this role works is illustrated in a case study on Coca Cola which follows this chapter.

The presence of two roles in any consumer product company, trade marketer and brand manager, is likely to cause conflict within the company. The role expected of a trade marketer is one of a coordinator, linking many aspects of the commercial activities of the business together (Jackson and Walker, 1980), but a similar role is traditionally recommended for the brand manager (Luck, 1969). Each has the role of coordinating many of the same activities but on behalf of the interests of different 'customers'. Smaller suppliers (and some majors) tend to employ the services of independent salesforces (Taylor, 1990). Here the problem of conflict is theoretically lessened as the supplier has no direct contact with the retailer and must concentrate on its brand franchise with the consumer.

Service

The management of the supply chain and its impact upon the service provided to both retailer and shopper were emphasised in Chapter 7. Indeed one perspective on the manufacturer/retailer relationship is to see the exchange not so much in terms of the products in the supply chain, but of the service the manufacturer can sustain to the retailer. If the product has been presold to the consumer, then the retailer is surely not that concerned about what the product is rather than whether it is there to be sold. Service, rather than physical product, is said to be the current focus in the search for competitive advantage (MCE, 1990). Much of the research into service management has focused on consumer rather than commercial markets, but the same issues are likely to be relevant in both. The intangible nature of any service makes it difficult to measure and service quality may be assessed by the customer by the tangible evidence provided by the supplier (Shostack, 1977) or by the customer searching detective-like for clues to indicate the quality of the service (Gronroos, 1980). Gaps can exist between what the retail customer wants and what the company provides, not only because of service failure but also because of lack of understanding of needs and poor communication of any understanding within the supplier organisation (Zeithaml *et al.*, 1988). Tools now exist for the measurement of service quality (Parasuraman *et al.*, 1988), and it should be a part of the role of the trade marketer to assess the retailer's perception of service quality, particularly in the delivery of goods.

Product variables

The product variables affecting the retailer rather than just the shopper include detailed questions such as:

- What should be the number of items in a case?
- Is the shelf space compatible with this?
- What is the shelf life?
- What are the arrangements over returned goods?

The list seems endless and is highly specific to the product being considered. But apart from managing a long list of such detailed points, is there a product issue that should take pride of place when considering manufacturer/retailer marketing? One issue that *should* be to the fore is that of innovation.

The potential weakening of a brand's franchise through price promotion, devaluing its psychic value through a thousand price cuts, has already been mentioned. The problem of evolving innovative advertising and getting it noticed within a plethora of promotional messages in our over-communicated age has been well made elsewhere (Ries and Trout, 1986). The fundamental problem facing the brand manufacturer remains the cost of developing and launching a new brand. Instead manufacturers have tried to extend the benefits of their existing brand names across a broader range of products, 'borrowing on the equity of the brand' (Farquhar, 1990). Line extensions, such as Mars bars as funsize products, or category extensions, such as Mars ice cream, are examples of the approach. Such a strategy can reduce or even eliminate the need for advertising support (Hastings, 1990), because of the association with the mother product and, increasingly, by astute use of public relations rather than advertising in the presentation and promotion of the brand extension to the consumer. Brand extension or umbrella branding is nevertheless a limiting strategy as the products a brand name can usefully be used for will be determined by the associations surrounding the brand itself. Sooner or later a manufacturer needs to consider substantial and radical innovation as an option (Anon, 1991a). While manufacturers claim to be concerned to launch new products how many are truly innovative?

Innovation

Innovation has two sources, the market place, 'market driven innovation', or technology, 'technology driven innovation' (Abernathy and Clark, 1985). Innovations involving brand extensions are essentially market driven. The retailer is well placed to compete with market driven innovations of its own, aided by better market information as to what is selling than that available to their suppliers. Own-label/brand is the most obvious example, where much is an imitation of existing, manufacturer's physical products. While many retailers do now sustain significant technology functions, their ability generally to innovate via the technology route is limited. The more attractive option for the manufacturer must therefore be innovation based on technology in combination with an understanding of the marketplace.

Innovation, even highly successful innovation, may not be enough in itself to compete in the coming years. The speed and rate of innovation and the distinctiveness of its output must increase for the manufacturer to compete with the retailer, who needs only to imitate, who can put a product onto its shelves within weeks of any decision to try for market innovation and at little cost or risk to itself. The process of innovation in the manufacturing sector needs to speed up and the level of technical content needs to be enhanced to reduce imitation. Interestingly some recent academic research has focused on the issue of reducing development time (McDonough and Spital, 1984; Gold, 1987; Rosenau, 1988; Stalk, 1988; Gupta and Wilemon, 1990) and on the need to coordinate technical development with marketing, but nowhere in the academic literature is there the realisation that the manufacturer is competing not only against other manufacturers but also against the lower cost, inherently faster system led by retailers. Time to market and technology driven innovation are the weapons the manufacturer must learn to use to compete with those who are also its customers.

From the author's personal experience much of the time spent by research and development personnel is on the D rather than the R in their function. Development activities include product line extensions, redesigning the successful innovation of a decade or more ago, and research into sometimes better but, more often cheaper, ways of making the product. Alternative but less expensive ingredients are substituted if consumer tests or just the judgement of the management indicates that the product is perceived to be the same as before. How much wishful thinking or short-term expediency has gone into the eventual undermining of the quality platform that *all* brands must contain to have the right to be thought of as brands (see also Chapter 6)?

Price in the trade mix

Pricing is the most complex area of the trade marketing mix but one of the least well researched. The pricing issue frequently descends to a wrangle over discounts in the negotiation between retailer and supplier, with the retailer trying to trade off margin against better display or better support in store. To avoid much of the conflict that can arise over price negotiations, suppliers in markets not subject to price maintenance legislation have attempted to impose standard discounts in open price lists. Thus every buyer 'knows' what everyone else is receiving in price support and that no one is obtaining preferential treatment. Such tactics seem to work where the manufacturer has a strong brand, where there is no alternative to their product, or where the threat to de-list is weakened by having other retailers, who would be willing to distribute the product who are not currently doing so. The pressure for better terms on price can also be resisted if the supplier can negotiate, other, non-price, issues. Fig 9. 1 lists some of the non-price factors that can be traded off in a price negotiation. The list could be made longer but there do not appear to be many issues the manufacturer can use. Many of those listed could also result in extra cost. By way of contrast Davidson *et al.* (1988) list nearly 40 types of 'assistance' that the retailer might request that involve the manufacturer in conceding margin. Professional buyers are well trained in negotiation skills and in the technology of the manufacturer's product, to the point where they can calculate their supplier's costs (Wingate and Friedlander, 1978). Negotiation is better seen as a process rather than a short discussion focusing on price, but if the trade marketer doing the negotiation does not understand the buyer's business well enough to introduce significant non-price factors, then the potential for realistic negotiation on other than price is reduced.

- The supply of own-label/brand.
- Change in logistics to reduce the retailer's stock levels and/or stockouts.
- Product presentation shaped to reinforce the retailer's market position.
- Training for retail staff.
- Quick-response systems.
- Returns policy on unsold goods.
- Sole agency agreement.
- Advice on more effective retailing, such as better space management.

Figure 9. 1 Non-price issues that can be used in negotiation

Stern and El-Ansary (1977) recommend unilateral action by the supplier in certain circumstances to head off the conflict that might result in any negotiation. For example, in times of reduced demand the retail trade might expect a price reduction to stimulate demand, even though volumes are down. A general announcement that the manufacturer is lowering prices can head off a protracted series of price negotiations. However the concession should be coupled with a clear indication of how the retail trade are expected to reciprocate, together with a statement about the purpose of the policy. In general such a policy by the manufacturer is only effective when the manufacturer is seen as the channel leader, and in effect is expected to take the lead on pricing. Where the retailer perceives itself to lead, the price reduction can be imposed on the supplier.

Much of the literature on channel management is American, written in the context of legislation that limits the price negotiating powers of retailers and in a marketplace where retailing is not as concentrated generally as in Britain. Retailers in Britain are in a more powerful position and probably more likely to see themselves as able to succeed in price negotiation. Ideally the manufacturer has to be capable of pre-empting price negotiation by moving the negotiation to one of the non-price factors. Where the supplier is competing with firms benefiting from lower costs than it can work to itself the need to avoid price negotiation is more pressing still. TEXCO *et al.* (1991) investigated how suppliers of 'soft goods', mainly textiles, within the European Community could compete with suppliers from low-wage countries. Of retailers, 41% were willing to pay up to or over a 15% premium to EC producers if the supplier could provide better service, quicker adaption to fashion trends, higher quality, risk sharing on price pressure and better marketing to the end consumer. Better service and quicker adaption are both achieved through the adoption of the quick-response methods discussed in Chapter 7. However for the manufacturer to be able to introduce non-price factors into the negotiation, the ability of the individual in contact with the retailer needs to match the role and that role needs defining carefully.

The negotiating role of the trade marketer

Bargaining or negotiation occurs in many areas within society other than distribution channels. Theoretically bargaining 'may occur in economic exchange relationships whenever imperfect competition prevails' (Young, 1975). In a situation of perfect competition, where all buyers are aware of all sellers and their respective prices and offerings, the market mechanism does prevail through open bid and counterbid. In practice negotiation tends to occur dyadically, one to one, with the buyer in particular using other parallel negotiations with alternative suppliers to extract concessions from the

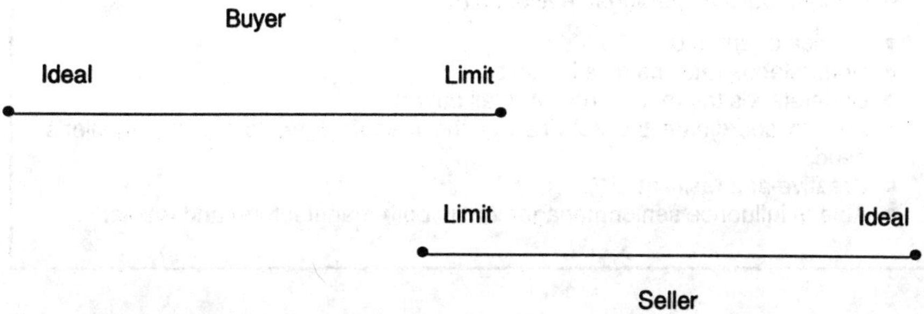

Figure 9. 2 Simple model of negotiation

supplier. In its simplest form the two parties will reach agreement if their negotiating continua overlap (Fig 9. 2). Such a simplistic model assumes that negotiation can be modelled in one dimension. In practice the buyer will have one negotiating agenda, the seller another.

Great emphasis is placed on personal skill in the many books written to advise the negotiator (Scott, 1981; Kennedy *et al.*, 1987; Mastenbroek, 1989). Few are based on formal research and most rely on the practical experience of their authors. That said some of their content reflects many of the same issues considered more formally by academic researchers, such as for example, Pruitt (1981), Raiffa (1982) and Bazerman and Neale (1992). Mastenbroek comments that negotiation occurs when there is 'not a vast difference in power', where the two parties are interdependent but have different interests. The two parties disagree but see value in reaching agreement. He sees 'cooperation' as behaviour between people sharing similar interests and goals; conflict might be a common problem but the relationship is open, information is traded freely and honestly in an attempt to understand the other's perspective. In addition to cooperation and negotiation, Mastenbroek identifies a third behaviour pattern 'fighting', epitomised by a permanent power struggle, little understanding and a desire to win. Scott (1988) reflects the same view of their being two different types of negotiation, constructive or competitive, but he links this more to the personality of the negotiator rather than to the situation. Whether the type of negotiation is a function of personality, context or both, one main message relevant to this book is that the strategy of the supplier should be to aim for a constructive relationship as a strategy and to employ well-trained negotiators as key account managers only as an insurance against competitive negotiation or fighting. The essence is either to gain power such that no negotiation is needed because the manufacture determines or where power is more balanced to avoid negotiation through cooperation. Extensive training of trade marketers in negotiation skills is almost an admission that the manufacturer's strategy has failed, yet skills training is advocated as one answer to developing trade marketing expertise. Others see the role as more strategic (Thomas, 1989).

Fig 9. 3 lists the attributes of the trade marketing manager identified by

- Capable of building long-term relationships
- Intellectual, usually graduate level
- A business strategist, numerate and financially literate
- Good presentation and inter-personal skills
- Good at building personal relationships
- Service orientated
- Understands retailing as a business
- Understands the motivations of retail buyers
- Able to coordinate the activities of the manufacturer to suit the retailer's needs
- Creative and resilient
- Able to influence senior management in both manufacturer and retailer

Figure 9. 3 The attributes of the trade marketer

Thomas and some of the author's own. One final issue is the level of authority given to such national account managers. In one survey buyers complained about the level of discretion delegated to account managers. It was argued that the ability to form a business relationship depended upon the level of authority vested in the individual (Tubridy, 1989).

Conflict

Fig 9. 3 mentions interpersonal skills as an attribute valuable to the trade marketer or key account manager. These skills are not only negotiation skills but include the skills needed to resolve conflict. Conflict has been mentioned throughout this book. Some authors see conflict as evidence of problems in relationships, others that it is evidence of a relationship. Moore (1989) reviews much of the literature on conflict and identifies a number of sources for conflict in the marketing channel but concludes that there is little research into what the business outcomes are that result from conflict.

Place

One element in the marketing mix that has received scant mention in this chapter is that of place, where the product is sold. Many manufacturers and retailers are national but fewer retailers than manufacturers are international in their operation. If manufacturers can develop international brands *and* if the physical product can be made the same, the 'market' can be defined as international. The balance of power swings towards the manufacturer who can better resist a threat to de-list if its production capacity can be used to fill orders from another country at will. At present few manufacturers can achieve this but many are aiming for this goal in the future.

One issue in the context of trade marketing is whether, in Europe, trade marketing should be organised on a national, regional or European basis. As trade barriers continue to fall in the EC, the logic of having separate production locations at the level of at least one per country is reduced. It may still be logical to retain separate brand managers for each country, although this often produces an unnecessary proliferation of stock items. Whether one needs trade marketers in each country/market is less clear. In the future in the EC it is possible to conceive of the need for a highly centralised trade marketing group responsible for developing relationships with larger retailers. Whatever the outcome, most large manufacturers need to evolve strong trade marketing functions if they have not already done so, even in markets where retail concentration is currently no real threat.

Keypoint summary

1) The trade marketing mix contains a number of elements:
    - *Promotion*, where a current issue is the balance between trade promotion and price promotion in general and consumer advertising designed to build the brand.
    - *Sales*, where the trend has been to reduce the real size of the salesforce while increasing the numbers of those whose role is concerned with trade marketing at head office.
    - *Service* is a key non-price factor (considered in earlier chapters). Gaps often exist between what the supplier believes is expected and what the buyer actually wants.
    - *Product*: while brand extensions or umbrella branding seem to offer the opportunity to develop the existing brand franchise, technical innovation, at a faster pace, holds the key to the future.
    - *Price* can be the main focus for negotiation. The aim of the trade marketer is to avoid this happening.
    - *Place* can offer the manufacturer an option for resisting retailer power, if the supplier can switch resources between markets.
2) *Trade marketing* has become a key role to rival that of brand management. The personal skills of the trade marketer, particularly in negotiation, may be crucial if the manufacturer's strategy fails to balance retailer power.

Note

The two case studies that follow illustrate radically different strategies to the supply of consumer products. That on Coca Cola identifies how a company with a very strong brand has even so sought to build relationships with retailers. The second on Ryecroft foods details the activities of a company who specialise in producing own-label products. Notice how in the Coca Cola example the role of trade marketing is separate from key account selling.

References

Abernathy W. J., Clark K. B. (1985) Innovation: Mapping the Winds of Creative Destruction, *Research Policy*, No 14, p 3.

Abraham, M. M., Lodish, L. M. (1990) Getting the Most out of Advertising and Promotion, *Harvard Business Review*, May/June, p 50.

Anon (1991a) The End of a Trade Promotion Paradigm?, *Discount Merchandiser*, Vol 31, No 4, p 62.

Anon (1991b) Caution is the Watchword, *Marketing Week*, 6 Dec, p 39.

Baum, H. M. (1990) Shock Treatment needed to revive brands in the '90s, *Marketing News*, Vol 24, No 25, p 12.

Bazerman, M. H., Neale, M. A. (1992) *Negotiating Rationally*, Free Press, New York.

Borden, N. H. (1965) The Concept of the Marketing Mix, in Schwartz, G. (ed) *Science in Marketing*, Wiley, Chichester, Chapter 13.

Buzzell, R. D., Quelch, J. A., Salmon, W. J. (1990) The Costly Bargain of Trade Promotion, *Harvard Business Review*, Vol 68, No 2, p 141.
Cobb, R. (1988) Press the Issue, *Marketing*, 9 June, p 5.
Curhan, R. C., Kopp R. J. (1987) Obtaining Retailer Support for Trade Deals, *Journal of Advertising Research*, Vol 27, No 6, p 51.
Dagnoli, J., Freeman L. (1988) Marketers Seek Slotting Free Truce, *Advertising Age*, Vol 59, No 8, p 12.
Davidson, W. R., Sweeney, D. J., Stampfl, R. W. (1988) *Retailing Management*, (6th Ed) Wiley, New York, pp 489–90.
Farquhar, P. H. (1990) Managing Brand Equity, *Journal of Advertising Research*, Vol 30, No 4, p RC7.
Gold, B. (1987) Approaches to Accelerating Product and Process Development, *Journal of Product Innovation Management*, Vol 4, No 2, p 81.
Grant, A. (1988) The Death of the Salesforce, *Admap*, April, p 37.
Gronroos, C. (1980) Designing a Long Range Marketing Strategy for Services, *Long Range Planning*, Vol 13, p 36.
Gupta, A. K., Wilemon, D. L. (1990) Accelerating the Development of Technology-based New Products, *California Management Review*, Winter, p 24.
Haselhurst, L. (1988) How Pedigree Pet Foods Evaluate their Advertising Spend, *Admap*, June, p 29.
Hastings, H. (1990) Introducing New Products Without Advertising, *Journal of Consumer Marketing*, Vol 7, No 3, p 19.
Hollis, N. S. (1990) Separating Advertising from Promotional Effects with Econometric Modelling, *Journal of Advertising Research*; Research Currents, Vol 30, No 3, p 6.
Holstius, K. (1990) Sales Response to Advertising, *International Journal of Advertising*, Vol 9, p 38.
Hooley, G. J., Lynch, J. E. (1985) How UK Advertisers Set Budgets, *International Journal of Advertising*, Vol 4, p 223.
Hume, S. (1988) Spending Heads Back to Consumer, *Advertising Age*, Vol 59, No 10, p 29.
Jackson, D. W., Walker, B. J. (1980) The Channels Manager: Marketing's Newest Aide?, *California Management Review*, Vol 23, p 52.
Johnson, W. C. (1988) Sales Promotion: It's Come Down to Push Marketing, *Marketing News*, Vol 22, No 5, p 8.
Jones, J. P. (1990) Advertising: strong force or weak force? Two views an ocean apart, *International Journal of Advertising*, Vol 9, p 233.
Joyce, T. (1967) What do we know about how advertising works?, J. Walter Thompson, London.
Kennedy, G., Benson, J., McMillan, J. (1987) *Managing Negotiations*, Hutchinson, London.
Liesse, J., Dagnoli, J. (1991) Brands in Trouble, *Advertising Age*, Vol 62, No 51, p 16.
Lodish, L. M., Lubetkin, B. (1992) General Truths?, *Admap*, February, p 9.
Luck, D. J. (1969) Interfaces of a Product Manager, *Journal of Marketing*, October, p 32.
Mastenbroek, W. (1989) *Negotiate*, Basil Blackwell, Oxford.
McDonough, E. F., Spital, F. C. (1984) Quick Response New Product Development, *Harvard Business Review*, September/October, Vol 62, No 5, p 52.
MCE (1990) *Service: The New Competitive Edge*, Management Centre Europe, Brussels.
McGoldrick, P. J. (1990) *Retail Marketing*, McGraw-Hill, Maidenhead, p 266.
Mintel (1988) Retail Advertising, *Retail Intelligence*, No 1, p 4.1.
Moore, R. A. (1989) Conceptual and Empirical Developments of Marketing Channel Conflict, *Journal of Marketing Management*, Vol 4., No 3, p 349.
Moran, W. T. (1982) Insights from Pricing Research in Bailey, E. L. (ed), *Pricing Practices and Strategies*, Conference Board, New York, p 7.
NCH (1990) *Coupon '90*, NCH Promotional Services, Northants
Parasuraman, A., Zeithaml, V. A., Berry, L. L. (1988) Servqual: A Multi-Item Scale for

Measuring Consumer Perceptions of Service Quality, *Journal of Retailing*, Vol 64, No 1, p 12.
Pruitt, D. G. (1981) *Negotiation Behavior*, Academic Press, New York.
Raiffa, H. (1982) *The Art and Science of Negotiation*, Harvard University Press, Boston, Massachusetts.
Ries, A., Trout, J. (1986) *Positioning: The Battle for Your Mind*, McGraw-Hill, New York.
Rosenau, M. D. (1988) From Experience Faster New Product Development, *Journal of Product Innovation Management*, Vol 6, p 282.
Schroer, J. C. (1990) Ad Spending: Growing Market Share, *Harvard Business Review*, January/February, p 44.
Scott, B. (1981) *The Skills of Negotiating*, Gower, Aldershot.
Scott, B. (1988) *Negotiating, Constructive and Competitive Negotiations*, Paradigm Publishing, Avon.
Shostack, G. L. (1977) Breaking free from Product Marketing, *Journal of Marketing*, April, p 73.
Stalk, G. (1988) Time the Next Source of Competitive Advantage, *Harvard Business Review*, July/August, p 41.
Stern, L. W., El-Ansary, A. I. (1977) *Marketing Channels*, Prentice-Hall, Englewood Cliffs, NJ.
Sylvester, A. (1992) What Works, What Doesn't, *Admap*, March, p 45.
Taylor, R. K. (1990) Manufacturer's Representatives; the March to Professionalism, *Journal of Personal Selling and Sales Management*, Vol X, Winter, p 53.
TEXCO *et al*. (1991) *Encouraging the Competitiveness of the Soft Goods Industries Through Cooperation in the Post 1992 European Community*, TEXCO International and Kurt Salmon Associates for the EC.
Thomas, H. (1989) Grand Nationals, *Marketing*, June 1, p 29.
Tubridy, G. S. (1989) More Authority for National Accounts Managers, *Federation of American Health Systems Review*, Vol 22, No 2, p 53.
Vaughn, R. (1979) How Advertising Works: A Planning Model, *Journal of Advertising Research*, Vol 20, p 27.
Walters, R. (1989) An Empirical investigation into Retailer Response to Manufacturer Trade Promotion, *Journal of Retailing*, Vol 65, No 2, p 253.
Wingate, J. W., Friedlander, J. S. (1978) *The Management of Retail Buying*, Prentice-Hall, Englewood Cliffs, NJ., pp.283–4
Young, O. R. (1975) *Bargaining, Formal Theories of Negotiation*, University of Illinois Press, Urbana–Champaign, Ill.
Zeithaml, V. A., Berry, L. L., Parasuraman, A. (1988) Communication and Control Processes in the Delivery of Service Quality, *Journal of Marketing*, Vol 52, April, p 35.

Case Study: COCA COLA AND SCHWEPPES BEVERAGES LTD

The market

The British market for soft drinks is substantial. By 1990 the equivalent of 8,390 million litres were being consumed, of which half were carbonated drinks. However the carbonated sector represented over two thirds of value. Over the decade sales had more than doubled in volume and much of this increase had been achieved through the grocery sector. In 1980 grocers retailed the equivalent of 58.6% of all volume, by 1990 some 70%. Increased consumption of carbonated drinks had been encouraged by the introduction of the larger, lighter bottles made from plastic making two- and three-litre bottles a practical possibility.

On the world stage Coca Cola had been a leading player for many years. By 1992 its worldwide revenues exceeded $12,000 million through brand names such as Sprite, Fanta and Coca Cola itself. Coke was the leading brand in the grocery sector in Britain where the product was distributed by Coca Cola and Schweppes Beverages (CCSB) – a joint venture formed in 1987 between the confectionery and food group Cadbury and Coca Cola. CCSB produced and distributed a range of brands, including those of the Coca Cola Company. The turnover of CCSB had reached £660.7 million by 1990, up 48% on 1988.

Organisation

Coca Cola and Schweppes divided their sales and marketing function into two. The Trading Division had four sections: Grocery, Impulse (Wholesale, Cash and Carry), Leisure and the Licensed Trade, each serving a different retail sector. The Marketing Department itself included four roles, Brand Marketing, Trade Marketing, Sales Promotion and Public Relations, and New Product Development. While Trading Division handled the day-to-day negotiations with their opposite numbers within the buying departments of individual retailers, Trade Marketing was responsible for a wider role, designed to develop the product category by working with, rather than selling to, the retailer.

The aim of the trade marketing manager was to present the image of a category specialist, able for example to forecast consumer demand for the soft-drinks sector as a whole. Trade marketing managers worked with managers in their respective retailers to maximise the sales of the product category to both companies' mutual advantage. The origins of the role had been to identify anomalies in individual retail stores, such as significantly less space being allocated to soft drinks than the local market would support. As the task of allocating selling space within retail companies became more centralised and the retailer's head office controlled space allocation by issuing planograms for each store, the role had evolved. Within each retailer a number of trading directors competed for the finite amount of shelf space in each store. Decisions on relative space allocation could be made by assessing the relative profitability of product categories but this was no guide to the potential for the category, if substantial increases could be made to shelf space. The trade marketing managers' role was to assist their opposite numbers in arguing the case for increased space allocation to the category. Once achieved, the role involved presenting the best case for maximising the display space given to CCSB products.

CCSB looked to building relationships and partnerships between specialist departments in retailers within their own company. Strong links had developed between planning managers who worked together to reduce mutual stockholding and achieve just in time delivery using electronic data interchange (EDI), a concept that was particularly important in managing promotions. Forecasting was a joint activity.

Contact between Trade Marketing and their opposite numbers was perhaps once a fortnight face to face but far more frequently by other means, including electronic messaging. While conflict might still occur, over for example price negotiation between the retail buyer and national account manager, relationships in Trade Marketing were of a different nature and the strength of this mutual dependency probably provided the framework that assured conflict would be resolved. In effect the trade marketing and trading director roles in supplier and retailer formed part of an informal organisation that straddled both organisations with the goal of developing the product category for mutual benefit.

References

The Grocer (1991) Focus on soft drinks, May 25, p 61.
The Grocer (1992) Soft drinks and mineral waters, May 23, p 67.
Euromonitor (1992) Concentrated soft drinks, market research GB, May, p 89.

Case Study: RYECROFT FOODS

The market for breakfast cereals in Britain is large and well established. The British led the world in relative consumption in the 1980s, eating on average some 7.5 kg per head each year (KeyNote, 1990). Cereal products were eaten, particularly by children, at all main meals (not just breakfast) and as a snack.

KeyNote suggest segmenting the market into three main product types:

- *Staple products* such as Kellogg's Cornflakes, Weetabix and Shredded Wheat.
- *Health products* such as Alpen, various muesli-style mixes and bran products.
- *Children's products* such as Kellogg's Frosties and CocoPops.

Staple products accounted for nearly half the market by volume and health products a third of the market by 1990. The latter sector had seen the greatest growth, due to concern over healthy eating and the publicity given to the benefits of increasing the amount of roughage in the diet.

The manufacturing sector for cereals was highly concentrated, with four companies controlling over three quarters of all sales. The largest single manufacturer was the international company Kellogg's, with about half the market. Their British base was in the north of England in Manchester; other leading suppliers were Weetabix, Cereal Partners and Quaker Oats. Beneath these very large businesses were a plethora of smaller concerns although many were part of larger groups.

Some, such as Jordans and Cheshire Wholefoods specialised in health products. Some, such as Viota, specialised in supplying own-brand products, which together accounted for 20% of all cereal sales.

The distribution of cereal products was almost entirely via the grocery sector, which had a similar level of concentration to that on the suppliers' side. Six retailers accounted for over 70% of cereal product sales. Sales of own-brand products were buoyant, despite the substantial advertising of the branded manufacturers and the refusal of market leaders Kellogg to provide own-brand. Some own-brand suppliers were themselves substantial businesses or subsidiaries of conglomerates, Viota for example belonged to Cereal Partners.

The technology of much cereal production dated from the end of the 19th century. The processes used to produce some of the leading brands were often lengthy, secret and capital intensive. Attempts by companies to imitate leading sellers often failed to achieve the same taste and texture. Nevertheless a number of companies were attracted to the sector in the early 1980s, not only because of the margins that could be achieved but also following the introduction of new technology that promised to revolutionise methods of making cereals. The new 'extruded' processes offered a much faster and cheaper way of manufacture but the taste and texture of the resulting products rarely matched those produced by traditional means.

Ryecroft Foods

The City of Manchester grew after the industrial revolution by processing and trading cotton. As other countries increased in importance as centres for the cotton trade, the industrial and commercial structure of the Manchester region changed, but the large mill buildings, built to house the textile industry, remained. One such mill, in the town of Ashton-under-Lyne just outside of Manchester, was converted to a bakery which traded under the name of John Hill & Son (1906) Ltd, around the turn of the 20th century. Fifty years later the business had changed to producing biscuits. In the mid-1960s the business was sold to the confectionery manufacturer Mackintosh (who were themselves subsequently purchased by Rowntree).

Perhaps because the biscuit business was quite different from that of the confectionery business, Rowntree-Mackintosh decided to sell what was now called Hill Biscuits to an ex-director of Nabisco and the food processor Whitworth. The 1980s saw the business, with about 1.5% of the biscuit market, struggling to make substantial profits and the owners looked to other sectors for greater potential. The cereal market was attracting attention and Ray Blakely, Research and Development Manager of Nabisco, was invited to set up a small private breakfast-cereal company.

Blakely's philosophy was simple enough: to duplicate one or more of the products produced by the leading manufacturers, match their quality and sell the production as own-brand to the leading grocery multiples. The bran sector was growing and Kellogg's Allbran was a significant product. A number of imitations existed, often made using the extrusion process that Blakely regarded as producing an inferior product. Premises adjacent to the Hill's biscuit factory were leased and 'state of the art' production equipment was installed. The company undertook much of its own engineering work and often purchased equipment (such as its flour silos) second hand. Productivity levels in the plant, which operated 24 hours a day six days a week, compared with those of much larger cereal companies. By 1992 turnover had reached £8 million a year, and 100 employees worked for the business which had now acquired a second site in Hastings on the south coast of England. Ryecroft held an estimated 1.8% of the cereal market by 1992 – remarkable growth for a small company that started in 1984.

Sales had grown steadily since the company achieved its first order from Safeway and Ryecroft supplied a range of bran-based products to most of the large retailers by 1992, but relationships with retailers had not always gone smoothly. One company had sent a buyer and a technologist to discuss the supply of own-brand. The technologist had suggested some changes and promised to work with Ryecroft's own development team. Ryecroft's management expected a negotiation on price with the buyer, but instead the buyer handed across a piece of paper with a single price written on it. The price was considered too low compared with the existing pricing strategy of the company, and as no negotiation seemed possible no agreement or orders ensued at the time.

Blakely commented that Ryecroft was still too small to be proactive with the large retailers: 'I wouldn't say we work together, we are still suppliers, they are our customers. They tend to take the lead and the bigger they are as a customer, the more power they have'.

However the relationship with at least one major customer showed signs of maturing. Contact was more with the retailer's technologists than with their buyers. Communication was shifting towards greater use of EDI (electronic data interchange) with the prospect of using the retailer's sales data to plan production even before the order was confirmed. Payment would be made without resorting to paperwork.

In Blakely's opinion Ryecroft owed its existence to three factors in the market: Kellogg, because they chose to ignore the own-brand sector (a strategy they adopted worldwide); large retailers, because they wanted to and could afford to develop own-brand; and Ryecroft's technology, which allowed them to match or exceed the quality of branded products and to better the quality of other own-brands.

Reference

KeyNote (1990) *Breakfast Cereals* (7th End) KeyNote Publications, Hampton, Middx..

10

TRADE MARKETING STRATEGY TODAY AND TOMORROW

The purpose of this chapter is to draw together many of the ideas from earlier chapters and to use them to produce some pointers for the development of trade marketing strategy. In doing so some of the more widely accepted concepts in business strategy will be challenged. A different approach will be proposed that it is believed is more appropriate to the changing relationships between many manufacturers and retailers and a number of analytical tools will be discussed that can aid the trade marketing manager.

In Chapter 1 an historical perspective was adopted to show how radical change has occurred at least twice in the distribution of consumer products. Well before the industrial revolution manufacturers or farmers were often retailers and vice versa. Wholesalers existed, as merchants, but retailing as we know it today was virtually non-existent. The changes wrought by the industrial revolution in the 18th and 19th centuries, over a long time period it must be emphasised, were based upon changes in technology but the social changes that resulted, particularly urbanisation, were equally significant in the shaping of manufacturer and retailer roles. Finally changes in the law towards the end of the industrial revolution, making branding feasible for example, enhanced the potential for manufacturer control and protected both manufacturer and wholesaler from any growth in retailer power.

The separation of manufacturing from retailing as activities after about 1850 was the first major change. Retailing gradually became reduced in status but the fragmented nature of both the new retailing and manufacturing sectors led initially to wholesaler rather than manufacturer power. Wholesalers were needed to provide the channel links between the manufacturer and retailer at an economic cost. As manufacturing became more concentrated and branding more significant an era of manufacturer power dawned. Wholesalers still existed but their power in the supply chain reduced. The main message from Chapter 1 was that technological, legal, economic and social change have a major impact upon the distribution of consumer goods, particularly in the relationships between the various members of the distribution channel/supply chain.

In Chapter 2 the rise of manufacturer power was considered in more detail both in terms of branding and from the perspective of academic research, particularly research into the concept of power. Between the two chapters the case study of Marks & Spencer illustrates not only some of the detail of how one retail business has evolved but also the power that modern retailers can hold and how this power has grown steadily over the decades. Retailing has become, particularly in Britain, more concentrated giving the larger companies increased purchasing power.

The manufacturer/retailer relationship

A modern retail multiple's source of power can lie simply in its share of a manufacturer's sales volume, as illustrated by Fig 10. 1. The scales on both axes are logarithmic, indicating that power is an issue once either party accounts for about 10% of the other's business.

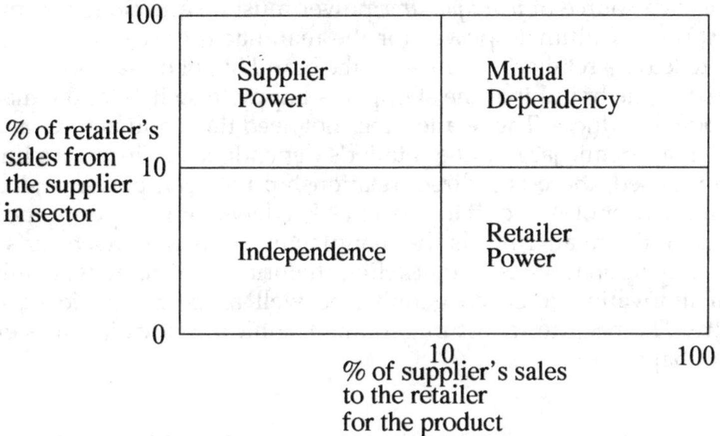

Figure 10. 1 Sources of dependency

A car dealer with a Ford franchise would fall into the top-left quadrant, because the few chains of dealerships mean the manufacturer is still in control. Marks & Spencer dealing with a small manufacturer and purchasing most of their output would fall into the bottom right hand quadrant, retailer power. More and more manufacturers are finding themselves locked into this particular box.

In the 1980s MFI retailed most of what the furniture manufacturer, Hygena, made but Hygena products represented a substantial proportion of MFI's turnover. MFI and Hygena at the time would have both been in the top right hand quadrant of mutual dependency. Many retailers and manufacturers would fall into the independence quadrant. The two businesses operate at arm's length. Relationships are not close, as can be seen in the case study of Emma Somerset that followed Chapter 3.

The locus of power will depend upon the level of concentration in the retail and supplier sectors generally but what matters is the power in the relationship between individual firms. So if the level of concentration in the retail sector is higher than in the supplier sector, as is now the case in the British grocery sector for example, power is *more likely* to be vested in the retailer. However the situation may differ with individual products particularly where there is a strong brand. Thus Pedigree Petfoods or Coca Cola, who have both brands with a strong consumer franchise and a large market share of their market, can still be in the 'supplier power' quadrant. Even here manufacturers are now regarding their relationships with retailers as 'partnerships' as was illustrated in the case study following Chapter 9.

Who holds one further source of power, the consumer franchise, is an important issue. In Chapters 5 and 6 two factors were discussed that appear to reduce the manufacturer's ability to retain a consumer franchise. The trend towards greater inner-directedness in society reduces the perceived value of branding. The treatment of own-brand much as any brand by most if not all customers is another factor reducing supplier power. Add to this the growing cost of establishing a brand for a manufacturer (because of a proliferation of brands and the dilution of the advertising media) and the relative ease in which retailers can develop their own products, and the future for branding as a source of *manufacturer* power must be questioned. A brand is only a source of ultimate power for the manufacturer if the shopper feels obliged to leave a retailer's premises if the brand in not on sale. Once alternatives exist to the brand that the shopper is happy to switch to, the manufacturer's power reduces. The retailer does not need the manufacturer as much, if at all. In academic jargon, the retailer's dependency reduces. As Emerson (1962) proposed, there is a direct relationship between power and dependency, the power of A over B increases as B's dependency upon A increases.

To ensure the retailer needs the manufacturer, the manufacturer's brand needs to rely upon more than marketing rhetoric to sustain it. Its quality and level of innovation must be genuine as well as perceived to guarantee longevity. The need to invest in genuine technical innovation was emphasised in Chapter 6.

Conflict or power?

Conflict is another of the more useful academic concepts introduced in Chapter 2 and relevant to our discussion at this stage. Conflict or the potential for it is likely to exist when the goals of two parties to a relationship are in opposition or just different. Gaski (1984) associates power with conflict, pointing out that the use of power has been found or has been assumed to cause conflict. Mallen (1967) proposed that for the maximisation of channel profits and consumer satisfaction, the channel must act as a unit. Where all members of a channel accept one member as being the leader then it is less likely that conflict exists. Leadership has been associated with power (Rosenbloom, 1990), although more complex models exist of what leadership is about (Price, 1991). But most theory still seems aimed at the traditional view of an administered system where the manufacturer is involved in the 'design of control procedures to ensure compliance' (Bucklin, 1973). The same philosophy can be applied to a situation where the retailer is 'in control', although it must be repeated that retailer control is rarely the perspective adopted in published research on marketing channels. But what if there is no clear leader?

The alternative view of the supplier/retailer interface from that of power, conflict and control was discussed in Chapter 3 – that of a relationship. A relationship implies mutual dependency, the top right quadrant in Fig 10. 1. While the supplier may not be a major supplier to the retailer as a whole, it could be a significant player in one sector and be seen as a major supplier by the retail buyer responsible for that sector.

A relationship implies a clear definition of roles and a mechanism for resolving conflict. One of the interviews following Chapter 2 illustrated the difference between an arm's length posture and the beginnings of a true relationship. This concept was developed in Chapter 7 using the idea of supply chain management, the notion that it is advantageous to see the movements of materials needed to make the product and the product itself as a single system, extending from raw material to end consumer. True someone has to be responsible for coordinating the supply chain and this probably involves leadership and possibly even power, but not necessarily. Many organisations work together with varying levels of formality in what have come to be called 'strategic alliances'.

Strategic alliances

The term strategic alliance often implies a large-scale 'joint venture' between two or more organisations. Indeed the two phrases tend to be used as synonyms to describe substantial, often global, associations of interest in the growing academic literature on alliances (Ohmae, 1989; Lyons, 1991; Lei and Slocum, 1991). The joint venture is often a distinct and separate organisation from that of its stakeholders (Datta, 1988; Borys and Jemison, 1989), with its own clear structure (Devlin and Bleackley, 1988). The term 'collaborative venture' has been used to distinguish those where the association is looser in nature (Lyons, 1991) or 'cooperation' where the arrangements are short term (Devlin and Bleackley, 1988). Lorange (1988) sees *any* joint activity as needing a clear architecture and competitive posture, a value-creating role for each participant, compatibility between partners and a balance in power. Nielsen (1988) points to the need for any cooperative venture to produce benefits for all parties. Jarillo (1988) examined a number of more fluid forms of cooperation including networks, where a number of often small firms work together almost opportunistically, coming together as and when the market opportunity requires.

To be an alliance therefore does not necessarily require a high degree of formality in organisation or large size. The word 'strategic' implies some measure of permanence. A supply chain can be usefully regarded as a strategic alliance between manufacturer and retailer.

To be effective a strategic alliance needs a clear architecture, involving the definition of goals and roles. Common goals for supply chains in general would be to improve overall profitability by increasing total sales and/or reducing cost. The costs in a supply chain will include stock, transport, raw materials, space costs in retailing, labour costs and other transaction costs. Each partner can contribute to cost reductions; often in fact each needs to make a contribution, for a saving to be made. To expand the sector also requires cooperation between the two.

The retailer's fundamental role in a supply chain includes selling and providing sales data and forecasts. The manufacturer's role includes prompt and appropriate supply. One or both will be responsible for promotion. Increasingly these roles are clearly defined and allocated in those markets where retailer and manufacturer are independent. The manufacturer presells the branded product, the retailer provides the utility of place for the shopper to buy. Only once the relationships become closer do the problems of conflict seem to become manifest and some mechanism is needed to resolve the tensions that seem to result. Chapter 9 discussed some of the issues in trade marketing and the role of the trade marketing manager. The point was made that relying upon the personal skills of the individual, particularly his or her negotiating skills, was tantamount to an admission of a lack of a clear trade marketing strategy. As the case study on Coca Cola/Schweppes illustrated conflict can still exist over the specific issue of price negotiation but this will not prejudice a relationship built at a different level in both businesses.

So, how should a trade marketing strategy be appraised? There is likely to be a need for both long-term and short-term planning, the latter being designed to suit the market situation as it is. A longer-term view will require a more fundamental examination of a manufacturer's or wholesaler's business. In the shorter term a suitable starting point is a channel map, similar to that shown in Fig 8. 3.

Channel mapping

Fig 10. 2 shows a simplified view of the channel map for a consumer-durable sector, based on a real example. Manufacturer A, to the left of the map, supplied the retail sector in three ways, via wholesalers to independent retailers, directly to independents (some of whom also dealt with wholesalers) and directly to large multiple retailers. Their main competitor, B, sold only via its solely owned retail outlets. A large number of smaller manufacturers sold to a plethora of small independent retailers.

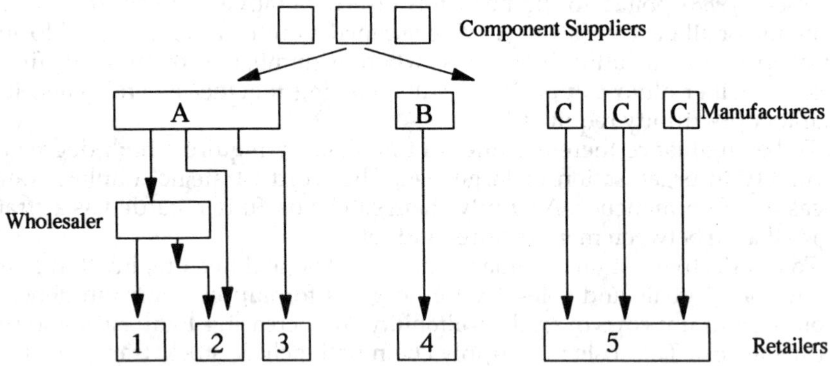

Figure 10. 2 Channel map example

As a major supplier, Manufacturer A had to ensure that all three of its main channels performed well. Problems had occurred particularly with the retailers supplied both by a wholesaler and by Manufacturer A. The wholesaler itself also felt threatened and was known to be looking for a second source of supply from abroad. The large multiples were constantly demanding special deals to give them a price advantage over the independents.

The manufacturer's strategic response was to create three profit centres, one for each of the main channels. Each were allocated different designs and model numbers to sell under different brand names. All three still used the same manufacturing base to source from.

Drawing up channel maps helps to focus attention upon issues that require attention. Once the channel strategy has been clearly defined, the tactics of how to manage each channel can be worked through, using the marketing mix as discussed in Chapter 9. In the example shown in Fig 10. 2 it was possible to create three trade marketing roles and to allocate separate brand names and products to each, even though the products were fundamentally similar. The option to imitate Manufacturer B and open its own retail outlets was not selected by Manufacturer A as it was felt this might threaten existing retail relationships. Interestingly the three channel managers began to see each other as competitors even though they worked for the same manufacturer. They began to insist on greater distinctiveness between the products they sold, by for example going back to component suppliers to have different sub-components designed for them.

One point needs to be emphasised from this example. Competition is often better seen as between *channels* not just between manufacturers. As Manufacturer A's trade marketing managers built their own relationships with component suppliers, the competition could even be seen as between supply chains *within* the same company.

Before moving on to consider the wider implications of competition between supply chains, there is one further level of analysis which should be added to an appraisal of how to serve different parts of the same channel. Fig 10. 2 represents a simplified picture. In reality there are a plethora of different retailers and ways of reaching them. Dickson (1983) suggested constructing a portfolio map where every retailer customer could be positioned according to the manufacturer's share of the retailer's total sales of the product under analysis, and according to the real growth rate of the retailer. This takes account of the dynamic nature of the retail sector where different companies and different formats are coming and going. Fig 10. 3 adapts Dickson's framework to a more conventional matrix which can be considered as

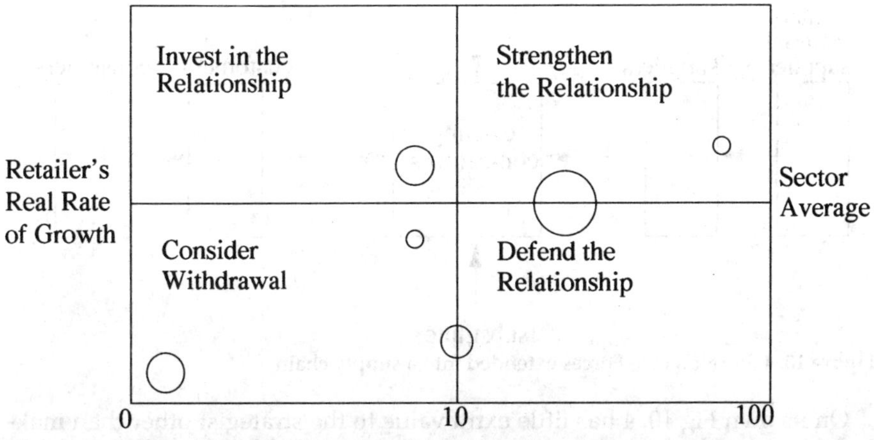

Figure 10. 3 Manufacturer's share of retailer's sales of product type

an extension of Fig 10. 1.

An analysis of a completed Fig 10. 3 can reveal those retailers the company needs to move closer to, those in the top left-hand quadrant, where the manufacturer is poorly represented, and those where greater effort may be wasted as the retailer is in relative decline, those in the bottom left-hand quadrant. A customer-account profitability analysis would provide further evidence of what actions to take in individual circumstances and the profit from each retailer can be represented by the size of its circle in Fig 10. 3. Interestingly, Dickson offers an example of a relatively small retailer obtaining the best deal from the supplier, indicating that large customers are not always the most demanding.

A new way of thinking about business?

Academic and practitioner thinking about business strategy has evolved rapidly since the 1960s. Writers then and since have tried to identify those factors that determine success in business and ways of analysing business to make better decisions. Many ideas can still be criticised as anecdotal, not based upon a genuine theoretical understanding of business and therefore prone to being less than universally applicable or predictive.

The work of Michael Porter published in the 1980s was capable of predicting success or failure. This broke new ground because he provided a number of universal frameworks which had a theoretical basis. His was one of the first approaches to business strategy that emphasised competition or rather the need to plan within a competitive environment. The output from the PIMS data base and Boston Consulting Group's experience curve have added other perspectives and models to a new generation of ideas that have general applicability.

The most widely quoted model of competition is probably Michael Porter's Five Forces, the five relationships that need to be addressed by the strategist. This can be extended to include other relationships up and downstream in the same supply chain as shown in Fig 10. 4.

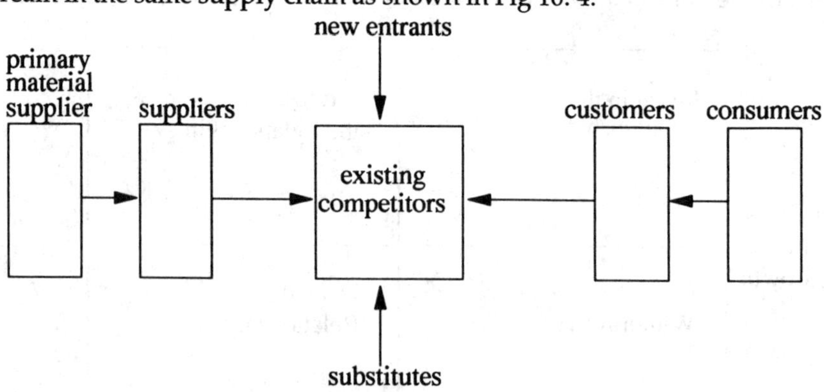

Figure 10. 4 Porter's Five Forces extended into a supply chain

On its own Fig 10. 4 has little extra value to the strategist other than making the point that any supplier to a business probably has suppliers of its own that can affect the profitability of all companies in the supply chain and that the company's own customers have their customers in turn who must be influenced, particularly if they are end consumers. Fig 10. 4 still implies that competition means 'other firms'. What if the basis of competition is taken not as *all* competing firms but as *all* competing supply chains? If a firm is a member of more than one supply chain, then each such chain has the same status strategically as all others, irrespective of whether they belong to the firm or not.

Fig 10. 5 presents the concept in graphic form, by representing the same structure as in Fig 10. 2 but as a series of supply chains. Each supply chain

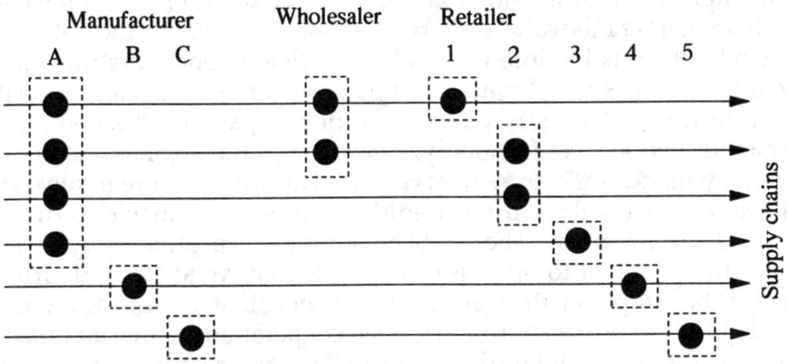

Figure 10. 5 Competing supply chains

represents its own series of relationships, its own power structures, its own sources of conflict and its own profit opportunities. If the same business is a member of more than one supply chain, then it merely collects from more than one revenue stream. In effect each chain is an example of both cooperation and a network but more an example of cooperation between individuals and a network of individuals than between firms. The key individuals within each supply chain are the trade marketers and the retail buyers. What should cement their relationship is a mutual dependency to achieve the goal of maximising supply chain revenue and profit. Revenue and profit flows accrue to each employing firm as a consequence of the flows that accrue to the supply chains that each is a member of. The more memberships, the more profit. The more channels any manufacture can sustain the larger its profitability (see Chapter 8). The more supply chains a retailer can accommodate, the larger its business can become.

The concept of organising around supply chains which extend between and across businesses rather than organising within businesses is made a practical proposition by modern communication techniques, and in particular by electronic data interchange (EDI). Each business in the supply chain must be willing to adopt something approaching an 'open systems' approach, one that allows sharing of sales data, forecasts and product plans. The two main parties to the process, manufacture and retailer, must appear to act as a single organisation, the seamless system as envisaged in Chapter 7.

A case has been made for analysing manufacturer/retailer relationships as supply chains, single systems melding the skills of two businesses into one cooperative alliance. While this may make sense for situations of mutual dependency (Fig 10. 1) what of those where supplier or retailer power prevails?

Supplier power

Manufactures are well placed to hold power when they own leading brands and loyalty to those brands is strong enough to prevail over source loyalty to the retailer. A branded strategy, as discussed in Chapters 2 and 8, involves supporting the brand with advertising, the judicious use of price promotion, and an emphasis on differentiation. New brands should rely upon technical rather than market innovation wherever possible to counter the potential for imitation by the retailer. International rather than national branding should become the norm. Strong brands exist in many sectors that cannot easily be imitated or duplicated; examples from different parts of this book include newspapers, petfood, confectionery, entertainers and are often the first comers to many markets. Their owners can often afford to ignore totally retailer power and treat retailers in the traditional way, as channels to distribute their products for them. The problem with such a philosophy is that it removes the potential to optimise the profits that could be made from the market if the supply chain were properly coordinated. For example, total sales could be increased through closer cooperation. If the manufacturer holds power, it may still be advantageous to coordinate the activities of the supply chain and act as its leader.

Price (1991) suggests that leadership in a channel must involve the aim of improving the performance of the marketing channel as a whole. A leader's behaviour influences the other channel member(s) by affecting their role perception, motivation, ability and environment. The roles of each channel member need to be defined clearly. Any ambiguity needs to be reduced by better communication and participation. Expectations of each need to be clarified and the leader must support the other channel members.

If the manufacturer decides to have little to do with the retailer, relying on the strength of its brand to sell through what it aims to achieve, it misses the opportunity to expand its total sales by working with, rather than just selling to, the retailer. A partnership, even for the most powerful of brands, can result in increased sales for the product category or supply chain as a whole.

Retailer power

Where retail concentration is high, where the potential for own-label is high *and* where the retailer's strategy is not to stock just the manufacturer's brands, then the larger retailer is likely to hold power in the channel. To regard the typical multiple retailer as holding power in a similar way to that held by a manufacturer would be wrong. A retailer is likely to act more as a supply chain manager, seeking to organise the supply of what it perceives its customers want, rather than a channel leader. The perspectives are different. One looks up the supply chain to organise, the other down the supply chain to control. The perspectives of the supply chain is still valid. However retailers can also be controllers, particularly if selling own-label.

Many manufacturers are shy of producing own-label. Strategically this may not make much sense. Own-label is a growth market and a substantial one at that. Growth markets are generally more strategically attractive than static ones as they offer easier potential for increases in sales and market share. Suppliers do, quite correctly, point to the dangers of supplying their own competitors, but should the question be more *how* they supply own-label rather than whether?

Taking the supply chain model, the supply of own-label is in competition with the supply of the national brand. The two supply chains are radically different, different enough to be operated as separate businesses. The case study on Ryecroft Foods illustrated the very different nature of a business supplying own-label.

The own-label supplier needs to concentrate on being the lowest-cost provider of the products it aims to make. Price positioning, while it does not dominate own-label in Britain any more, is still important (Shaw *et al.*, 1992) but as the retailer is now responsible for adding any brand imagery, the responsibility and role of the manufacturer is mainly to produce an appropriate quality at the lowest cost.

Service is likely to be a particularly vital factor in dealing with the retailer, particularly delivery performance. The largest problem will be managing the relationship in such a way that the retailer cannot damage the manufacturer's business by a sharp reduction in orders or by the termination of contract. Sole supply to one retailer is unlikely to be the best option. Raising the exit costs of the relationship to the retailer by investing in EDI and hard and soft physical distribution systems generally is another way to protect the own-label producer's business.

The formal integration of the European market presents significant new opportunities to all business, but establishing a brand that was once national as a European brand could be very costly. Alternatively, the manufacturer could seek to expand by using the market presence of the retailer and produce own-label.

Because the own-label supply chain is radically different from that of the manufacturer's brand in terms of the division of roles and focus on cost, it is unlikely that both businesses can be operated together. Furthermore, as pointed out in Chapter 6, offering both products to the retailer simultaneously invites the retail buyer to trade one business off against the other. Only where the manufacturer has a weak brand, where the retailer may not accept it without the simultaneous offer of own-label, is there much logic in providing both from the same organisation.

Culturally a brand and own-label provider are likely to be different businesses to work for. The creativity and innovation needed in the one may be counterproductive in the other. It should be the retailer's role to manage market innovation not that of the own-label provider. Technological innovation in the own-label supplier can be limited to following the market, not leading it. The picture of a frugal business, stripped back to the basics of its role of manufacturer, may dismay. If own branding is to be a partnership, an alliance with a clear architecture and definition of roles, then the role of brand management needs to be vested in the retail organisation whose name appears on the product and not with the supplier.

Understanding the retailer as 'customer'

What is remarkable about the academic research on channel management and about the conversations the author has had with manufacturers in preparing this book is the prevalence of the word *conflict*. It pervades the academic literature and the views of trade marketers and retail buyers. Gattorna is possibly unique (see Chapter 2) in seeing conflict as potentially beneficial between companies, arguing that at least it shows that a relationship exists. If Dwyer *et al.*'s and Arndt's analogy (discussed in Chapter 3) between business partnership and marriage is valid, then perhaps conflict should be expected and the emphasis placed on methods of resolution rather than avoidance. Talking problems through may be as sound advice to firms 'married' together within the same supply chain as it is to those in more traditional marital partnerships.

Chapters 3 and 4 were written to aid understanding of retailing as a business and retail buying as a process. In fact this book would not have been written at all were it not clear to the writer that retailing was rarely understood as a business by the majority of managers working for suppliers. One of the issues here is that the typical retailer has itself changed from being a member of a fragmented sector with a reactive stance of only a decade or so ago, to the larger, more centralised and proactive business of today. Retailers are learning the need to think longer term and to manage themselves as brands or branded experiences. Retailers have recognised that their relationships with the consumer are often just as strong or stronger than those of the manufacturer – they are certainly less tenuous and physically closer. One only needs to stand inside a retail store to see what is selling and to listen to customers to understand why the relationship is so commercially valuable.

What retailers *sometimes* lack is an analytical approach to their business. Their proximity to the customer leads to a fast-moving but also to a highly reactive approach to marketing issues. Manufacturers can still benefit by providing advice to a retailer, for example on space allocation through the provision of planograms, or the potential for a product category in the longer term.

The retail buyer is still appraised more on the gross margin achieved rather than the net profit made, because the costs of selling do not fall within their control and are difficult to allocate to individual lines. DPP techniques are changing matters and it is likely that buyers will become appraised more on the true profitability of the products they buy in the future. Manufacturers may have a vested interest in promoting this trend but they will only achieve such a goal if they genuinely understand the business of retailing, so that their advice is couched in ways the retailer can understand.

The future

In Chapter 5 the distinction made by Pierre Wack between what is predetermined and what is still uncertain was mentioned as useful in deciding how the future might look. Business planning normally involves an environmental scan where the main issues are economic, legal, social and technical change; the competitive environment; and the detail of the competitive position the business finds itself within. The purpose of this final section is to look forward by considering some of the points made earlier in the book and how they might shape the supply chain in the future by concentrating on what is predetermined and what is still uncertain.

Legal trends

In the author's view legal issues dominate the potential for power of the large scale retailer. Legislation such as Resale Price Maintenance, Robinson Patman in America (anti-discriminatory discounts), planning legislation and procedures restricting larger shops, such as the Piano Regulatore in Italy, are fundamentally intended to curb the power of the retail multiple and to support the independent retailer. By restricting the retail multiple, and directly or indirectly their negotiating power, the legislation also favours the supplier. Robinson Patman has even been nicknamed the anti A and P law (Hollander and Omura, 1989).

Gradually these legal constraints are being removed throughout the world. What perspective will dominate the legal framework within the EC after full integration is as yet unclear but if the concept of free trade means anything, then legislation designed to fetter the large retailer is unlikely to stand the test of time. In America, Robinson Patman appears to be being progressively ignored. In the longer term any shift in the legislation making it easier for multiple retailers to expand and to negotiate more favourable terms will increase the potential for retailer power at the expense of the manufacturer. Wholesalers will find it progressively more difficult to survive if the levels of concentration among retailers *and* manufacturers or producers increase.

In the author's opinion the trend in legislation is 'predetermined' and the effect will be to enhance retailer power in those sectors and/or countries where retailer power is still low.

Economic trends

Disappointing as the recessionary beginning in the 1990s has been for business, economic growth has been a long-term feature of the business environment for centuries. Assuming that human beings do not suddenly stop being acquisitive and stop buying, then economic growth is another predetermined factor – people will have more to spend in the future. Whether they will buy more or better is an issue that is returned to in the next section. However there has been a trend to spend proportionally less on objects and more on experiences in developed economies. Sales of services such as holidays, meals out and entertainment have grown faster than those in many product markets. The manufacture and retailing of products is therefore unlikely to grow as fast as the rest of the economy, adding further to pressures within the supply chain to increase profit by reducing costs rather than by increasing sales. This is again predetermined. What is uncertain is whether manufacturers and retailers are willing to work together to achieve cost reductions, to counter the effect and improve their profitability, or to fight back against the general trend and, by better marketing, increase sales.

Social trends

An ageing population in most developed countries raises its own problems of allocation of resources to health care and caring for the elderly of immense proportions. Older people are also consumers and supply chains need to respond to the sometimes different needs of the 'grey' market. Growth in home shopping is a distinct possibility.

The growth of inner-directedness in society as a whole may mean less affinity towards brands, more self-confidence in buying own-label/brand and more individualism. This will favour the retailer with an own-brand but not one with an own-label sold on price with less than convincing quality.

High levels of unemployment and under-employment in many countries contrast with higher levels of employment generally as more women have entered the employment market and for longer periods of time. The distribution of individual wealth and income has changed little in recent years in Britain but the differences between households has become marked and this will continue to grow. In some households no one has paid employment, in others two work and have no plans to raise a family. The prospect of a permanent underclass of the disadvantaged is very real as is the development of a superclass of smaller households containing two high-wage earners. The latter have disposable income, less time to dispose of it and are poorly served by a retail sector located in the wrong place and available at the wrong times (Davies, 1991). If retailers are unable to respond, then manufacturers will need to become retailers again to ensure that shoppers are offered what they want, not what retailers and planners want to provide.

The environment

Environmentalism is potentially the most significant social trend of the decade. Important as they are, the effects of an ageing population and a more individual consumer are nothing to the impact that a greener attitude to consumption would have on the typical supply chain. Concern for the environment is again a predetermined trend, but how the consumer and supply chain will respond is not yet clear, although there is evidence of fundamental change as illustrated in Chapter 5. It is possible that society might revert to a subsistence economy, consuming only what it needs to consume. In the author's opinion this is unlikely. It is possible that we will consume in the same but more 'responsible' way. Products will cost more as they will have to be produced in an environmentally sensitive way. In the author's opinion this is highly likely, as it allows for economic growth while being compatible with the already evident trend of spending proportionally less on buying products.

One of the central themes in a green economy is conservation and one implication is greater pressure to recycle. Gone are the days of the returnable bottle but bottle banks are now permanent features outside shops and in local amenities. Products are being labelled to aid recycling, for example Boots have been labelling their products telling the consumer what materials the bottle and cap are made from. BMW label their car parts and have moved towards the idea of recycling entire cars. DIY retailers Wickes tell their customers that their hardwood products are from forests which are replanted.

In Germany excess packaging is penalised and there are restrictions on the amount of refuse a household can dispose of.

More and more products will have to be produced in a truly environmentally conscious way, and distributed with the same ethos. In Figs 10. 4 and 10. 5 supply chains were shown as being linear. Fig 10. 6 shows the supply chain of the future, almost circular in shape as materials used in producing products are returned to the beginning of the supply chain or to various stages therein. There is a new role emerging, that of a recycling agency,

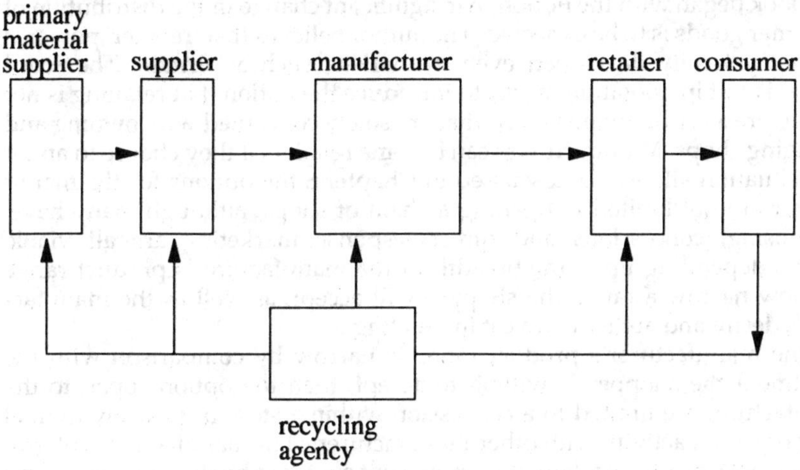

Figure 10. 6 The supply chain of the future

which may be part of one of the supply chain members or more likely be independent of it and acting for many supply chains. Recycling can be made an economic proposition if consumers will pay more for products designed to be recycled and accept lower standards of presentation, in packaging for example when such is made from recycled material.

Recycling can become the norm even without extra cost. The economics of recycling steel products are more favourable than refining iron ore to make new steel. Metal and glass are however inherently easier to recycle than paper or plastic and natural fibres, and significant advances are needed in technology for Fig 10. 6 to represent the majority of products.

Information technology

If the technology of recycling is one uncertainty, there is another technology that will affect the supply chain if companies allow it to, EDI. Earlier in this chapter EDI was seen as an issue relevant to the short to medium-term planning of companies. It is also a factor that could affect the long term. Fundamentally EDI makes communication between firms and individuals easier. Companies are already experimenting with automatic reordering and EDI forms a central part of the quick-response philosophy. Well used, EDI can be part of a move towards far lower stock levels and the far faster supply of merchandise within supply chains. Thus far prompt delivery has been associated with high stock. Better information means that safety stock can be reduced or eliminated and that what is produced is what the customer wants, thus reducing redundant stock and the need for sales or clearances. EDI can also reduce the transaction costs between manufacturer and retailer, lowering prices for the consumer and thus stimulating economic growth.

The competitive environment

This book began with the notion that significant change in the distribution of consumer goods is to be expected. The author believes that 'retailer' power is still not yet fully developed even in markets such as Britain. The word retailer is put in quotation marks to introduce the notion that retailing is not just the preserve of organisations that are solely concerned with owning and managing shops. Manufacturers can become retailers if they choose to and if their situation allows. As discussed in Chapter 8 the options for the manufacturer are not limited to opening a chain of shops, although many have. Franchising, concessions and direct response marketing are all viable options depending upon the breadth of the manufacturer's product range and how narrow a range the shopper will accept, as well as the manufacturer's desire and ability to invest in retailing.

If the manufacturer's product range is narrow by comparison with the assortment the shopper is willing to accept, then the options open to the manufacturer are limited to a concession within a store or possibly to mail order or a joint activity with other manufacturers. For manufacturers of grocery and DIY products where the assortment expected by the shopper is very wide (20,000 product lines in many grocery superstores and over 500 in a convenience store) the manufacturer is poorly placed to become a retailer. In fashion the options are much greater and a growth in the number of manufacturers entering retailing in this and similar sectors such as furniture and cars can be expected.

It is possible to conceive of alliances between manufacturers opening their own outlets, but further into the future home shopping may offer the manufacturer greater opportunities to enter 'retailing'. Home shopping reduces the role for a retailer and increases the opportunities for an alliance of manufacturers to deal directly with shoppers through electronic means.

The coming years will see the maturing of an age of retailer dominance over the distribution of consumer products. As with all generalisations there will be significant exceptions but the lessons of history suggest that it is dangerous to assume immunity to a general trend. Trade marketing as a function will increase in significance and brand marketing will experience relative decline. Successful suppliers will often be those with a clear view on how to deal with the new environment, and of which option to choose, whether heavier branding or better retail relationships or even retailing itself.

The nature of competition will change from competition between firms and within supply chains to competition between supply chains and within firms. New accounting systems will be needed to control organisations where the emphasis is less on the profits made per product and more on the profits made per retail customer.

References

Borys, B., Jenison, D. B. (1989) Hybrid arrangements as strategic alliances; theoretical issues in organisational combinations, *Academy of Management Review*, Vol 14, No 2, p 234.

Bucklin, L. P. (1973) A theory of channel control, *Journal of Marketing*, Vol 37, p 39.

Datta, D. K. (1988) International joint ventures: a framework for analysis, *Journal of General Management*, Vol 14, No 2, p 78.

Davies, G. (1991). Aspects, *Retail Week*, 27 March, p 9.

Devlin, G., Bleackley, M. (1988) Strategic alliances – guidelines for success, *Long Range Planning*, Vol 21, No 5, p 18.

Dickson, P. R., (1983) Distributor portfolio analysis and the channel dependence matrix: new techniques for understanding and managing the channel, *Journal of Marketing*, Vol 47, Summer, p 35.

Emerson, R. M. (1962) Power-dependence relations, *American Sociological Review*, No 27, p 31.

Gaski, J. F. (1984) The theory of power and conflict in channels of distribution, *Journal of Marketing*, Vol 48, p 9.

Hollander, S. C., Omura, G .S. (1989) Chain store developments and their political, strategic and social interdependencies, *Journal of Retailing*, Vol 65, No 3, p 299.

Jarillo, J. C. (1988) On strategic networks, *Strategic Management Journal*, Vol 9, p 31.

Lei, D., Slocum, J. W. (1991) Global strategic alliances, payoffs and pitfalls, *Organisational Dynamics*, Vol 19, No 3, Winter, p 44.

Lorange, P. (1988) Cooperative strategies: planning and control considerations, in Hood, N. and Vahine, J. E. (eds) *Strategies in Global Competition*, Routledge, London, p 370.

Lyons, M. P. (1991) Joint ventures as strategic choice – a literature review, *Long Range Planning*, Vol 24, No 4, p 130.

Mallen, B. (1967) Conflict and cooperation in marketing channels, in Mallen, B. (ed) *The Marketing Channel*, Wiley, New York.

Nielsen, R. P. (1988) Cooperative strategy, *Strategic Management Journal*, Vol 9, p 475.

Ohmae, K. (1989) The global logic of strategic alliances, *Harvard Business Review*, Vol 67, No 2, p 143.

Price, R. (1991) Channel leadership behaviour: a framework for improving channel leadership effectiveness, *Journal of Marketing Channels*, Vol 1, No 1, p 87.

Rosenbloom, B. (1990) *Marketing Channels* (4th Ed), Dryden Press, Chicago, Ill. p 281.

Shaw, S. A., Dawson, J. A., Blair, L. M. A. (1992) The sourcing of retailer brand food products by a UK retailer, *Journal of Marketing Management*, Vol 8, p 127.

INDEX